"Nothing gets one's attention like one's imminent demise," writes Gene O'Neil in *An Upraised Chalice,* a book that chronicles the remarkable travels, adventures, and near-death experiences that have marked his quest to discover the meaning of life. O'Neil's practical insights, born of experience, cut across religious boundaries to convey a vibrant spirituality in plain, accessible language... O'Neil's compelling book offers a clear road map for both what he calls the greatest and most exciting journey one can take (the journey within) and the greatest discovery one can make (our true identity as divine love).

— *Awarded Five Stars from* ForeWord Reviews

Reading Gene's book has been a remarkable time for me to reflect upon and to question what we consider as reality in this day and age. It felt like being in "a moving retreat" with him throughout his arduous journey through mysteries, near-death experiences, shocks, conflicts, joys, and revelations—only to discover the light of the Ever-present Self. Gene stands bold like a warrior with superb courage, yet with sublime surrender to the Will of God. His enthusiasm, awareness and words soar through the ever-present field of Consciousness that is beyond time and space. I thank him on behalf of humanity.

— *Roop Verma, Master Sitarist and Professor of Music, Vedanta, and Yoga Philosophy at Hartwick College, Oneonta, NY*

There's no better place to begin, for true spiritual revelation, than with one's own personal experience, and so, *An Upraised Chalice* sets the tone for anyone ready for their own "journey of discovery." Those who would drink from O'Neil's chalice of understanding will find its contents full and complex. Add a travelogue to the world's spiritual places and you have a fascinating blend of self-inspection, pilgrimage, and revelation that will resonate with many readers.

— *D. Donovan, Midwest Book Review*

The remarkable story of a lifetime quest by a modern-day mystic of his world travels and then integrating his experiences back into professional life in America. But what is really interesting here are the practical disciplines that he incorporated into his life that paved the way for his survival in multiple near-death experiences. A fascinating and thought-provoking read.

— David Tame, author of "The Secret Power of Music" and "Beethoven and the Spiritual Path"

Rarely do you find a book that is both an amazing-page-turning adventure as well as a truly heart-felt exploration of a sincere search for oneness with Divinity. I was amazed at the sincerity of Gene's spiritual search and his tenacity in following the voice/ knowing of his "Inner Presence. I marveled at his hair-raising experiences and also at his tenderness toward his inner discoveries. Readers will love this book and will also appreciate the wisdom it contains as Gene unfolds his life adventures and his spiritual discoveries. Excellent tool for growing and learning on one's spiritual path.

— Meredith Young-Sowers, D.Div., author of "Agartha: A Journey to the Stars" and "Spiritual Crisis," Founder, Stillpoint School of Integrative Life Healing

This is a personal story that somehow taps into each of our own. While Gene is weaving his cosmic travelogue, it is unavoidable that you will see your own reflection within it. Accounts of sacred journeys are often stilted, flaky, or indistinct but An Upraised Chalice is none of these. It is authentic and heartfelt. His adventure offers a clear roadmap to a higher consciousness, unapologetic in its forthrightness, determined in its execution. I have placed it on my recommended reading list—you will too.

— Dr. Dennis Perman, co-founder of The Masters Circle

# *An* Upraised Chalice

## Adventures *and* Near-Death Encounters *in my* Search *for the* Brotherhood of Light

# Gene O'Neil

**ASEMC PRESS**
UpraisedChalice.com

ASEMC
PRESS

# An Upraised Chalice

### *Adventures and Near-Death Encounters in my Search for the Brotherhood of Light*

## By Gene O'Neil

*Foreword by David Tame*

Copyright © 2015 by Gene O'Neil and ASEMC Press

pages cm
LCCN 2014901477

ISBN 978-0-9912635-2-3 (Print)
ISBN 978-0-9912635-1-6 (eBook)

1. O'Neil, Gene
2. Spirituality
3. Near-death Experiences
4. Adventure Travel
I. Title

BL624.O54 2014     204'.2     QBI14-600066

### Published by ASEMC PRESS

P.O. Box 44
South Newfane • Vermont USA 05351

*Cover art by Damian Bland*
*Editing, design & layout by Denis Ouellette*

*More information, addition copies and formats,
and cover art prints available at*

## UpraisedChalice.com

*Printed in the United States of America*

*For Azure and Jesse
who have taught me so much
about love.*

# Contents

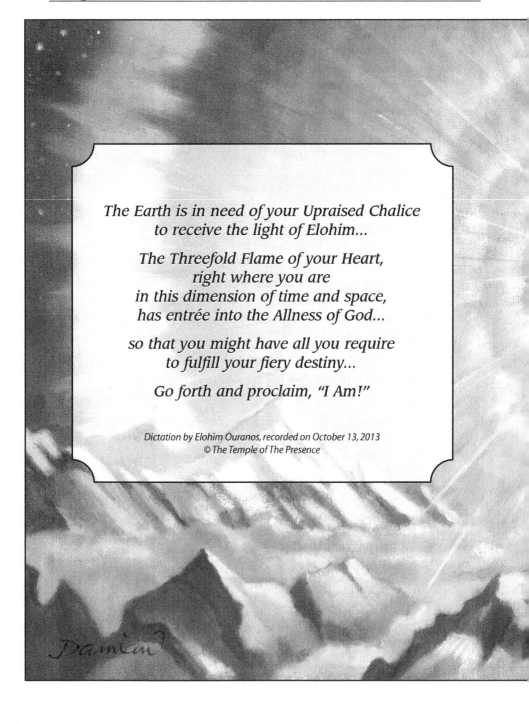

The Earth is in need of your Upraised Chalice
to receive the light of Elohim...

The Threefold Flame of your Heart,
right where you are
in this dimension of time and space,
has entrée into the Allness of God...

so that you might have all you require
to fulfill your fiery destiny...

Go forth and proclaim, "I Am!"

Dictation by Elohim Ouranos, recorded on October 13, 2013
© The Temple of The Presence

*An Upraised Chalice* ~ Cover artist Damian Bland
Color prints available at <u>UpraisedChalice.com</u>

# *Foreword*

*By David Tame*

E xtraordinary lives are usually lived by extraordinary people. Gene O'Neil is, without a doubt, an extraordinary person who became that way because of his many unusual, miracle-filled and frankly stunning experiences. Gene wouldn't call himself exceptional; in his words he's a regular "hard-headed" guy who was chosen, for some reason, to experience life in a most unusual way. Until he set his experiences down on paper, I didn't quite know just how profound his stories were. They transformed me and they probably will you—in fact, Gene intends his life story to be a prologue and a stepping-stone for you to look at your own life in a new light.

Gene's experiences propelled him onto a spiritual path, although not of the monk-in-a-cave variety. These days, we can find mystical people of all kinds anywhere. Gene is here to show us that anyone's life becomes mystical when it is lived as "an upraised chalice." Be open to God's Presence in your life—place that first—and all will be well with you. In fact, miracles may become quite ordinary.

I first met Gene in the closing days of June 1999. I was due to arrive from England at a point near his home in Vermont and to be picked up by him so as to stay overnight, after which it was arranged we'd both go the next day a few hours further to a twelve-day spiritual retreat. I'd flown into Boston and then caught a bus into the green, wooded hills of New England. And being English, perhaps in the back of my mind, I had expected some formal greeting as Gene drew up in his car. Well, Gene is a man of action, very much anchored in the physical world. And while our meeting was fine, my baggage was in the trunk and we were underway within mere seconds, Gene also introducing me to the NASA employee, Alex, who was with him.

Upon reaching his 100 acres of land in the Vermont hills, with its beautiful brooks and waterfalls, before ever reaching the house or getting my head under a roof, Gene prevailed upon us that we must first visit his special waterfall swimming place. A few hours before, I had been 30,000 feet in the air. Now, again a fair distance above sea level and in the slightly chilly and drizzly late afternoon, I found myself climbing down rocks surrounded by thick woods in the wake of Gene and a NASA scientist to go skinny-dipping in a deep, natural pool, fed by a magical waterfall and its refreshingly cold, mountain water!

That evening, and on many evenings to come, I got to know Gene better. We soon discovered that we had in common the challenging overland journey young people used to take in the '60s and '70s, from Europe to India and the Himalayas. We'd both undertaken this life-changing rite of passage at exactly the same ages of 21–22, but Gene ahead of me by three years. I held the special knife, with the sun inlaid on one side of the handle and the moon on the other, given to him in the Himalayas by a Buddhist lama.

And I heard from Gene's own lips—as you'll read here—of the astonishing encounter with a creature, with it on the outside of the barred door of a yak-herder's hut and Gene and his friend on the inside. When he writes of this encounter in this book: "We threw ourselves up against the far wall and grabbed for our knives, terrified as to what would surely come next," it is this ceremonial knife from that Tibetan lama that Gene had in his hand.

Gene isn't an air-headed visionary; he doesn't make up stories. So when he relates, for instance, that Archangel Michael spoke to him and saved his life, I believe it's the solid truth—and one that is, in fact, more real than ordinary and mundane experience, because it reveals to us the exalted Reality beyond this one. Such experiences afford us important glimpses into a way of life that has an expanded purpose and perspective—a life lived as an upraised chalice.

Gene believes his extraordinary life was indeed renewed more than once for higher purposes. One of these purposes is most assuredly the recording of his experiences and collecting them here in a labor of love and gratitude—to God and His emissaries, for posterity, but more directly and most sincerely, for you. ൠ

*David Tame is the author of*
The Secret Power of Music *and*
Beethoven and the Spiritual Path

# *Dedication*

This work is dedicated to those pure, beautiful children (of all ages) who have incarnated in these times to play their part in the great awakening of humanity—that they may know that they are not alone in the quiet, unformed yearnings of their hearts.

It is understood, at the inception of this work, that some will find the very concepts herein and many of my experiences detailed here to be astonishing, even unbelievable (depending on one's frame of reference). I assure you that it's all truly stated, with no literary license or exaggeration.

There are many thousands of others who have also had firsthand experiences in these matters and who have, through the purity of their lives, experienced direct interactions with their Divine Presence—the *I Am That I Am* within—and encounters with the Great Ones, be they angels or masters, similar to what I have detailed here.

It is also true that there are many more who are on the verge of remembering, in the purity of their hearts, that they are more than the sum total of their experiences in this lifetime—that they have come here for a sacred reason.

It's for all of you that this accounting is written. Although it's a road map of my long journey, my hope is that it will assist you in your own journey of discovery that you might experiment with these Great Laws yourself, and see what fruit they bring to your lives. The Great Ones have stated that each individual's Path is unique but they all proceed from the pure aspirations welling up in the Silence of the Heart, eventually merging in the great reunion with the Individualized Presence of God, the *I Am That I Am* within.

Lastly, this accounting is written for those who love, because it is only through the purity of loving that we can truly perceive. ⚘

# *Acknowledgment*

On this Christmas Day, 2013, now that this project is completed, I express my endless gratitude for all who have made this long story possible.

First and foremost to the Divine Presence, the *I AM That I AM* within, to Archangel Michael, and to our elder Brothers and Sisters Ascended whom I refer to as the Great Ones—all who have assisted me in so many ways.

To Heaven-sent Joanne, the mother of our son, who has held the Mother Flame and nourished the altars here with her love, and her prayers and adorations, these past twenty years. Her compassion, grace, and organizational abilities have touched many and assisted in creating a home of Light that has been a refuge from the storm.

To Denis, Damian and David—my three spiritual-warrior brothers-in-arms. Denis Ouellette was the primary editor and layout artist. His support has been another example of divine assistance in smoothing out the concepts, the flow, and the look that I sought to present.

Damian Bland has painted the artwork on the cover that depicts the vision that I was first given in a meditation with Archangel Michael, and seen independently by Damian himself, and now may be experienced by many—the vision of *An Upraised Chalice*. (Color prints of this painting can be obtained at UpraisedChalice.com.)

David Tame was the first to give me the support and literary direction that I needed on the first draft of the story. His Foreword graces the opening of this book. ❧

Recorder/Chuck Blake

One of two cars involved in the Factory Hollow accident Tuesday is towed from scene.

# Factory Hollow crash claims life of Athol man

By CHARLES L. KELLER
Recorder Staff

GREENFIELD — A two-car crash on Route 2 in Factory Hollow at about 12:30 p.m. Tuesday claimed the life of a 30-year-old Athol man and hospitalized the other driver, a 35-year-old man from Wilmington, Vt.

It was the second fatal auto accident in the county in as many days, the fifth in the past three weeks and the 20th in 1985.

William P. Carlson of White Pond Road, Athol, was taken to Franklin Medical Center by Mercy Ambulance where he died about 30 minutes later. Mercy personnel found Carlson alive at the scene, but had a difficult time at one point finding a pulse.

Dr. Albert B. Giknis of Turners Falls, Eastern Franklin District medical examiner, said an autopsy on Carlson was to be performed this morning. Carlson suffered severe head and chest injuries.

On Monday, Lawrence R. Waldron Jr., 37, of Wilmington, Vt., died when his car left Colrain Road in Shelburne and struck two trees. Dr. Giknis said today that an autopsy showed Waldron died of multiple injuries. "He could have survived any one of them," Giknis said, "but put them all together and he didn't have a chance."

In Tuesday's accident, Carlson was driving west on Route 2 when he collided with a car being driven east by Eugene J. O'Neil, 35, of Newfane, Vt.

The accident occurred at the junction of Route 2 and Factory Hollow Road.

Greenfield police officer Roger S. Kisloski said O'Neil told him the Carlson car "just seemed to turn into his lane." That observation was corroborated by Michael Wellington of Swanzey, N.H., who was driving a Coca Cola vehicle behind the Carlson car. Neither could tell why. John Roberts of Attleboro, who was driving a Sysco truck behind the O'Neil vehicle, said he thought he saw Carlson turn his

See ACCIDENTS Page 16

Article from the Greenfield Recorder (Greenfield, Massachusetts) dated Dec. 4, 1985, showing my car being towed away after the fatal accident.

# Introduction

For over a month now the premonitions got stronger almost every day. Something very unpleasant was approaching. I knew that I was going to have to be physically alert and supercharged with the Light of my Presence if I was going to be able to deal with whatever it was that I was feeling. My morning meditations were strong and clear and the mantras that I used seemed even more powerful; still, I knew within that this appointment was coming and could not be avoided. I told my family about these premonitions and made sure my affairs were in order. I thought the plane I was flying would crash.

On December 3, 1985, at around noon I was driving my car about 70 mph on my way to the airport to conduct a flight lesson for two of my students. My outer consciousness was busy with reviewing the flight plan that we would follow for the long training flight to Maine. Suddenly there was a soft explosion of Light immediately in front and to the side of me, a sphere of fire perhaps a foot in diameter appeared in front of the dashboard stereo of my car. In this sphere of fire that was before me, yet enveloped me, like a thunderclap, Archangel Michael commanded me to do a decree, a fiat of protection. I was shocked, dazed by this all-encompassing experience, time seemed to slow down and I reduced my speed to perhaps 50 mph instantly engaging in the powerful prayer that I was commanded to give. It was less than a minute later that a car in the opposite direction lost control, crossed into my lane, and hit me head-on. Both drivers, myself and the man who lost control, were killed. I was sent back, repeatedly.

The story that you are about to read details the lifelong chain of events that brought about Archangel Michael's intercessions, the reasons why I believe they happened, and the prior and subsequent interaction with the Great Ones that have so shaped my life. As remarkable as this may be, there is a deeper story here—one that is vast in its implications and that contains a challenge to all who seek to know the Truth. That challenge involves the discovery of the answers to those penetrating questions: *"Who are we?"* and *"Why are we here?"* ଔ

# 1 ~ **Looking at the Big Picture**

I am a hardened man with little patience for mediocrity—a multi-professional man who is well versed and applied in the physical sciences. I live on a homestead that I carved out of a forested mountaintop. I still wear the body of a warrior many years younger than my 62 summers. I am a father, a lover, a builder, a teacher, and I have always been a seeker of the ancient wisdom. This story is about the life-long yearning and striving of a boy to remember, to awaken to what he could only dream about through the mists. As you continue to read about these great adventures, remember that I am taking no literary license here—it all happened as it is stated.

Looking at the big picture gives most of us pause for concern. For many decades now, we have watched the world we live in become more unsettled. Populations have increased dramatically; food and shelter throughout the world, even in the United States, are concerns for many. Many areas of the Earth are experiencing climate change, punctuated by extreme weather conditions. Severe drought, heavy rains, and extreme temperature-swings threaten world food production. The world economy seems to teeter on the brink of insolvency, experiencing one crisis after another. This makes it difficult for many to make ends meet, which in turn, serves to fuel more credit-card debt, which exacerbates the debt crisis. The worldwide geopolitical conflicts, often fueled by extremist religious dogmas, seem to envelop more countries and produce unimaginable horror year after year.

Many feel a cultural malaise has settled in. Exposed to continual media broadcasts concerning these disturbing worldwide events, many become used to it, numb, and indifferent to what is happening around them. We cringe as our children grow up in this environment, exposed to all of this. They seek to emulate the lifestyles that are presented to them by the so-called entertainment industry and by corporate advertising. This in turn outpictures in our children's lives, effectively steering new generations into lifestyles that give less importance to altruistic behaviors and ideals and great importance to materialistic pursuits. Our children are confronted with an almost irreconcilable gulf between the innocence they know in their hearts and the cold and too often violent images that are served up by the media. Tragically and more and more frequently, this outpictures in actions of undreamed horror that in some instances can bring an entire nation to its knees. There is a growing sense among many that something major is missing in our civilization—a lack of moral compass, a lack of direction. Many are looking for answers.

With all the above as background, we are caught up in our daily lives. The days turn into weeks and the months into years. Before you know it, we're not kids anymore—relationships, careers, families, and responsibilities have arrived. For many in this culture, it's almost a frantic pace of doing, doing, doing, for both us and our families.

The years move forward and everyone is attending to their life's priorities, focusing on how to be happy, make a living, raise a family. The years turn into decades and sooner or later, (hopefully later) sickness or accidents happen and all are again confronted with the big questions: Why? What's next? What has this life that I've lived been about? As one begins to consider their own eventual departure: What have I been able to do to make things a little better? What have I passed along to make others' lives more beautiful?

Some, hopefully many of us, know that somewhere, way deep inside, that there is a reason for our life that still encompasses what every parent wants for their children, but goes beyond that. Perhaps it is what we felt in the idealism of our youth, before we became jaded by life's responsibilities, that comes closest to touching this sense of a life mission.

As a child there was a sense conveyed by family, and by perhaps a more innocent world around us, that God was guiding our lives. However, as the years rolled by, many started asking questions that could no longer be suitably answered by the simplistic dogma of organized religions.

The counterculture of the 1960s and 70s led the way to my generation's questioning established authority symbols and organizations that governed our lives, from our government right down to the church. Did these times make the new generations smarter, less willing to be led by a ring through the nose? Many of us have, by this phase in humanity's slow awakening, walked away from the hollow dogmas found in most religions, feeling that God is more evident in a child's smile, in the kiss of the beloved, or in a beautiful place on a beautiful day.

Some whose thirst for understanding could not be sated by this culture's materialistic activities have explored other options.

This is the account of one such person's journey, seeking to understand what this life is all about. The story details my first outer contact with the concept of the Brotherhood of Light—the organization of the Great Masters of Wisdom comprised of those who have "graduated from Earth's schoolroom" and become the immortal Great Ones. Then as the years went by, my burning drive to obtain first-hand experience with these Masters and their Teachings—not just from book knowledge, but through physical-plane, concrete integration with the Great Laws of Life and the transformative power that the wielding of this knowledge brings into life's experiences—a power that transcends and supersedes physical limitations.

What makes this story perhaps a bit more interesting is my adamant, unrelenting drive to make sense of it all, come hell or high water, no matter the outer cost. I'll recount the long scope of the journey, including the repeated physical intercessions of the Ascended Masters, including Archangel Michael in multiple life-and-death circumstances (including all the details of the fatal car accident I mentioned earlier). All of this has led to an ongoing crescendo of

Life that leaves me awestruck and completely humbled by the glorious majesty of God's Master Plan, and which has propelled this accounting forward so that others might benefit. ❧

# 2 ~ **The Point of This Exercise**

W e are at a critical junction in our civilization's history. There are many in embodiment now who have been prepared for many lifetimes to take part in what is now unfolding across the face of the Earth. Due to the veil of forgetfulness that is lowered upon each individual's memory, prior to their physical incarnation, we all most must go about our lives until some event occurs that jars our memory. Hopefully it's a beautiful and peaceful event that does this. Somewhere there will be a key that will begin to part the veil and the individual will begin the process of remembering that they are more than just the experiences of this lifetime—that there is a Great Plan unfolding.

This is a delicate process, easily thwarted or stopped by the pressures of the outer world; so what to do to assist in this process— to reinforce such a personal, gentle awakening? My response to the question that I've posed here is what has been burning within me for decades. I have long known that I must get my experiences out there. I've got to use the sheer immensity of the telling of the Masters and Michael's intercessions in my life, coupled with all that is chronicled here that has forged this lifetime, to paint a vivid picture of how these Laws work in an individual's life. A prayer that some will recognize as truth, in the quiet spaces of their heart, what is stated here.

I will not hold back in the use of strong language and descriptions to convey these experiences and concepts. The weight and the record of this lifetime's experiences should dispel any thoughts that what is contained herein is mere fantasy. The forging of this lifetime's experiences has directly prepared the way for this work to come forth now. It is my deepest prayer that what I will relate in this work might benefit those who are unwilling to accept the status quo of *Samsara*. (The Sanskrit word *Samsara* means "journeying." In Buddhism,

Hinduism, and Jainism, *Samsara* is defined as a cycle of birth, death, and rebirth.)

We are all Sons and Daughters of God and yet, the Great Laws of Life are immutable. The difficult circumstances of our lives, the problems that we face, individually and collectively, are a direct result of our ignorance of these Laws. It is imperative that we awaken quickly, those of us who are ready, and, that we work within the framework of these Laws for our liberation and for the quickening and healing of humanity and our planet.

This work will not leave the reader high and dry without a place to go. At the conclusion of this accounting, I include recommended reading list where the reader will be able to obtain more information on the history of the Brotherhood of Light's work. More directly, it introduces The Temple of The Presence, which is the accelerated and present-day work of this Brotherhood.

What is very interesting is that many of the accounts with the Great Masters appeared in the current era within a few decades, on either side of 1900s. These books arose on four continents, and all contain accounts of this same Brotherhood of Light, written by individuals who made contact with the Masters and sought to bring their teaching to greater public awareness. There were several major thrusts of the Brotherhood's outer work over the past hundred years or so—each laying the foundation for those that were to follow. From the Theosophical Society (circa late 1880s–early 1900s) to the I Am Activity (circa 1930s and 40s), to the Bridge to Freedom (circa 1950s), to The Summit Lighthouse (1960s–1990s), to the current, vanguard activity of the Brotherhood that is ongoing today, known as The Temple of The Presence.

The reader will discover as this story unfolds that I'm not talking about a "book knowledge" of the Ancient Sacred Sciences here, but of a physically tangible way of living life that produces wonderful and far-reaching results. The Masters have made the statement that if an individual wishes to know of and experience the Path for themselves, they may employ a specific series of exercises, which I will detail later in this work. When these simple exercises are undertaken for a period of time, so much change will be evident in the individual's life that they will apprehend with certainty the reality of what is now opening before them. This Sacred Wisdom will enable them, by their free-will choice, to purify and accelerate their being, to begin the process of pushing back the veil of forgetfulness, and integrate more and more with the Teachings of the Ascended Masters. The end-point of this sacred process is the reunion with our Individual I Am Presence. As such, we will reach our full potential as Sons or Daughters of God wielding the absolute Love, Wisdom, and Power of the *I AM That I AM* within, just as Jesus and so many others have done. ∞

# 3 ~ **Preparation for What Is to Come**

Perhaps it's due to cultural differences, perhaps due to women's more intrinsic intuitional faculties, but it seems to me that most men are far less inclined to consider, let alone seek an understanding of, the great Mysteries of Life that are beyond the stone walls of culturally imposed dogma. So how to present this material to those whose focus has been upon making their way in the world, those who have been too occupied with their outer life to take a deep breath and pause and take stock of it all? (Certainly a major challenge—and perhaps why I've put off this accounting for a very long time.) Because of the unusual (at least to most in this society) experiences detailed in this accounting, it may be helpful for the reader to have a bit of background to establish a better understanding of what follows.

The brief biographical overview included here primarily deals with the outer world circumstances and life experiences that are similar to what most people have over the course of their life. However, over the course of my "adult life" there were at least three instances where Divine intervention kept me in this body, or brought me back into it. One of these (the car accident already mentioned) became somewhat well known—all of which, when one takes into consideration the mechanics of the situation and the reasons why these experiences occurred, are truly remarkable and, more importantly, contain aspects of the Great Laws in action from which others might surely benefit.

Though little in this material world captures one's attention like the instances of one's imminent demise detailed here—the width and breadth of the unfolding experiences conveyed in the bulk of this work (from Chapter 7 on, right through to the present day) framed by such outer beauty and perfection allude to a much bigger picture and a greater design than just the chance happening of fate. It is for this reason that I set this forth now—that others, no matter how deeply enmeshed in the pains and joys of the material world, might know of the teachings of the Masters and the great Laws that govern all.

## *Outer Background*

After the military and three semesters of college, I left college for a year and a half to embark on a life-altering quest to find out who I was. I traveled solo throughout Europe, Israel, and then throughout southern Asia. I was aware throughout this period that I was on a mission. The detailed, remarkable experiences that took place during these adventures provided a framework, a new perspective, through which I have lived this life.

I returned to the states and to college and immediately started flight training. Within a few years, I became a professional pilot, and a few years later, a flight instructor. Flying was a perfect fit for me. Taking off from the Earth and climbing thousands of feet into the sky, traveling hundreds of miles and then coming back to the Earth again was exhilarating. Watching the amazing beauty of the Earth, the rivers, the cities and the farmlands pass by beneath the aircraft I was piloting conveyed a sense of peace and order that was not so present for me on the ground.

Flying in and out of the major airports in the northeastern United States, especially in IFR conditions (Instrument Flight Rules), that is, when weather conditions make flying by outside visual reference impossible, was always an extremely rewarding technical challenge. As wonderful as professional aviation is, I was completely enthralled with hang gliding. Strapping into a hang glider and running off a several hundred foot high cliff to soar like a bird without any sound save the rushing of the wind is the closest thing to heaven that I've experienced in my physical body.

From India forward, the beginning of every day, the most

important part of my day, began in prayer and meditation. It was in my morning meditation that I sought to align myself with my Presence, to keep that perspective, to go about doing the things that needed doing that day centered in that peace. I used the techniques that I had learned in India from my experiences with the teachings from the great Indian masters including Sri Aurobindo (1872–1950) who was considered the Thomas Jefferson of India, from Yogananda (1893–1952) the Indian sage who brought the spiritual traditions of India to America from 1920 up to 1952, when he made his transition, and from the Theosophical Society's writings (1875–forward), the organization mentioned earlier and later in this accounting, which was an early thrust of the Brotherhood of Light to convey the teaching of the ancient wisdom to the western world.

The biggest challenge for me upon returning to this country after a year and a half was to be able to hold to the deep peace, the inner attunement, that I learned how to draw forth while living in India. In order to do this, I had to place myself in a harmonious, rural environment—cites and large towns felt too chaotic to me. After moving around for several years, I knew that I had to find a special piece of land and build a homestead.

Flying around the northeastern United States several times a week in the course of making a living gave me a clear perspective on the lay of the land and I found there was always something special about southern Vermont. In 1977, I was led to a magical piece of land that met my criteria, a large parcel situated in a mountain bowl with southern exposure, amazingly beautiful mountain brooks and waterfalls with deep swimming holes. Between the two brooks were beautiful, rolling, forested hills and an area that had a special feel to it, an amazing fragrance that I first inhaled that summer day in 77. I just sat down and went into meditation on this spot, listening to the soft roar of the two brooks that surrounded me, the fragrance of the summer forest transporting me. It was here that I would build a home.

After a lot of research, I built a passive-solar home on that spot and the next year, again after a lot of research, built a hydroelectric system on the larger of the two brooks to provide all of our power. Both of these were immense projects for me in fields that I had next to no experience. I hired a friend who was a builder to teach me how to build, and I hired another friend who was an electrical engineer to help me design the hydroelectric plant. This consisted of 1000 feet of 6-inch plastic pipe that was buried through the forest beside the brook so that it wouldn't be noticeable or disrupt the sacred, pristine beauty of the roaring brook. Over this 1000-foot run of pipe (called a penstock) we had to use dynamite several times to blow up rock ledge that blocked our excavation. Over this 1000-foot run, the penstock dropped 100 feet in elevation, creating 45 psi (pounds per square inch) of pressure at the turbine house. I ran wires from the generator in the turbine house for a half-mile up to my home and fed the power directly into a large battery bank that supplied our electrical requirements. This was our only source of electricity for 14 years.

But there were "complications." Three or four years after the hydroelectric plant was up and running 365 days a year, the newly elected town "officials" decided to sue me, pressing legal charges against me for not getting "their permission" to build this hydroelectric plant on the large tract of land that I owned. They ordered that I dismantle it completely—the 2-foot by 20-foot concrete dam, the 1000 feet of penstock, and the turbine house. They levied a $250 fine upon me for every day that the system was still in place. They told me that I didn't get their permission to build it. I told them that I asked God and God told me that it was OK, so I built it. Oh well—they didn't like that very much.

A few weeks later, I was inundated by state and federal officials who began surveying, measuring, and testing every facet of the system, since the town officials told them that my system was a hazard to the community. (My nearest neighbors were a mile or more away.) The officials all agreed that my system was a model of efficiency and couldn't understand the town's objection. A few days later, I met the Governor of Vermont while she was campaigning for re-election and told her of my predicament. She became very interested and asked her aide to get all the details. A week later, I received a notification from the town that all charges were being dropped. I was then asked by the Governor's Office to draw up a set of guidelines that were incorporated into a new law for the state of Vermont encouraging the development of small hydroelectric systems.

Fast-forward now. I was turning 40 and getting tired of flying around for a living. After a year of research, I designed and built what became known by those in the field as a state-of-the-art aquaculture facility. Using the abundant pure water on this land, I built a large enclosed building on 3 levels. Each level had three 15-foot by 42-inch circular rearing tanks in which thousands of trout were raised. Utilizing pure oxygen and ozone injection, the passive-solar hatchery allowed our fish to grow from fry (baby trout) to 12 inches in under a year. This was the most technically difficult and demanding project that I had ever been involved with.

Although I loved the science and all the engineering involved in this business, it was immensely labor intensive and after a few years I was asking myself, "What did I get myself in to?" Finally, I got the business to start making money and soon couldn't supply the demand I had created for our fish within southern Vermont. Our smoked trout got top honors at the fêted Taste of Vermont Food Festival.

Still, I knew that I had to get out of that business. For years in my morning meditation, I presented that question to my Father, my Presence, in my prayers and meditations. Finally after several years in this business, right after I finally found someone who loved doing the work who would be the manager of the facility, my desire unexpectedly manifested. I got a call from my friend who ran Vermont Fish and Wildlife fisheries, the regulatory agency that governed all aquaculture in the state. They told me that the 50,000 fry, which I had purchased from another out of state facility to raise in my operation, were contaminated. The other company had forged federal- and state-mandated inspection reports, knowingly committing fraud, and had sold me fry that were not allowed to cross state borders.

In the space of a fifteen-minute phone call, my showcase

aquaculture facility was shut down and I was ordered to kill all the fish, dismantle the entire structure and sterilize everything with toxic chemicals! Seven years of intensely hard work was over. Now I was confronted with how to pay off the loans that I obtained for the business, using my home and land as collateral. Then, on top of that, I needed to figure out how to make a living at the age of 47.

I can clearly recall that, while listening to my friend from Vermont Fish and Wildlife tell me that my facility had to be closed, I knew it was the direct answer to my yearning to be free of this aquaculture business. I knew that I was to be faced with a huge challenge of orchestrating a legal action against the company that committed federal fraud for the sake of divesting themselves of a few thousand dollars of sick fry. I knew it was literally going to be a trial-by-fire and that the only way that we (my family) would prevail and not lose our home to federal and state foreclosure was to go deeper and deeper into meditation. I needed to charge myself so full of Light that I would be able to navigate through these very troubled waters and stay clear of all the chaos and fear that such a dire financial legal situation was bringing to me and my world.

Immediately after this phone call with the state, I went out and sat in meditation by the pond where I would meditate every morning when the weather was nice. I offered it all up to whatever was the will of my Presence, whatever was the greater plan for me and this lifetime. I knew it was way beyond my outer abilities to orchestrate what I was about to go through. With all sales over, no money would be coming in to buy food for my family, no money to pay household bills and mortgage, no money to pay the much larger notes to the federal and state governments for this business that was now over. My consciousness was reeling with the implications of this. It was all such an immense shock, but still, I knew it was all part of the Master Plan and that we would prevail.

From my first meditation after getting this news, I knew that somehow this would all work out but that I had to stay constantly centered in my Presence so I could direct what needed to happen. I had to trust my Presence and the Masters who were involved in my life that no matter how greatly loomed the appearance of these dire circumstances, we would get through it, because "I Am the Only Presence Acting Everywhere." This is a very powerful affirmation taught by the great master Saint Germain in the 1930s. The "I Am" is the I Am Presence individualized within each person who is giving this command, not the human consciousness, and therefore Perfection must come forth.

The aquaculture facility that I designed was a huge, complicated operation but it was extremely efficient. All the byproducts of the hatchery were composted so there was no environmental pollution even though I was raising thousands of pounds of fish every year.

Because we were a showcase operation for the state of Vermont, we had people coming from all over the northeast to learn how we were able to grow our fish so large in such a short period of time with so little water. A representative of the United Nations who heard about what we were doing visited us and I was asked if I would consider working with the UN to develop this type of aquaculture facility in the developing countries of Africa and Asia as a local, high-protein food source.

As I shared, I had every penny I had tied up in this business and I wasn't about to lie down and let the legal threats and positioning from the other company's attorneys deter my adamant resolve to be justly compensated for the loss of my business. I was then 46 and had to figure out a new way of making a living to support my family—as many of you know, not an easy task at that stage of the game.

The state of Vermont had the actual "smoking gun," the forged inspection document that proved the fraud of the other large company. I knew of a few lawyers in the local town and engaged one of them to represent us. After this attorney told me that we might get a settlement for $10,000, I laughed and fired him. I retained a second team of attorneys who seemed more interested in developing this complicated case, but after a few months with them, seeing their mediocre performance, I realized that they just didn't have the ability to go up against this large company's team of attorneys, who were trying to intimidate us into accepting a very small settlement. So I fired the second team of attorneys and hired a larger firm whose track record with large cases appeared more convincing.

Still we ended up doing much of the investigative work for these attorneys, leaving them to deal with the never-ending legal documents that such a complicated federal suit produces. We obtained all of the documents from the state that proved our case. We provided all of the supporting documents about our business and even researched and obtained hidden information that the other side didn't wish to reveal to the court.

The case was then moved from the state to the federal court because of the interstate fraud. Still, our attorney tried to get us to settle for a pittance. In a federal mediation, he told us to accept less than a $40,000 settlement, which wouldn't even cover half of our business loans. I got up and walked out of the room after telling several attorneys that I'd see them in court.

This back-and-forth between our attorneys and the other side's attorneys became very intense and bitter. The other side was trying to discredit our business by every means imaginable. I was put into the position of having to justify my business that I had spent several years and all of our money building. The entire experience was infuriating. Still, throughout it all, I was able to maintain my morning meditations and inner attunement throughout the difficult days and the months of this two-year trial.

Finally, in the last few months before the federal-court trial, the other side's settlement offer began to increase in size. Our attorney was very upset when I angrily refused a $75,000, and then a $100,000 settlement offer. He was getting 33% and was very concerned that he might not get his money.

Over the next few months, the process became very intense as the settlement offers increased. I thought our attorney would have a stroke he was so upset. Still in every meeting with the other side, I was resolved to go the distance come hell or high water. This large corporation destroyed my business and put my family in jeopardy and I just wasn't going to back down and whimper and gratefully accept their offer. It went on this way right up to the night before the trial began. My attorney called me during a family dinner.

The other side, in their desperation, made a large offer that would allow us to pay off all the notes, get out of debt, and have a little money to start a new life with. Our attorney said it was the largest settlement offer he ever heard of in this state in a civil trial and that I would be crazy not to accept it. He reminded me that even if I won a larger award at the trial, which was to begin on the following day, it would take me a long time to get the money with appeals, and then the company might go bankrupt. After weighing everything, I reluctantly accepted the offer.

Thus ended this aquaculture chapter of my life. It was perhaps a year after we began the legal ordeal that The Temple of The Presence moved to Vermont.

Now at this early point in this story, with my outer physical plane background laid out, the reader will have a much better idea of the physical-plane sciences and drive (and challenges) that are the cornerstone of this outer lifetime. Keep this big picture in mind as I relate the formative experiences that forged this lifetime, which eventually opened my heart, my consciousness to a greater reality that I could only just touch in my younger years. I wish the reader to have this co-measurement as the more intense and magical events unfold in the timeline of this life, for this sets the stage that helps to understand why I was miraculously protected in multiple near-death encounters detailed in this work. ଔ

# 4 ~ The Bigger Picture

There comes a time in the life-cycle of every Son and Daughter of God when it's time to wake up as to why we are here and to what Life is all about. For some, this awakening progresses gently throughout their lifetime. For others, this process is born out of seeming misfortune, often associated with traumatic events, or occurs in the final years (even the moments) of a particular lifetime. Then as the individual confronts their sense of self, the great mystery descends upon them, sometimes with a crushing weight of sadness, as the reality of the impermanence and unpredictability of this physical life can no longer be ignored.

For a long time this drama has taken place over and over again for all of us. In the East, it's called *Samsara*—the Wheel of Rebirth. In the West, the doctrine of reincarnation was taught in the earliest books of the Bible, in the foundations of Judaism, and sprinkled throughout the New Testament and the Gnostic Gospels chronicling Jesus' great victory. The fact is that reincarnation is a consistent theme throughout most of the world's religious traditions, although veiled or blocked in the outer branches of Christianity, but not its mystery schools.

So now, in the dawning of the 21st century, life goes on. But now there are many, scattered across this beautiful planet, who have stepped outside the bounds of organized religion in their desire to integrate this relentless urging from within their hearts. This deep, unformed need is the inborn drive to comprehend, to be integrated with this Supreme Reality that they can touch within their hearts, in the quiet moments of their lives. This thirst for a closer relationship with God outside of the mold of organized religion has given birth to myriad forms of spiritual expression.

The profusion of new-age mysticism, the interest in eastern religious traditions, and an increasing fascination with angels, are all outward examples of this great inner quickening. Even the media has taken note of this expanding interest in things of the spirit. It is almost as if these aspirants seek to "take Heaven by storm," using every possible means available to get there.

But then, as with all things under Heaven, there is a rhyme and a reason to it all. While this is not apparent to those who are so caught up in the physical aspects of their lives, it becomes more and more apparent to those who were born into this lifetime with a sense that they had something that they were supposed to do—that there was something deep within them that spoke, oh so softly, of the cause behind the effect. Some of these individuals grew up in this world, often thinking that they were alone, that they were the victim of such a sensitivity of heart that they had to learn, at an early age, how to protect themselves from the harsh experiences that growing up in this world brings to many.

Unfortunately, this learned behavior, motivated by self-preservation, served to also harden their heart, dampening the innate sense of love, joy, purity and innocence of the child, which in Reality is their Divine birthright.

Thus the child grew up, propelled here and there in life's circumstances by the actions that they had initiated in previous lifetimes (karma). Now such an individual knows deeply within their heart of the Omnipresence of the Divine. They lead their lives according to the dictates of their hearts, seeking to live in harmony and peace with as much love as any of us can get. And on their journey through life's highways, knowingly or unknowingly, they have the ear of their consciousness cocked to listen for a certain vibration— the vibration that they once knew very clearly as young children, the vibration of Home, and Purity, and Innocence, which is the vibration of the Love of God.

Somewhere in time, God willing, these individuals (Individualizations of God) will either meet someone, pick up a book, hear a broadcast, attend a presentation or have a dream where again they recognize that oh-so sweet vibration that they once knew so long ago. This sacred experience is meted out by their own I Am Presence and the Ascended Hosts and determined by the preparation and purity of the individual's heart. At such a time, the Great Ascended Masters through the Grace of God, open the aspirant's consciousness and heart and allow for the quickening of the individual into the precepts of the Great Laws that they can safely outpicture in their lives at the present moment. Thus the individual has arrived in the lifetime where they are so blessed to be able to consciously engage upon the Path for which all of their lifetimes have been in training. Now they are consciously on their way Home.

Then comes the awareness that this is what they've known all along, since their earliest remembrances in this lifetime and sometimes before that. There is the vague recollection that this Divine Order and Perfection that they can just barely perceive has been with them, in the background, for a very long time. There is a sense of Holy Awe as to the purpose that is opening and unfolding as if through the mists before their consciousness.

To many, when the knowledge first comes that there is a very real, tangible, celestial (or extra-dimensional) association of Great Beings who have been charged with the overseeing of the affairs of humanity, it is not such a surprise. In fact, all cultures and religions point to such a Divine organization; albeit, it is called by many different names, depending on the cultural/religious tradition that refers to it. Many of us who have been searching for this Ancient Wisdom and connection with our Divine Source for many, many years have come to know these great beings as the Great Masters of Wisdom or the Ascended Masters.

Would that all could know of the great love and assistance given to all, especially to those on the Path of self-awakening, by the Great Ones known as the Ascended Masters, who have walked this Earth, just like you and I, in their various embodiments prior to their Ascension. The Ascended Masters are the Great Ones, who have brought forth the initial purity of all the world's great religions, as well as all of the achievements of humanity. They are those who wield the unlimited Love, Wisdom, and Power of God for and on behalf of all life everywhere. The scope of their service to Life is all but impossible to assess, for indeed, they have become One with God through the initiation of the Ascension, just as Jesus demonstrated almost two thousand years ago.

From that absolute Union with their own I Am Presence, the Ascended Masters minister, with the limitless love of a parent for their child, to the awakening Christ Identity in all. Their Great Work is the awakening of mankind to the reality of the Mighty Presence of God I AM, individualized in every person. The Masters assist in the nourishing and the expansion of that identity into the fullness of each one's Divine Plan. In this process, the Divine Spark known as the Threefold Flame of Love, Wisdom and Power within the heart expands and one's world begins to become transformed. Gradually our outer lives take on those patterns of perfection that is "on Earth even as it is in Heaven."

Now, by the Grace of God, humanity is at the point in its evolution where this Ancient Wisdom can be shared with many. As recently as eighty years ago, this Sacred Teaching was only available to those initiates who had the inner attainment to be able to travel to the Retreats of the Great Masters in their finer bodies while asleep. For countless centuries this Knowledge was passed down to those few among humanity who had the wherewithal to follow the soft promptings of their hearts in search of the reason for it All.

Now the cycles have turned. The Piscean age has concluded and the Aquarian age has come. The Great Lords of Life have given the Dispensation for the awakening of humanity to the reality of their Divine birthright. Heaven has again sent forth its Messengers to remind us of all that we've forgotten over centuries of lifetimes. That we are indeed Sons and Daughters of God, just as Jesus said in the Sermon on the Mount. The call has gone forth for Knowledge of the I Am Presence and the Violet Transmuting Flame of Mercy's Grace to be made available to those among humanity who have "eyes to see and ears to hear," and I might add, a heart to feel the quickening, as the Sacred Fire from our own I Am Presence descends and the process of the Re-Union unfolds. ❧

# 5 ~ **How to Convey?**

How does one begin to convey an early childhood memory of perfection and love that finally took form with my first conscious reminder at thirteen that there always was a Brotherhood of Light comprised of the Great Masters of Wisdom?

How does one describe this yearning that was always in the background of my early experiences, a yearning to discover, perhaps to remember, why these Great Masters were so important to me?

How does one begin to compile the instances of such a quest that has taken place over five decades, a quest that has done away with the boundaries that have imposed such imaginary gulfs between life as it is lived in this material world and the higher worlds?

How does one begin to convey the promise, the hope, and the purpose that these events could have, to a humanity so unconsciously jaded by materialism, the realities of making a living, and the non-stop effluvia of the media and the mass consciousness that lay upon the heart's pure yearning like a cold dense blanket of smog.

How does one craft the sentences that awaken the sleeping one and open the heart, so that others may tangibly, physically experience this perfection for themselves—becoming once again aware of these ancient Great Laws that govern all aspects of life? When this perfection is even glimpsed, there is a quickening that touches every facet of one's life.

This has been the lofty goal of this exercise—one that many others have endeavored to convey in one form or another over tens of thousands of years in Earth's long history. ❧

# 6 ~ How It Began for Me

Just the other day, and yet a long time ago, a little boy wondered why. His earliest memories are of being in church and loving the singing, of feeling a closeness to something that seemed "of home," but yet at this early age, was intangible. He remembers the conflict he felt when looking at the horrific image at the front of the church of the person strung up on the cross. He couldn't reconcile the sense of home and peace and joy with the sterile, cruel atmosphere of the church.

Through these early years, there was often a background sense of being out of place. What brought him the greatest peace and joy was this: he remembers so clearly swinging on a swing, by himself, and singing one particular hymn that the nuns taught at school—something like, "God Father, praise and glory..."

He remembers feeling such a rush of love, joy and power that he would swing to the highest point of the arch and then let go of the swing, flying through the air perhaps eight feet off the ground in complete joy-filled abandon, flying with the Angels. Then he would crash back onto the ground, laughing, getting up and doing it again and again. It was just wonderful. I was probably seven to eight years old then and I can still remember the comfort and the sense of being "home" that this activity provided when I couldn't understand life about me.

### *"The Search for Bridey Murphy" and Edgar Cayce*

Aside from this sense of connection with the Angels, growing up was probably very similar to what other kids experienced up until my twelfth or thirteenth year. I'm not sure at what age my sense of being "out of place" first began. I do recall that when I read my first book on reincarnation, around the age of twelve or thirteen, I wondered if all those images that I had of another life in the mountains far, far away was due to a previous lifetime. I can still remember my Mom handing me the book and telling me that I might find it interesting. I devoured that book, *The Search for Bridey Murphy*, by Morey Bernstein, in probably less than a week. My mind was spinning with all the implications of reincarnation and how it folded into my current experience. It was at this point that I realized that the Catholic Church wasn't telling the whole truth. I knew that Jesus, Mother Mary, and the Angels were real, but I knew that there was something very wrong about the message that I (and so many others) were spoonfed up to that point.

Some kind of awareness that there was "more" to be understood was added to my consciousness. It was almost like an indefinable background hum that I became aware of but didn't know how to even begin to describe, or understand why it was so compelling. I remember going to the library and trying to find out as much about reincarnation as I could. In the early sixties, there wasn't a lot of material available on the subject. Eventually I was able to get a book about Edgar Cayce where his experience was described in fascinating detail. This was my first encounter with the concept of karma and reincarnation and the concept of Great Masters. I can still remember the realization—the profound sense of "I know all this." It was like the top of my head lifted off with a great rush of electricity.

At that moment, somewhere around 13 years old, I knew that I was not only my parents' son; I knew that I was someone who had many lifetimes. I also knew that I had to find out why I came back into this world, into such a culture that was so alien and uncomfortable to me. At that moment, I felt like a million years old, and so wise, I felt a sense of freedom, but then again how much freedom did a thirteen-year-old boy have in this society in 1963?

It was at this time that I began to feel auras around people. There was absolutely no interest by my family or peers in anything I was experiencing, so it all just stayed as background experience. I had this sense that I had lived many times before, but was now stuck in this place that I didn't like very much. Conflict seemed to be everywhere one turned. I remember watching a neighbor building a bomb shelter in their back yard; it was the period around the Cuban Missile Crisis and my parents were scared.

## *High School*

My high-school years seemed fraught with more seeming conflict and a complete lack of direction as to where to go with my life. In my high school, compared to what my own children now receive, someone might see a "guidance counselor" once or twice a year. It was my sense of "self" and my strong physical presence that brought me the respect of my peers and an increasingly strong desire to get as far away from my "home-town" atmosphere as I could possibly get. Early in my high school experience, I became very involved in scuba diving, just loving the sense of adventure that went along with this new world. It was this that compelled me to pre-enlist in the Navy so that upon graduation, I would be going right into to active service. The Naval recruiters told me that I would have to pass a series of tests if I hoped to qualify for Special Forces. I began in my junior year to build up my physical body in preparation.

There was one other event that in some way played a part in my development at that period. In my senior year, I was very loosely involved in the student government. Somehow, I became the point man in organizing a student rebellion against a few inconsequential unilateral decisions that had been made by our despotic high school principal. To make a long story short, I was being suspended from school by this principal for "fomenting dissent." Because of this suspension, it was doubtful that I would have been able to graduate from high school.

When my friends found out that I was in the principal's office being suspended for the stand I took in promoting the "rights" of the high school students, they began a protest in the high-school cafeteria, which soon involved the entire student body from that lunch period. Several hundred students began chanting and some even threw their food at the cooks. The "overseers" locked the doors, trying to contain all the students, which only served to inflame them more.

I remember being in the principal's office, getting thrown out of school, when his phone rang and his face went ashen. He looked at me and told me that I had "ruined him" and that the students were rioting. Somehow the students got out of the cafeteria and the protest spread throughout the entire high school of approximately 2000 students. They all emptied out of the building and gathered on the front lawn of the school, on the main street of the city. Police and television cameras showed up.

The principal, very shaken, implored me to speak to the students of the entire school over the public address system, asking them to be calm, to go back into their home rooms, and assuring them that their grievances would be honored. Over the next several days, I was thrust into a position of negotiating with the principal and a school committee on behalf of the students. I remember being interviewed by the FBI at school. They were concerned that the school protest had something to do with the SDS (Students for a Democratic Society), a leftist organization that was protesting the Vietnam War and causing a lot of problems in colleges on the west coast. At any rate, that was my first involvement with taking a stand that was not popular with the governing authority and barely averting dire consequences for it.

### *The Military*

The next phase of my life after graduation was involved in the military. Suffice to say that this experience crystallized my self-discipline and my resolve to follow the promptings of my heart, even when they were seemingly opposed by the temporal powers of the society in which I lived.

Prior to being sworn in to the Navy, I was a scuba instructor and a member of the underwater local civil defense team. I had put myself through intense physical training for a year in preparation to becoming a Navy diver. I was given physical and written exams to determine my qualification for the Naval Special Forces program. I passed with flying colors and expected to enter that training once I was formally part of the U.S. Navy. Upon enlistment, I soon discovered that I was just another number and was told that I would not go into that program because of a deficiency in my color vision. The Navy recruiter knew this, but needed me to increase his enlistment quota, so this information was kept from me. Now, I had the shock of looking at four years in the military, doing something that I didn't wish to do.

I made the best of it until the Kent State massacre occurred in 1970. I was horrified that the U.S. military (members of the Ohio National Guard) had shot and killed those students who were protesting the Vietnam War. This bothered me so profoundly that I determined to get out of the Navy. I was angry and horrified at my government for all of the above, but even then, I knew that America had to stand for Freedom and that the U.S. military was the means by which the human rights of those less fortunate in other parts of the world might be protected. Still there was a burning sense that I had something very important that I had to do and it wasn't in the U.S. Navy.

I used the knowledge that I had obtained at naval administration school to process my request to be discharged from the service. It was denied and I had to go through a formal military board of review. My quarterly marks where all 4.0, the highest you could get, and it was obvious that the entire country was reeling with the Vietnam war protests and the horror of Kent State. I stood my ground for those long weeks totally alone and made my case.

I was 20 and my disillusionment with the U.S. government and the political system led by Nixon was great. When I was finally honorably discharged and walked out of the gates of the military base on that cold, grey November day, the clouds parted and a ray of intense sunlight poured forth all around me as I walked away into my new life. I clearly remember at that very instant saying, "Thank you, Father." There is no doubt that this was a huge turning point for me. If I had ignored what I had felt so strongly within and stayed in the military at that crossroads, my life would have been much, much different. Would I have still been drawn to the Path? Of course—but what of the timetable of the sacred events that unfolded thereafter?

Now, looking back on this from the vantage point of almost four decades, that period truly was a fork in the road for me. The fire and determination that I had to summon in order to deal with that system as a 20-year-old enlisted man served me well in later years. In my latter years of high school and in the military, it seemed that my outer awareness of the Eternal that had so permeated my early life was clouded over by my having to make my way through a society that outwardly (at least to me) was full of conflict and had few redeeming qualities to it.

## College—The Masters Resurface

After the military, I used the GI Bill to go to college. I still had no idea of which course my life would take but college was the obvious next step, especially since the government paid it for. It was a new life that was a lot more fun and purposeful than what I had ever experienced before. It was here in my first year of college that my awareness was again drawn to the mystical side of life. I remember getting a book, *The Ultimate Frontier*, that detailed an account of a young boy's involvement with the Great Masters. It was here that I first outwardly heard of the Great White Brotherhood. At this point, in college in the early seventies, there was quite a bit more information on reincarnation available to me. In fact, there was a profusion of material, so much so that it was easy to get bored just looking through the titles.

The problem for me was to find something that spoke to my heart so that I didn't have to wrestle with heady, intellectual concepts to understand—I didn't have the patience for any of that. Now and then I would find very interesting books that would start to fill in a lot of information about the world's mystical traditions. I can still remember reading Krishnamurti's *First and Last Freedom* when I was twenty-one and the sense of peace that I felt in meditating upon his words.

One particular statement comes to mind. When he was asked what he believed in, he said, "The space between the period at the end of a sentence and the capital letter that started the very next sentence...," implying that this space of silence was what he considered to be the most important thing in life. In that silence everything was contained.

## My First Experience with the Allness

In my twenty-first summer, I was dealing with the end of my first major relationship, meditating on a mountaintop in the Colorado Rockies just outside of Aspen. I was emotionally spent and confused as to what the next step was in my life. At that time, I was pondering whether to go into the family insurance business, the thought of which made me cringe, or just casting my fate to the wind and watching where it landed. All of this was brought to a head when my lady friend decided to end our relationship. After a 3-day hike, I can so clearly remember walking through a meadow of wildflowers in the high Rockies and then climbing a bit higher to the mountain's summit (approximately 12,000 feet) surrounded by great vistas.

I can remember the confusion and the despair that I felt within, juxtaposed to the grandeur of being on this summit overlooking the continental divide and seemingly all of creation. I was awed by the majesty of the view and the perfection before me. Slowly I began to feel a sense of purpose in my life that I had been bereft of for a very long time. I bent down to pick up an interesting-looking rock, so that in the future, I could remind myself of this point of clarity that I was experiencing. Around me there were scattered thunderstorms that I could see amongst the incredible sweep of the mountains. Now looking back on this I can still see and hear the lightning and thunder reverberating between the mountains and the valleys.

Against this backdrop, the Sun was shining and there was a light drizzle in the pure, supercharged air. As I bent down to pick up that rock, a very clear strong voice said to me, "Gene, you don't need that rock to remind yourself of this moment, you have this within you forever..." At this point I reeled back against the side of the cliff, in astonishment at what was unfolding around me. My body seemed electrified as I saw seeming tidal waves of Light rolling across the Continental Divide that is the grandeur of the Colorado Rockies. The lightning and thunder off in the distance, shafts of sunlight through the clouds illumining the mountain peaks in golden glory—it was magnificent. As these tidal waves of Light approached closer to me, (they began on the horizon perhaps a hundred miles away), I began to have incredible realizations about my life.

When the tidal wave of Light hit me, it plastered me against the rock cliff with the force of it. The realizations that blasted through me seemed to lift the top of my head off. One after another, these tidal waves of Light came rolling across the Continental Divide, each carrying with it another encyclopedia of understanding. Tears of joy and thanksgiving were pouring down my face. I knew with utter certainty that I had come into this world to do a certain work. I knew with utter certainty that I would never go into the family business. I knew with utter certainty that my life was being guided by these Great Ones, whom I still had only a vague conscious knowledge of, and that I only needed to be true to myself and all would be revealed in God's Own Good Time.

After a seeming eternity being plastered against that mountain-summit cliff by these glorious tidal waves of Light, this blessed experience began to subside. Giddy and feeling new, completely altered by what had happened, I made my way back down through the wildflower meadow just below the summit. All the wildflowers were radiating this self-luminous Light and this incredible fragrance. I was rolling in them, in tears, completely overcome with what was happening to me. Everywhere I looked, the world was transformed by what I had experienced. Everything was radiating this Light, seemingly from within out.

I now knew that I was part of all of this grandeur, the sense that there was purpose to my life, that I would eventually discover, was the most incredible blessing to me. And there was peace—the conflicts that I had for my entire life were no more. I smiled at my lady friend and our other friends when I arrived back at the campsite several hours below the summit. I picked up my backpack, said goodbye, and very happily walked down the mountain into my future.

## A New Perspective and the Dream

When I started back at school in September after my mountain-top experience, I had a new direction. I went into Special Education and started working with the handicapped. Everything had changed; I liked what I was doing. I proceeded along this path for the next two semesters, when I had a dream that changed my life even more than the tidal waves of Light on the Continental Divide had.

I dreamt that I was in a bar in the hometown that I couldn't wait to leave all those years ago. Feeling stagnant and doing the same old things: drinking beer, the women and the boredom, when there was a major earthquake. Then running out of this bar, the earth shaking so much, the city hall collapsing, the ground splitting apart, and the stars falling from the night sky. There was this sickening sense that I had blown the purpose for which I had taken incarnation. I woke up, totally wide awake, knowing instantly that I was quitting school and that I was leaving the country, first for London and then on to points and times unknown.

That very day, I applied for my passport and put my motorcycle and stereo up for sale. I knew that I had an appointment somewhere in life that had to be kept and that it wasn't here. With every fiber of my being, I knew that I had to find out exactly who I was—who I Am. Southwest England, Rome, Greece and Israel called to me; the East called to me. The mountains of Tibet, Nepal and India that I had seen so clearly as a little boy—when I began to remember "home"—called to me.

I didn't know if I would ever come back to the United States again and I didn't really care. The only thing that mattered was to do what I had to do. It was two weeks after this "dream" when I said goodbye to my family and friends and departed the life that I knew, on a jet heading to London. There was no apprehension in the least; I felt such a thrust of purpose. It was surreal rushing to the airport for the overnight flight from Boston to London. It was surreal getting moved from coach to first class because there was an open seat, given a glass of champagne. It was as if the Powers That Be were congratulating me on making the right decision. I knew what was before me was part of my destiny and that it was sanctioned by the Great Ones who were now more frequently in my outer awareness. It was in that state of understanding that I closed my eyes and fell asleep, knowing that my tomorrows would be very different.  ଔ

# 7 ~ **The Quest Begins**

I will skip my accounts of Europe. While southwest England (Glastonbury), Ireland, Southern Italy and Greece were very familiar, even comfortable, the magic didn't start until Israel. My destination in Israel was Jerusalem—period. Fabled Jerusalem. Unlike any other place I've visited, pronouncing the very name was almost a mystical experience in itself, producing a flood of feelings that I could just barely perceive on the perimeters of my consciousness. I just had to get there as quickly as possible and made a beeline for that ancient city as soon as my flight arrived in Tel Aviv in the wee hours of the morning.

I remember walking through the stone arch gate into old Jerusalem before dawn that morning—the incredible antiquity that seemed to just pour out of the cobblestoned, serpentine, little streets and alleyways that cut through the jumble of ancient, dark buildings like a maze. I remember seeing a few of the Arabs and the Jews going about their pre-dawn chores in preparation for the day's business. So clearly do I remember the palpable, heavy weight of the city, of all that happened here over thousands of years, as it descended upon me like a heavy blanket.

Later I found that navigating through Jerusalem, even with a map, is quite difficult—the tiny streets and alleyways just go about in circles. But now, the faint light of pre-dawn only served to highlight the drab, ominous surroundings. Yet on this first pre-dawn morning in Jerusalem, I was far from lost; my steps had a purpose and a direction that I, in my daze, was dimly aware of. It was like my feet knew where I was going but my consciousness didn't. Making my way through these very narrow cobblestone streets, a left here, a right there, and then I rounded another corner and found myself standing in a line of hooded, dark-robed Greek monks. They were waiting, standing in a single-file line on ancient stone steps, descending into the basement level of some ancient, large structure. They looked at me and I looked at them, but perhaps save for a slight smile, no words were conveyed.

After a while, the iron hinges on the huge, heavy, wooden door creaked open and these priests walked down the stone stairs. These steps were concaved, worn by millennia of use. The line of monks proceeded through the doorway into the darkened building, with me following. We walked into this large cavernous space only lit by candles; it appeared to have been carved out of the stone that the building was erected upon. There were religious icons on the carved, stone walls and then, finally, some writing in English. It was then with a seeming thunderclap of understanding that I realized by the inscription on the walls that I was in the basement level of the Church of the Holy Sepulcher.

In the background of my awareness, my mind raced in astonishment to make sense of what had just transpired. How and why I was drawn like a magnet to this place, but around this consciousness, there was the undeniable charge of purpose that I felt buoy me up the stairs into the main body of this ancient, sacred place. Then, up the stairs again, to the small altar area that was built over the rock that had a split in it, from the Cross.

Why was I directed to this place this very early morning, with such sure steps? Why did I enter through the basement level with the priests, before the main doors were open to the public? Looking back on it, all these years later, I am once again sitting there in the upper level of the Church of the Holy Sepulcher in meditation. I am aware of my astonishment, not so much for the fact of my early morning guidance to this place, but for the sense of God's Hand so strong in my life. For the first time, I felt with absolute concrete certainty that I was at the right place at exactly the right time, to begin something that I had to do, and that I had not a clue as to what was going to happen next.

I recall sitting in the pews in the uppermost level of the

church in meditation upon the events of the past few hours. Eventually tourists begin to enter and exit on the periphery of my vision, I noticed that the priest who was sitting by the altar, the very altar that was erected over the place where the crucifixion was supposed to have occurred, acted differently. My attention was again drawn to this priest and I discovered that he was reading some kind of girly glamour magazine that went quickly under the table when the tourists came in, then the magazine came out again when they left. He took no notice of me as I'd been there for some time by then.

This blaring dichotomy reverberated through me. A month or two before, I had visited the Vatican, which to me, aside from the great art, was like a lifeless mausoleum of desiccated dogma. Now here, at the very place where it all began, the hypocrisy that I had sought to find surcease from was ever-present. The juxtaposition of these experiences propelled me deeper into meditation there, in the upper level of the Church of the Holy Sepulcher. I was aware of the question, "Why was I experiencing this—for what purpose?"

### *Jesus and the Aquarian Gospel*

How do I put into words what happened next? Sometime later, I was pulled from meditation by two of these priests on either side of me. One of them said in broken English, "Get out! You have been sleeping here most of the day." In astonishment, it was at this moment that I realized that I had been out of my body in full consciousness, watching Jesus teach and heal people in Jerusalem. The vantage point that I had was perhaps twenty or thirty yards above and to the side of the scene, watching Jesus as he exercised his great love and mastery. I was stunned by this realization at what I had witnessed. This was no dream—it was so real I could taste it.

The priests escorted me out of the building, leaving me standing on the steps of the main entrance of the church in the mid-afternoon sun. My head was reeling—trying to understand what had happened this day, trying to understand what it all meant. I walked through the now crowded streets of old Jerusalem somehow feeling altered—a different person than when I had walked through the gates of this ancient city before dawn that morning.

The storied history of this place and just about everything else in my life didn't seem important any more. I felt so stretched out, so expanded. I knew then enough about the mystical side of life to know that this experience was a great blessing, that I had seen a portion of the Akashic Records of Jesus' life. (The Akashic Record is a Sanskrit term that refers to that substance upon which is recorded all the events that happened in a person's lifetime. In the Old and New Testament, this is referred to as the "Book of Life" that one reviews at the conclusion of a lifetime, in which all of a person's actions are recorded.)

A few hundred meters from the church, I walked into one of the numerous sidewalk cafes that fill the streets of old Jerusalem. I was parched by the dry heat of this ancient city that late summer day. Making my way through the crowded café, I fell into a chair and ordered a cold drink. A moment later a young man in some kind of clerical clothing sat down in the chair across from me, smiled and started talking. "You look like you've just been through an intense experience," he said. With a slight smile I nodded and with an incredulous look I said, "That's for sure." He identified himself as an American studying to become a Jewish rabbi. One subject led to another and then somehow we were discussing what had taken place this day. I related to him my pre-dawn arrival into the subterranean level of the church and then my experience watching Jesus teach and heal. He smiled, "I've got something for you," he said. He then pulled out a book from his satchel and laid it on the table before me.

The book, *The Aquarian Gospel of Jesus the Christ*, by Levi, was recorded by an American minister in the late 1800s, and was revealed to this minister by an Angel. It was taken from the Akashic Records and describes a very different Jesus than what is chronicled throughout the New Testament. This book subsequently had a great impact upon me. Over the next days and weeks that I read this book, I knew that this was an affirmation from my Presence and the Great Masters, presented to me on that incredible day after my experience in Jerusalem. This indeed was a very physical indication that I was at the right place, at the right time. It was like I was given an ancient road map to the greatest of adventures, at the conclusion of which awaited the greatest of treasures. All I had to do was learn how to read it and summon the wherewithal to make it happen.

Over the decades I've often wondered about that person who put that book into my hands that late afternoon. How did he know to come up to me and begin a dialogue? How did he happen to have the absolutely perfect book to place into my hands? Was he really an American rabbi student? From my vantage point now, I wouldn't be surprised if he was directly employed by the Brotherhood of Light to play that brief part in my Jerusalem experience.

This book talked about how Jesus awoke in this lifetime to a mission for which he had been preparing for many lifetimes, that he traveled around the world for years seeking to find and then study under the Great Masters that comprise the sacred Brotherhood of Light. I had always known that Jesus' true teachings were far different from what the Christian dogma taught, that they were edited and re-edited by men, and that for almost two millennia had shaped the culture of the west. However, getting this book put into my hands on that specific day, after the extraordinary events that happened in the Church of the Holy Sepulcher was like a lightning-bolt affirmation from the Powers That Be that I was on the right course and that my quest was about to greatly accelerate.

As I stated before in this work, I was familiar with the concept that there were Great Masters from an early period of my life. My first conscious understanding of them came from a book about Edgar Cayce's life that I read when I was thirteen or fourteen. Then in my late teens and early twenties, I read several other accounts of this Great Brotherhood, from several different sources. It made all the sense in the world that Jesus was intimately connected with these Great Masters and that his mission was to convey that wisdom to the world. I would have to be pretty dense not to understand that "someone" was trying to tell me something here in this place in my 22nd year of this incarnation.

## *Israel*

E very day throughout the next three months, as I traveled across Israel, the experience that happened in the Church of the Holy Sepulcher unfolded in my awareness. Many times throughout those days I was drawn back into the wonderment at what had happened. Because of the magic of this place, I decided that I needed to spend some time living and traveling in Israel to integrate what I was experiencing. In those days, many young people from around the world would choose to spend a few weeks or months in the various kibbutzim, collective farms, which were all over Israel. If you were accepted by the kibbutz, you were required to work 5 to 6 days a week in exchange for room and board and a small stipend. It was a good way to experience the culture of this place and conserve money, while still being able to travel extensively on weekends. Because Israel is so geographically small, weekend trips would take you to many different corners of this ancient country.

I was attracted to Masada, that ancient mountaintop fortress adjacent to the Dead Sea, which is as a national shrine for the people of Israel. It was here that the Jews held off the Roman army for years until finally the Roman army built a great ramp and stormed the mountaintop fortress only to find that the Jews had all killed themselves rather than be killed by the Roman army or go into slavery. With a few traveling companions from the kibbutz, we decided to sleep up there that night beneath the stars. You could feel the charge of energy from all that had happened in this place and that night, the slight breeze added to the somber atmosphere, moaning through the ruins. All around us lay the great desert, the Dead Sea, and the history of Israel.

Demonstrating the power of this place, a decade or two after I was there, the President of Germany was on the first tour to Israel by a German head-of-state since the Holocaust. When visiting Masada, his helicopter crashed there on one of the small outcroppings that form a shelf several hundred feet above the desert floor. None of his party was hurt. It was a not-so-subtle reminder of what had happened.

After visiting several kibbutzim, I arrived at Kafar Blum in northern Israel, a beautiful place on the Jordan River, just south of Kiryat Shmona with wide, rolling fields and hills, extensive orchards and fishponds. There were flowers everywhere and the actual kibbutz living quarters, a network of little buildings, was interconnected by flower-strewn pathways. I have so many wonderful memories of this place and the beautiful people who lived here. It was here that I found the space to integrate the events of my life up to this point. It was here that I began what was to become my formal meditation practice. Every day at dawn, usually picking apples along the Jordan River, I would pause in my work and walk over to a place near the river, away from the other workers, to meditate as the Sun crested the mountains to the east.

Here in this place where so much had happened, I would call out to Jesus and to my Presence, that I could dimly perceive in my heart, that I knew as Father, asking to be shown why I had experienced all that I had experienced and what I was supposed to do next. It was here that I knew that I was going to travel overland across Asia to India, just as Jesus had done almost two thousand years earlier (as recorded in *The Aquarian Gospel of Jesus the Christ*, by Levi Dowling (1908) and *The Lost Years of Jesus: The Life of Saint Issa*, by Nicolas Notovitch (1894), and other works).

Looking back on this period, I've often described the sense that I felt connected to my Presence by a thin gold strand of Light, and that my Presence pulled me from experience to experience, from country to country, by this thin strand of Golden Light. This strand was to increase in size and power over the next months and years of my life.

The days turned into weeks and the weeks into months in this beautiful place, until the day that the terrorists killed the Israeli athletes in Munich at the Olympics. I can remember that morning so well. I was in the orchards by the Jordan River with several other Israelis and Europeans picking apples. One of the Israelis was listening to a portable radio and told us that the Israeli athletes were killed. Not a minute later, wave after wave of Israeli jets screamed up the Jordan River valley directly overhead, not 50 feet above the apple trees that we were working in, knocking us out of the trees with the thunder of their engines. We watched in amazement as they swooped up the valley and then split into two formations around Mount Hermon, with one formation going into Syria and the other into Lebanon. We could hear the bombs dropping from where we were.

This was my first taste of war. The next morning, it seemed that the entire Israeli army was parked outside the entrance of our kibbutz. There were armed soldiers everywhere and men and women who lived full-time on the kibbutz actually patrolled the flower-strewn walkways, riding bicycles with Uzi machine guns hung over their shoulders. That night, the Syrians launched some missiles into northern Israel not far from our kibbutz. The peace of this place was shattered quite completely; it was time for me to leave Israel.

## *Istanbul and Asia*

Within a few days, a short flight from Israel brought me to Istanbul. Although I had been in Greece several hundred miles west of Istanbul only four months prior, Istanbul seemed a very different world. There was no mistaking that I was finally in Asia. The buildings, the people, and the culture were unlike anything I'd ever experienced at that time. Looking back on this period now, I realize that I had no thought of staying in Istanbul or any part of Turkey, Iran, Afghanistan, or Pakistan, for even a day to visit different places. I was a driven young man and I had to get to India as soon as possible. It was almost as if I was on some kind of schedule and I was not going to be late. This sense of "an appointment to keep" continued to increase in my awareness.

The familiar culture of the West that was my only experience in this lifetime (other than for my time in Israel) was now very much behind me. Now, every day brought me further and further into Asia, which in most cases, except for the few cities, had not changed for thousands of years.

I can remember when crossing the frontier into Iran, that the border guards were very aggressive with their machine guns. They would order everyone out of the ancient bus that was the only means of travel and with their automatic rifles at the ready, inspect everyone's passports and belongings. It was a threatening situation that only increased the oppressiveness of these countries. I was required to obtain visas from the embassies of the countries that I was about to enter prior to entering those countries. This was done in Istanbul for Iran, in Tehran for Afghanistan, in Kabul for Pakistan and India, etc. It usually took a few days for the visas to be processed so, in this way, I did spend a few days in each capital city but was very happy to finally have the visa to be able to leave those countries and continue east.

## *Iran ~ Afghanistan ~ Pakistan*

These endless rickety bus trips from one ancient Asian city to the next were the only method of travel other than the camel caravans that I frequently saw passing outside the bus windows. Everywhere, with the exception of the major cities, the buildings, the people, and the culture and landscape seemed thousands of years old. Mud and stone huts without running water were the norm. The landscape was sun-blasted; the buildings were drab earth tones. All the Muslim women were covered in oppressive black robes (burkas) save for a little area over their eyes where they could look out into this very bleak, parched world in which they lived. This oppressiveness was only heightened as the days changed to weeks and then to months as I made my way across Asia.

The nature of my experience in crossing Asia can perhaps be best summed up by one particular experience that I had while traveling across Afghanistan. As noted, the only means of public transportation was in very old, run-down buses. In most cases the

**Kandahar, Afganistan.** This picture, taken in late 1972, depicts life in the center of town. Note the bus on the left. It was here that I saw a group of boys pull an ox into an alleyway between the buildings. They tied a noose around its neck and threw the rope over a tree branch, then tied another rope around its front feet. There were several boys on the rope slung over the tree and several on the rope tied to its front legs. They pulled and the ox had its head pulled up and its front feet pulled back. Then the boys got on a large, two-person tree saw, in this case, two boys on each side. They cut off the ox's head from the bottom. In the space of ten minutes, they had it butchered in the dust and brought the meat to the numerous cooking fires that lined both sides of the street. The brutality of this scene, all the missing-persons pictures of westerners in the embassy, and the uncomfortable looks from many of the people here, underscored my desire to leave this place quickly. This was life in Afganistan.

buses had few windows and were filled with goats, chickens, pigs and people. The dirt roads were in poor condition, which resulted in the bus lurching this way and that. At that time there was one main road that went from Herat in the west to Kandahar in the south and then on to Kabul in the east.

When the bus departed Herat for Kandahar, or Kandahar for Kabul, they didn't stop (except briefly) until they reached their destination. These were overnight journeys that seemed never to end. I well remember the endless blasted landscape of desert and alien-looking mountains slowly passing by, the ceaseless noise of animals and humans in the bus and the all-too-brief respite when finally falling asleep for a few minutes or hours, however the case may be.

It was in one such period of brief, unsettled sleep, somewhere in Afghanistan, that dimly, through a fog, I felt something like a rat scratching at my side. As I instantly became wide-awake, I slapped at this "rat" only to find that it was a human hand. The hand belonged to one of the locals sitting in the seat immediately in back of mine. This guy had cut a hole in the back of my seat and was reaching his hand through the seat in an attempt to remove my satchel that was carried across my shoulder resting on my right side. The satchel carried my passport and some of my money. (The rest of my money was hidden in my boot.)

As soon as I realized what was happening, I was up on my feet and spun around ready for whatever was going to happen next. It seemed that the entire back of the bus was full of these Afghanis, staring unkindly at me. I was about a foot taller and 50 pounds heavier than any of them. I wasn't too happy as I turned around and sat back down in my seat looking to get off at the next village that we stopped at.

I had a much clearer understanding now of why I was warned in every embassy to stay on the well-traveled routes while traveling across Asia in this manner. In the entrance foyer of each embassy, there were hundreds of pictures of missing Americans and Europeans who had "disappeared" while crossing Asia in the same manner in which I was. There were rewards offered by their families for any information leading to contact with them. Nonetheless, I still felt very much focused and perhaps propelled toward my goal, which was to get to India as soon as possible.

Every day since my experiences in Jerusalem, I started my day with my own form of prayer and meditation. My prayer was simply seeking to know and follow whatever was God's Will for my life. Then, with this thought formed in my heart, I would try to be mentally and emotionally silent so that I could perceive whatever might be perceived as an answer. I was very often aware at this point that there was a thin gold thread connecting me to my Presence. This gold thread seemed to be increasing in size and was pulling me from one experience to another, from America to Europe, to Israel, and now Asia. Perhaps it was here in Afghanistan in that instance on the bus that I first became aware of the Protection that this tangible connection to my Presence afforded me.

While I'm sure that there must be nice places in these countries, I had no interest in stopping anywhere in Turkey, Iran, Afghanistan, or Pakistan longer than I had to in order to obtain visas or get a bite to eat. It was with relief that I saw the Hindu Kush Mountains and the infamous Khyber Pass begin to rise in the distance to the east, relief because I knew that beyond those mountains lay Pakistan and then after a day's journey through Pakistan, India.

## Coming Home to India

After traveling through the Hindu Kush Mountains, the world began to change again. Pakistan was much different than the rest of Asia that I had been traveling through all these long weeks. The people seemed to have more energy, the buildings were more dynamic, and there were a lot more people, especially in the cities. It was only a short day's journey passing across this narrow piece of Pakistan and then we were at the Indian frontier.

Never before could I differentiate anything other than a political border when crossing from one country into another but there was something definitely in the air now that I was in India. It was like a dream after crossing Asia for these past months. Within a few minutes of crossing the border, there was luxurious color everywhere. The people, the buildings, and the landscape—all were alive in a way that I had not seen in Asia or anywhere else before. The women were not veiled in drab, black burkas with only little holes to peer out into their bleak surroundings. Here in India, they were dressed in beautiful, colorful saris—you could actually see them and they would even smile at you when you passed by.

There was a quality and smell in the air that was so different

**Golden Temple of Armritsar.** This clearly conveys the magic of India one
experiences after traveling overland across Asia.

from anything that I had ever experienced. Never before have I felt
my heart thrill as I was now feeling; all the fatigue of traveling and
having so little sleep over the past months washed away from me in
an instant. Something wonderful was happening. There, shimmering
on the banks of the river was the Golden Temple of Amritsar. Some
consider this sacred place to be one of the Wonders of the World. For
me, compared to the long, tedious months of traveling through Asia,
the Golden Temple was an appropriate metaphor, an introduction to
the rich beauty of India.

In Amritsar I boarded the first of many trains that I was to ride
in India. The British had built thousands of miles of tracks crisscrossing India and it was the most convenient way of getting from one
place to another. It was perhaps here, on this first train ride, that I
began to take note of the people. Those who lived in the other Asian
countries that I had traveled through seemed almost imprisoned by
the poor quality of their lives and their religious dogmas; here in
India, there was so much beauty and so many smiles.

The train ride was quite an experience, one that I would get
more accustomed to over the next several months. While the people

45

were so polite, there was also the obvious undertone of great poverty. I didn't at first understand why all the train windows had bars across them until sometime later when we pulled into a city. All the cars of the train were literally mobbed by every type of vendor, selling everything from chai (a sweet-tea beverage), to chapatis (flour tortillas), and just about everything else one could imagine in this land where everything is possible. They would thrust their wares through the barred windows after a few rupees were supplied.

What was most sobering though was what happened when the train pulled away from the station. Apparently the police kept the unfortunate ones away from the train, but as soon as the train started to pull away from the station, dozens and dozens of people jumped up and grabbed onto the window bars. Some fell off as the train gained speed; some climbed onto the roof of the train for a free ride to another destination.

Writing about India's juxtaposition of great beauty and great misery is quite difficult; perhaps only those who have actually lived in this country for a period of time can best relate to what I am attempting to convey. It was perhaps on my very first day that I saw the first of many dead people just lying on the side of a street. It was at the Delhi train station that I saw the first of many lepers; those who were more able would approach me begging *baksheesh* (charity) with their infected hands thrust out for whatever they could get. Then in the next few feet, you would see a beautiful woman wearing a sari, going about her business, completely ignoring the beggars and the sick. I had never seen leprosy before. The images that I recalled from early Christian stories were scary but actually seeing a person approach you with terrible, large open wounds on their faces, and much worse, and not being able to provide anything to help other than a few rupees, was an experience I don't wish to repeat.

Even then in 1972, going into Delhi was not a nice experience. It was a huge south-Asian city with all the ills that every big city has, and more, because it was the capital of India. The rickshaws (foot powered, bicycle powered and scooter-powered) were everywhere. There were people everywhere. It seemed to me that more than half of them were very poor, with many homeless living on the streets. In some parts of Delhi, many people, as is the case everywhere in India both then and probably now, make their home on the streets. There were cooking fires alongside the streets; they lived there and slept there, and many relieved themselves there when they needed to.

I needed a place to stay on my first night in Delhi. I had heard of an inexpensive hotel that was frequented by westerners in the center of the city so I made my way there. It was a large building, three or four stories high, with a large, outside porch on each level. As soon as I walked inside, I knew that the dormitory-style bunkbeds covering every foot of space were not for me. So I opted to stay on the third-floor porch where there was plenty of air and more open space around me. I eventually fell asleep in the wee hours to the sounds and smells of this bustling ancient city.

The next morning, I was awakened with a start just as the sky began to lighten. I had learned long ago that it was always best to be the first one in a public bathroom to get a shower and be gone; however, I wasn't prepared for what I saw when I left the porch and made my way through the hallway toward the bathroom. All over the floor in front of me, and seeming everywhere I looked there were pools of excrement. As I had learned, one of the first things that westerners have to overcome when they come to India is their reaction to the tainted food and water. Dysentery, or severe diarrhea, were common afflictions. Fortunately for me, I had long ago stopped eating meat, so I was somewhat protected. I say somewhat because later that day, prior to boarding the train for Agra, I was hit with severe stomach cramps that caused me to dive into the bushes at one of the parks that are scattered about Delhi.

Over the next seven months that I traveled through India, that was my only instance of any type of illness whatsoever. I believe that this was because of a sense of being "home" that I felt so strongly, an understanding that just so long as I maintained this contact with what I could only describe as my Presence, all would unfold perfectly. I was then beginning to somewhat understand that this vibration that

I associated with my Father was growing stronger. During the past several months, the pressure of this vibration increased, as I would pause more frequently to go within, to remember to be grateful for the experiences around me. I was becoming more aware of the changes of vibration that surrounded me as I went from place to place. I was beginning to sense this more frequently, and I would pause, as if to seek direction from this new sense.

This also resulted in me taking a moment before I ate to ask this great God Presence to bless the food and drink that I would take, so that I could do whatever it was that I was supposed to do. Anyway, this and my joy at being in largely vegetarian country kept me healthy from thereon and forward to this present day.

I'll never forget sitting in a restaurant in Delhi having dinner and then watching a great big ox walk into the front door and try to take some food off of the plate of a person who had just left the table. The owner of the restaurant shooed the ox away.

I have a strong dislike for large cities. I needed to get away from Delhi as quickly as possible. I needed to get into the country and see how the people lived. I decided to go to Agra to see the Taj Mahal. It was upon my dawn departure from the hotel via rickshaw being pulled through the back streets of Delhi that I became more aware of the vibration of this land and the people who lived there. The rickshaws that were everywhere in Delhi and throughout India, like the one I was traveling in, were powered by barefooted young, middle-aged or old men, picking up the poles that connect to the bicycle-wheeled rickshaw and running off wherever they are told to go, pulling it behind them.

It was on this pre-dawn trip to the train station that I again became aware of the incredible smells of India; even the very air felt different against my skin. I was in India, on the opposite side of the world from where I had lived the first 21 years of this lifetime. During that rickshaw ride in the monochromatic lighting of early dawn, I was once again very aware of watching myself experience what was happening around me. ∞

**Taj Mahal from inside the wall of the Red Fort.** This different perspective of the Taj was taken immediately next to the red sandstone fort wall that surrounds the Taj on three sides. Alongside the back of the Taj runs the Yamuna River. (High-resolution color pictures can be viewed at <u>UpraisedChalice.com</u>.)

# 8 ~ Mystical India

Of all the world's countries, India has a very special and very unique spiritual dimension; every day is a holy day in this land. Most of the people were brought up with an understanding of karma and reincarnation that is contained in the ancient sacred books of India—the Bhagavad Gita, the Upanishads, and the Vedas. Outside of the intensely crowded cities, in the smaller towns and villages, the temples are ubiquitous, as are the monks and Hindu sadhus (holy men) associated with them. Each temple is dedicated to this manifestation or that manifestation of the Gods and adorned with elaborate statues and paintings. The monks, priests and sadhus easily stand out with either their shaved heads and plain robes, or as is the case with the wandering sadhu renunciants, their

49

threadbare rags, oftentimes bizarre hairstyles and painted faces.

I can remember walking through small villages and seeing women making beautiful, geometric yantras on gravel roads in front of their homes (often small huts made of wood or straw) every morning. Yantras are colorful, intricate designs usually a meter in diameter, created with colored pebbles or grains. Prayers and mantras are recited while these yantras are being created. Immediately after these yantras were made, the foot traffic of the day would increase and the yantras would be walked over by hundreds or even thousands of people, by carts, rickshaws and animals. The purpose of the yantra is to remind the person who makes it and those who see it or walk upon it that the Divine is everywhere, in every person, every object, and every action.

## The Taj Mahal

I remember taking the train from Delhi to Agra passing through the long, endless plains. For hours I would watch town after town approach off in the distance, each with a mist of smoke from scores of roadside cooking fires drifting around them, making each village look even more surreal against the distant landscape we passed through. After a while, the Taj Mahal appeared off in the distance, shimmering like a huge, great, white dream on the horizon; it was amazing. As the train traveled the last several miles into Agra, I could not take my eyes away from the Taj. The closer I got, I was very aware that this was more than just a stunningly beautiful wonder of the world—there was a unique energy here that I wanted to explore. Outside of the tall fort that surrounds the Taj, on a small, forested hillside there was a sprawling village of huts that were full of various holy men constantly involved in their religious rituals. Here there was also an abundance of people who had every type of affliction imaginable, imploring their gods for relief.

I found myself developing a sense of becoming super-aware of my surroundings in such a place, of taking nothing for granted. It was nothing less than astonishing to see and experience this level

**Sadhu.** One of many sadhus (priests) and monks who live in the forested hilltop immediately adjacent to the Taj Mahal.

of religious devotion mixed with such human misery, juxtaposed to what one experiences when walking through the gates in the large stone-walled fort that surrounds the Taj. The majesty, the incredible beauty of the Taj, floating above the reflecting pools that surround it, is stunning. Truly this is from another world.

There's an interesting story of how the Taj was protected during the war in the 1940s. A large plane almost crashed into it, but at the last moment was magically deflected. It would be easy for one to just shrug that story off, but when one encounters the Taj, the very magic of this place seems to make all things possible. The Taj was built by the great Mughal emperor, Shah Jahan, as a mausoleum for his beloved wife, Mumtaz. Years later I discovered that Shah Jahan was a previous embodiment of one of the Great Masters, Kuthumi, one of the sponsors of the Theosophical Society (circa 1875, at which time Kuthumi was an unascended adept).

The Taj is made of moon marble and on the three nights surrounding the full moon, they would open the gates of the fort to allow people in. Walking through the gates that first night that I was there is forever burned into my memory; it was perhaps the most magical physical thing that I've ever experienced. The light of the full moon is somehow captured by the Taj and the entire structure radiates the moonlight somehow brighter than the full moon itself. The Taj seems to levitate, shimmering above the earth, reflected in the huge reflecting pools and fountains that surround it, like some celestial dream; there are no other words to describe it.

I became aware that gazing upon the Taj was a visual meditation, producing a deep peace and a soaring sense of the Divine. I sought to have my eyes drink in the memory of every graceful sweep of the perfect arches and the contrasts of the radiant, luminous moon marble against the dark of the night sky. I sought to etch in my memory forever every detail of this place that is so charged with Life. Again I became aware of watching myself having this experience, including a sense that I was at the right place at the right time. The great Love that permeated this place was so tangible. ❧

**Tibetan monks celebrating life in downtown Kathmandu.** Note the little boy in front. It is considered an honor for a Tibetan family to have a child become a monk. I learned here that every day is celebrated as a holy day, unlike the periodic holidays that I experienced as a boy growing up in the United States. Note the thatched roofs on the pagoda temple and buildings.

# 9 ~ **Nepal**

After visiting the Taj Mahal, I got back on the train and made my way to Kathmandu. The prolific trains of India, which the British built during their long colonial period that ended on August 14, 1947, is more than vast; it crisscrosses all of India and services seemingly every major town. The first-class section is for those with means, but I had to make every rupee count, so I always traveled in coach with the rest of India. I've already described theplethora of every type of humanity earlier on my first experiences with India; the train stations and trains were the melting pots of the dozens of different Indian ethnic cultures.

Unlike the homogenization of the culture that one experiences throughout Europe and America, the only thing seemingly guaranteed in India is that you'll experience such a wide diversity of people, ethnic groups, circumstances, poverty levels, diseases, life and death as to leave one astonished.

Then as the train picks up speed and leaves the station, making its way out of the town or city, it passes through such endless miles of timeless, rural vistas that haven't changed for hundreds or thousands of years. A water buffalo plowing the fields directed by a barefoot man wearing a simple cotton dhoti (cloth wrapped around the waist), thatched huts in clusters spread out across the villages with more permanent stone buildings toward the center of towns, women draped in saris gracefully carrying water jugs upon their heads, usually with a few young children in tow.

These people make their way through the days in their village life as they have for millennia. I remember the windows of the train being open most of the time. The smells, in some instances, the fragrances of India were pungent, almost heady, changing from region to region.

Inside the train, it's literally another world. People of every age, in every manner of dress, usually traveling in families, were going about their lives. Families all sitting together on the benches, seats and floors of the train would break out baskets of prepared food for their meals, sometimes even making their meals over a smoldering fire that would be contained in a type of grill sitting on the floor.

My travels crisscrossing India were always by train and those trips were usually measured in days or overnight trips, usually catching a few hours of sleep here and there on the benches, along with the other travelers. It was always a riot of activity when the train pulled into the station of one of the larger towns, for even before the train stopped moving, dozens of Indians would rush the train, thrusting their wares through the barred windows trying to sell their foods to the travelers.

### *Approaching Kathmandu*

I awoke at dawn with the increased noise and the jarring of the train as it came to a stop in the frontier town of Siliguri on the India-Nepal border. Here I had to board a very old bus for the full-day journey across the Himalayan foothills. The roads, like everywhere outside the cities of south Asia, were not paved. The winding road through the mountains that this careening bus took on the way to Kathmandu is not for the weak-hearted, with sheer cliffs often adjacent to steep curves, and the bus always traveling too fast. To this day, it seems every few years, I read about a bus going off the road and plummeting down the cliff in this part of the world, killing dozens of people.

After this endless, often harrowing journey crossing these Himalayan foothills that were still comparable to the Rockies, we descended into the mountain valley that holds the ancient forbidden region of Kathmandu—forbidden because this entire area was closed to foreigners until sometime in the early 20th century. As we approached this ancient city, I was confronted again with the fact that I was in a world so completely different in every way from where the rest of my life had been spent. But yet, this place, along with all of India, felt somehow comfortable or familiar.

The city of Kathmandu was stunning, surrounded by the high, snowcapped Himalayas, with numerous ornate wooden pagodas towering over the other very old buildings that were so cramped together. The people were very different here than in India. Kathmandu, Nepal, is a blending area of the peoples and cultures of India to the south with the strong, oriental Tibetan, Mongol and Chinese cultures to the north and east.

Finally the bus arrived. I can remember just walking around in amazement at the sights, sounds and smells; the architecture and craftsmanship that went into the towering wooden pagoda temples and the wood and stone buildings was so oriental and exquisite. The top floors of the building were residences, while the bottom floors

**Kathmandu produce vendors.** Shows the produce grown around the Kathmandu valley as well as the everpresent, large porting baskets that are carried by only a strap across the forehead. (The high-resolution color image on <u>UpraisedChalice.com</u> shows the finely carved detail in the posts on either side of the vendors.)

were usually open-air markets selling everything from piles of grains, vegetables and fruits, to ornate straw woven baskets, worn like backpacks, that both men and women used to port their belongings, usually attached by a strap across the forehead.

These baskets, as I later discovered, were used by most in Nepal and Tibet to port their cargo across the endless Himalayan foot-trails that served as the only roads for most of this region of the world. Later I would be amazed at the loads that both men and women carried in these large baskets as they made their way up and down the long, steep, rocky trails separating one village or monastery from another.

Whenever I arrived into a new city or town, the first thing I would do is to locate a base, a place to stay for a while, to plan out my next steps. Fortunately for me, though I had very little money, most of the population had even less, so I was always able to find a nice, clean hotel room still within my meager means. After assessing the security of my hotel room, I would leave my heavy backpack which contained all my worldly belongings that I schlepped around the world and carrying only my small, over-the-shoulder satchel with my money and passport I would set out to explore my new location.

To say that Kathmandu was magical, on that early morning day in mid-December of 1972, would be an understatement. I don't know (even now) if it was the refined and sparklingly clear Himalayan mountain air—Kathmandu is, after all, located in a valley that is 4600 feet above sea level—or the numberless beautiful pagoda temples that adorn every block of the city with their countless prayer wheels spinning aside them.

Even then, though I didn't know what the meaning of what was chanted when the prayer wheels were spun, it was still familiar to me—*Om Mane Padme Hum*. This script was written usually three times on the prayer wheel, so every time it was spun, the mantra

**The Boudhanath Stupa**, just east of Kathmandu, is one of the largest in the world, and is now a UNESCO World Heritage Site. Note the Eyes of God looking out at the four directions, the prayer flags, and the prayer wheels inserted around the base of the stupa.

**Ferocious snow dragons** like this statue guard the doors of most Tibetan pagoda temples. This one is a meter tall.

would be repeated three times per revolution. A rough translation of this powerful mantra was explained to me by a Tibetan in Kathmandu who spoke a bit of English. He said it meant, "Hail to..." or "I Am... the Jewel in the Center of the Lotus," which is further understood to reference the I Am that is the Sacred Fire—The Presence of God—anchored in the center of our Heart Chakra. In other words, the mantra is a salutation to and affirmation of the Divine Focus of our life in this incarnation.

It seemed that the people were more inclined to smile than not. There were monks in their red robes walking about everywhere, some of them twirling hand-held prayer wheels and chanting away. Though I was somewhat introduced to the vast spirituality of India over the past weeks in my travels across northern India, here in Kathmandu, I felt for the first time that I truly was in a very sacred, powerful and spiritually vast place. There was a purity here, perhaps best conveyed by the smiles on the people's faces when we made eye contact, that far eclipsed anything that I had experienced before in my travels.

**Two large Buddha statues** flanking the long steps to the top of Swayambhunath temple on a hilltop in the center of Kathmandu.

**The great Buddha,** perhaps 12 feet tall, inside the main temple atop Swayambhunath.

My first days here were spent exploring this enchanted place, learning about the temples, the influence of the Hindu and Tibetan cultures that came together and to some extent blended here. A new culture arose here in this mountain valley, just as the vast Himalayan mountain range arose from the colliding of the Indian and Asian tectonic plates. There

59

**The top of Swayambhunath Temple** with one of the monkey
guardians that freely roam whereever they wish, outside and inside
the temple grounds. [AmazingPicturesPlace.com]

was a dramatic starkness and a pristine clarity here—to this city, to
its people, to the architecture and the overall vibration of this place
that was entirely different from anything I had ever experienced. It
was as if the thousands of years of the hourly recitations of the great
mantra, Om Mane Padme Hum, had thinned the veil that separates
the physical world from the higher or etheric world of the Gods.

In the very center of this ancient city surrounded by the snowcapped Himalayas arose a large hill, on the top of which stood an
ancient monastery called Swayambhunath with commanding views
of the entire city below, surrounded by the snowcapped Himalayas.
Climbing up this steep hill was good exercise. There were ancient
stone steps all the way up to the monastery that the many pilgrims
used daily to make their offerings to the Divine Presence. As Kathmandu was a blending of various cultures, the Divine Presence could
be represented by the great, golden statue of the Buddha that was
located inside the monastery, or by Chenrezig/Avalokiteshvara/The
Buddha of Compassion (the radiant, white Buddha form that repre-

sents purity and power of the enlightened mind's loving kindness and compassion) or by Maha Kali (the fierce Hindu aspect of the Great Mother deity, often depicted holding decapitated human heads)—all aspects of the Divine were revered in this place.

As I began to climb the long steps up to the monastery there were signs with apparent warning messages. I could not read the script but the pictures were easier to understand. Apparently this mountain was home to many large monkeys (about 3 feet tall) that were known to harass the pilgrims as they made their way up to the temple atop the hill.

Over the centuries the monkeys had come to rely upon the pilgrims for their food so as anyone made their way up the mountain to the temple, they were approached by many monkeys—all looking for food. It was recommended that you not travel alone as the monkeys were quite aggressive. I was solo but there were many pilgrims also making their way up to the temple, so I quickly became familiar with the monkeys' antics. When several approached me, I made a quick feint toward them and they scattered, chattering away.

Atop the mountain monastery temple complex sat a large stupa, a domed structure with a large spire. Beneath the spire on the dome were painted the eyes of the Buddha facing outward toward the four directions. These stupas or chortens of various sizes appear at every temple, every monastery, every mountain pass throughout Nepal, Tibet, Sikkim, and Bhutan. These serve as a reminder to those who pass by of the omnipresence of God symbolized by the eyes of the Buddha looking in four directions.

Inside the temple atop the mountain was a huge, golden statue of a sitting Buddha, perhaps 15 or 20 feet tall. Draped over its shoulders was a large sheet of clear plastic that was somewhat soiled with monkey droppings. The monkeys had free rein throughout the temple and were actively climbing the walls and the timbers that supported the ceiling. I learned later that the monkeys were considered sacred in this place and were allowed to roam freely (similar to cows in India).

### *Inner Acceleration—The Himalayas*

In my morning meditations that began to take shape in Israel, I would always pose a question; perhaps it was more of a statement to my Presence.

This prayer was that I be guided throughout the coming day so that I would experience all that I was supposed to experience. Now here in the Himalayas, throughout the day I found myself slipping into a similar stream of meditation even while walking about; it was like a listening dialogue with the Presence, my Father. The fine, gossamer thread that led me from day to day back in England and throughout Europe to Israel, all those months ago, now had become more of a golden chain. I was so conscious of the growing strength of this golden chain that I knew was connected to my Presence, guiding me forward according to a timetable that I could not yet perceive. I had a sense that all I had to do was wake up in the morning and I would enter this stream that would take me to the next experience, whenever and wherever that was, as part of the Master Plan for this lifetime.

After being in this enchanted location for just a few days, this sense of the golden chain grew stronger. There was a sense of excitement in having this conscious awareness that there was a major event ahead of me that I was literally being pulled forward into. I had the strong and clear sense that I had actually started this process long ago, that I had made choices earlier in this life that were directly responsible for the acceleration that I was now experiencing.

By now in this quest, I had long since given up any sense of concern as to what the next hour, let alone the next days, weeks or months, would bring forth into this life. There was never for an instant a question of going back to the life that I had lived before I left on this quest. I could easily summon the terrible taste of that dream-experience that I had back in Amherst at the university before I left America—for what I knew not. Waking immediately after the dream, the utter devastation of the culture about me, the sense that I had failed at whatever it was that I had come into this life to accomplish. I clearly recall the sickening feeling, realizing that I had gotten so caught up in that material culture—despite the inner promptings of my heart that there was more to life. I knew then that it was my mission in this lifetime to find out who I Am and why I came into this lifetime.

### *The Archer*

Now, in the first days of being in Kathmandu, the sense of acceleration and the profound sense of being at home in India and now in Nepal seemed to throw a light upon so many turning points in my life. I had a clear sense of how everything before now had prepared me for whatever it was that I was about to embark upon. The crystalline atmosphere of the Kathmandu valley, the radiant smiles of seemingly everyone whom I had eye contact with, even though I couldn't consciously understand a word they were saying, the beautiful pagoda temples, so ornately hand carved, each one focused upon a different God, which I knew even then was a different aspect of the One Divine Presence. The chanting of the mantras that seemed to be non-stop—all of this was like the great reward to me—a reward for the right decisions that I had made up to this point in the game.

All of this was like a great bow drawn back with me as the arrow, ready for flight, though I didn't consciously know the target of this arrow. I knew that the Great Archer who drew back the bow knew well the target and I was excited beyond words with this understanding.

Walking the ancient streets of Kathmandu in this sense of revelry I had met some guys who had just returned from a journey to the Mount Everest region. They told me that their Sherpa guides stopped at various monasteries along the way for shelter. Over the early years of this life, I had read mystical tales about Tibetan Himalayan monasteries and the monks who lived there. I knew then in an instant that I was going to visit these monasteries, and the fact that they adorned the long trails to the highest place on Earth, like jewels set upon towering mountain cliffs, just added fuel to the fire of my desire.

I visited the only expedition shop (in 1972) that existed in Kathmandu; this was the place run by a few European or North American guys that provided supplies to the expeditions that were going to make attempts to summit Everest or the other Himalayan peaks. They also arranged for Sherpa guides and knew the various circumstances that had to be navigated to attempt a long trek up across the high Himalayan Tibetan frontier (as opposed to the several-thousand-foot-high Himalayan foothills where Kathmandu is located). It was here that I first learned that there is a difficult, long trail, hundreds of kilometers long, which stretches from just outside Kathmandu to the base camp of Everest. This arduous long trail is the route that the Everest expeditions take to further condition themselves for the summit attempt, and to acclimatize their bodies to the high altitudes.

## The Long Trek to Everest

On Christmas Eve, I was sitting near a pagoda temple sipping from a small bottle of Nepali rum that I had purchased in honor of the day. While I was musing on everything that was opening before me, I saw a guy nearby taking photos. We started talking and found that we had some things in common. He was from Seattle and was also traveling solo, just having flown in to Delhi. It turns out that he was also very interested in taking the long journey to Mount Everest. We met the next day at the expedition shop and started making plans to do this. He knew my primary interest was in visiting the monasteries along the way. I had heard that, by making a small gift to the head lama at each monastery, one could take shelter there from the freezing-cold nights.

We obtained our permits from the Nepali government to trek up along the Tibetan/Nepali frontier and started gathering supplies—medicines, dehydrated foods and very warm clothes. We were told that very few ever attempted what we were going to do without

The following pictures were taken during the 25-day trek from Kathmandu to Mount Everest. During this period we passed through several different climate zones as we ascended higher and higher in our journey.

**The lush agricultural stepped terraces** carved into the side of the lower Himalayas.

**One of the more sturdy rope and wood footbridges** that we had to cross every time we descended a mountain pass, before we started the ascent to the next mountain pass—and there were many of them.

**A Tibetan woman** carrying a large, heavy basket by the strap across her forehead. Note the size of my pack and that I'm wearing shorts. In the lower altitudes, it was often very warm; however, after ascending several hours it became much colder.

Sherpa guides and porters. We were told that it was approximately a three-week, arduous trek of approximately 250 kilometers across the grain of the Himalayas, just to get to the Everest base camp and that there were many places where the going was extremely treacherous. We were told that the trails were mere footpaths, sometimes just a few feet wide, which wound up and down the extremely rugged and dangerous terrain. We were told that there were many shaky foot-bridges spanning roaring Himalayan rivers and there was no room for accidents. The men who owned the expedition shop did their best to warn us about what we were up against and why we needed to have Sherpa guides and porters. However, that was out of the question, as we just couldn't afford that luxury.

Getting there was one thing, getting back another—we knew it would take over three weeks just to get there. Planning logistics for a six-week-plus journey seemed a bit too much. Considering options, I discovered that it was possible for a specially equipped plane, weather permitting, to land at a short 11,000-foot-high field where yaks foraged, called Lukla, five days south of Everest, at or around a specific date. We could not carry enough supplies for the three-week return journey back to Kathmandu, so I made arrangements for this plane to pick us up at Lukla on or about January 27, 1973.

The "on or about" was due to the fact that the plane may not be able to land on a specific day because of weather, and there was no means of communication (except by lamas teleporting their thoughts from one monastery to another). It was our plan to make our way to Lukla after reaching Mount Everest, understanding that we might have to wait a few days for the weather to clear so the plane could land.

The planning continued. Around Dec 30th, I sent a letter to my parents, which I knew would take 2 to 3 weeks to get to them from Kathmandu. I wrote to them that I had spent most of the remainder of my funds on supplies and clothing to undertake this 3-plus-week trek across hundreds of miles of the Himalayas up to Everest. That I would be back in Kathmandu somewhere around the end of January and that if they wished to see me again, would they please loan me several hundred dollars, or else I would effectively be broke on the other side of the world upon my return from Everest. I was quite OK with that decision, as I had long since given up everything in my life to this increasing sense that my Presence was propelling me forward from one experience to the next. I told my parents in that letter that they could wire the funds to the U.S. Embassy in Kathmandu. I mailed the letter and forgot about it.

On January 1st at dawn, we got on a bus for a short journey to where the dirt road ended and the long trail to Everest, through the roof of the world, began. Our backpacks were huge and very heavy with food, warm clothes and double sleeping bags. I had a map (that I still have) showing the hundreds of kilometers of this trail's course across the Himalayas with all the mountain passes and their altitudes, with the valley floors, the footbridges over the raging rivers and their altitudes, and the various Tibetan/Nepali settlements and monasteries.

A settlement, for lack of a better word, was two or more buildings; actually they were mud/stone/thatch dwellings that hadn't changed much in thousands of years. The bottom of these dwellings were where the family's animals would take shelter in the night, the top floor would be usually one room where the family lived. When there was not a monastery nearby, we were allowed to sleep in the lower portion of some of these structures with the animals; it was far better than being out in the cold.

There were a few occasions in which we missed taking the correct fork in the trail and after climbing and descending many thousands of feet over many miles, realizing the error and having to backtrack. I was told by the expedition guides in Kathmandu that one of the reasons you have Sherpa guides and porters is because they know the trails; often there are avalanches that take out the trails and bridges, requiring detours. At the bottom of the map was a note that "trails, passes and bridges are subject to change" according to the acts of the Gods—they may or may not be there when you arrive.

### Himalayan Perspective

Though I wrote a journal of the technical aspects of this 28-day period detailing the thousands of feet of daily ascents and descents as we crossed the grain of the Himalayas, I will not include that here.

The crispness, the fragrance, of the Himalayan air is still pronounced in my memory after all these years, the intense sense of elation that I experienced literally every moment of this long, arduous trek is so tangible. There is no way to describe the grandeur of the vistas, and they changed every few minutes, as we progressed on this long trek. I was already in very good physical condition, so my body just accepted the heavy load of my backpack. The magnificence opening before me mile-by-mile eclipsed the physical exertion of climbing up thousands of feet and many miles over one Himalayan pass, then descending down thousands of feet and many more miles to the obligatory raging river below. The shaky footbridges that we then had to cross were just part of the day-after-day experience.

As we ascended to each pass, the stunning views everywhere

**Taking a break** near the mountain pass with our destination, the high Himalayas, in the background.

one looked only expanded. After several days of this, every Himalayan pass that we went through seemed like a victory, an accomplishment, because it took so much to get to this point. The trail at the very top of the pass had been literally gouged out by thousands of years of foot-travel with the Tibetan people scuffing away at the gravel or bedrock as they crossed the pass. On some passes, the gouge was several feet deep and along both sides of this were erected Mani walls, large rectangle stones, perhaps a few feet wide by 3 to 4 feet tall, upon which were carved Tibetan Buddhist scripture. These Mani walls were, for the most part, quite ancient. On some passes they stretched out for a few dozen yards on both sides of the gouged-out trail.

There was always a relatively small stupa, or chorten perhaps 12 feet tall, similar to what I described at the top of Monkey Temple in Kathmandu. The stupa was situated at the very highest point of the pass, not in the depression made by the thousands of years of foot traffic, but to the side. The Eyes of God, painted on the 4 sides at the top of the stupa, glared out over the four directions keeping watch over the affairs of the Earth. Atop the stupa, the spire adorned with Tibetan prayer flags fluttered in the ever-present wind. On the ground around the pass were the remains of ancient Mani wall pieces, which were now eroding by the wind and the rain back into gravel, no doubt thousands of years old. There were also older prayer flags that were also going back into their basic elements.

I try to convey here the great sense of Majesty and the sense of sacredness that my surroundings almost glaringly demanded of my dawning awareness. The meeting of a group of Tibetan Sherpas traveling in the opposite direction along this trail heightened this sense. They would be trekking single file, each carrying the large woven cone shaped baskets on their backs held by the strap across the head. Sometimes they used heavily laden yaks carrying hundreds of pounds of cargo; however, most of the time the people did all the work.

It was in this manner that goods were hauled from one monastery or one settlement to another. As we approached, they would stand to the side and raise their hands, palms pressed together as if in prayer before their heart, bow their heads and smile saying, *"Namaste,"* or "I bow before the God within you." Seeing their smiling eyes I thought that nothing could be more appropriate, no greeting could be more perfect, in this spectacular setting.

Every day the almost month-long journey to Everest became more physically difficult but more rewarding in every other way. After several days on the trail, we both had multiple blisters on both feet and it was painful to walk. We had planned on spending a night at a Sherpa settlement that we learned about back in Kathmandu where it was possible to share some food and rest for a day. When we arrived at this place, we were in very rough shape. It turned out that this was kind of a way station for expeditions that were heading up to, or returning from, Everest. Here we were able to stay in a dorm-style room with actual bunks. The first thing we did was to drop our huge heavy backpacks and take off our climbing boots, limp over to a beautiful, clear Himalayan stream and soak our tortured feet. I had planned for this eventuality and had packed bandages and antibiotic cream for my blistered feet. We stayed here for most of the next day just resting and soaking our feet. I was amazed at how quickly the blisters on my feet healed; it was as if the mountain stream that I soaked my feet in for hours had magical properties. The next day, recharged, we set out again on the trail.

This trek was a few hundred miles long. Over this period we had ascended over 35,000 feet and descended over 22,000 feet as we made our way up and down the grain of the Himalayas, crossing numerous rivers on rickety footbridges. There certainly weren't any roads, so the rickety, narrow, wood-and-rope bridges only had to accommodate hikers and yaks.

On more than one occasion, as we got into the last half of the journey, we would be rounding a corner on the very narrow trail hacked into the side of a sheer rock cliff, when toward us came a huge yak. Scurrying up the side of the cliff before we were gored, trampled or pushed off the cliff, we watched as these huge beasts loaded with their packs lurched by. They were shorter than cows but much wider, longer and heavier, with long, sharp horns and very long hair.

### The Monastery

I shared earlier that my plan was to visit the monasteries that were the heart of the Himalayan Tibetan Sherpa culture. We planned the trek hoping to spend the night at various monasteries along the way. As we navigated a half-day's journey off the main trail, climbing up and up this great spur of the Himalayas to this monastery straddling a great mountain cliff, I wondered at all the work that it had taken to erect this building. It was sprawling, many times the size of the dwelling places of the local people. The building, set on a large terrace cut into the mountain cliff, was of a whitewashed, stone material with large brown timbers framing the stonework. The prayer flags radiated out from the highest point to the lowest points of the monastery like the spokes of a wheel. Aside the monastery stood

**Stupas with the Eyes of God** looking out over this ancient mountain pass. Note the tattered prayer flags and the antiquity of the stupa bases. These were rebuilt over the countless centuries. Also note the mani walls between the two stupas. These mani walls are a meter high indicating that over the centuries, the foot traffic has scuffed away a deep trench across the top of this mountain pass. We are beginning to approach the high Himalayas off in the distance.

again the ever-present stupa with the Eyes of God facing the four directions fiercely looking out over the Earth—the constant reminder of the Omnipresence of the Father.

We approached the actual building marveling at the crafts-manship and the ornateness of the carved timbers, the carved wooden prayer wheels, the colorful prayer flags streaming in the wind, the stunning view of the high Himalayas everywhere one turned, and the sense of the sacred everywhere. An ancient Tibetan lama appeared around the corner of the building, standing there in his felt-peaked hat and red-brown robes, his hands raised in prayer. His eyes twinkled in a deep smile as he greeted us with, *"Namaste"* and invited us in.

We walked into the great room adorned with magnificent *tangkas* (rich, ornate and colorful paintings upon a raw silk background depicting the Tibetan Gods and Goddesses). Each of the tangkas magically shimmering, the images of the Gods seemed to move in the late-afternoon sun pouring through the huge, arched window as it settled behind the Himalayan peaks across the high valley.

Beneath the tangkas, sliding cabinet doors revealed dozens of Tibetan scripture scrolls rolled up and bound in some kind of silk ribbon. The fragrances of incense and chai, of the oil lamps and smoke from the wood fire in the corner, were all so comforting. The smiling eyes of this ancient lama looking not so much at me but through me—how perfect this place was, how wonderful. It was at this point in my journey that I became aware of a sense of conversation ongoing with this ancient lama and his wonderful female companion as we sat there before their open fire sipping tea while the Sun set across the valley.

No words were spoken on the outer, as I wouldn't have understood them, but conversation there was—the serene, majestic peace and perfection was so pregnant with wisdom—my senses overflowing with gratitude to my Father, the Presence of God within, for this experience. My physical body was exhausted from the long day's climbing. The lama gave us chai and some type of stewed potatoes. We shared the food we had and watched the daylight fading through the beautiful, large arched window. As soon as night approached, in acknowledgement of the lama's silent direction, we unrolled our sleeping bags on the floor of this great magnificent room. I remember seeing the lama and his companion do the same on the other side of the fire.

My consciousness replaying the events of this incredible day trying to wrap my mental arms around what I was experiencing since arriving at this monastery, but it was hopeless. I had the sense that I was using a retarded intellectual process to ascertain an ongoing experience that was so far beyond the intellect as to be unintelligible by that means of comprehension. Laughing to myself at the senseless

**The Taksindu Monastery.** The smaller buildings are living quarters for the monks. The small white building above the monastery is an unheated single room (just like all the monk's quarters) that is used by monks for long periods of solitary seclusion, in some instances lasting several months.

**The interior of the main room.** These are cabinets containing ancient, sacred Tibetan parchment scrolls. The paintings of the Tibetan gods are luxurious; the actual paint is made with locally produced pigments just as it has been for many centuries.

**Detail of a Tibetan Tangka painting** on raw silk showing three Tibetan gods. The elephant carries some kind of rainbow-hued wheel on its back. On the horse's back is an object from which six heads, perhaps representing souls of different races, are ascending.

**Tibetan Lama.** This is the lama from the first monastery that we stayed at.

effort, I fell hard into a dreamless sleep.

I was instantly and alertly awakened as Helios (God of the Sun) set afire the top of the Himalayan peaks towering above us at the monastery. The lama was smiling and making chai. It was a celebration—I was beginning to realize that every day is celebration. The lama opened a small bag and poured some roasted ground barley flour into the chai making a kind of porridge. *"Tsampa,"* he said, and handed it to me. It was delicious. I walked outside with the lama around the perimeter of the monastery. He showed me a large ornate prayer wheel, the largest I have ever seen since or before, perhaps 7 feet tall and 3 feet wide. It was constantly moving, powered by a small water wheel in the stream beneath it, its little bells tinkling. Dozens of lines of *Om Mane Padme Hum*, graced with hundreds of beautifully painted images of the Tibetan Gods—thus my perfect day started.

There were so many precious experiences during this journey. Some days later, we were descending from a high mountain pass with towering snowcapped Great Himalayas surrounding us. As we rounded a ridgeline, we had our first view of our goal—Mount Everest, towering surreal in the distance. It was still more than a week's climb away. Then, a few hundred yards further along this narrow trail, along the side of a sheer cliff dropping off thousands of feet below us, we reached the tree line—except the trees here were all rhododendrons in full bloom—and there was a snow-squall taking place. It was a scene that dreams are made of.

Another memorable but very long day concluded after reaching a Tibetan settlement, nothing more than a few stone-age dwellings situated in a relatively flat area along the side of a great mountain range. As I walked closer, I began to smell a strangely familiar aroma that reminded me of being a kid at the movies. I was astonished to identify it as popcorn. As I walked up to the door I looked in and saw a Tibetan woman stirring raw barley in a wok-like pot over an open fire. After it started to brown and burn, she ground it into powder. This she called *tsampa*, the primary staple of these mountain people, this is mixed with their yak-butter chai to make a porridge, exactly what the lama had given us a few days earlier. We were able to purchase some of this from her to add to our morning chai.

One day led quickly into another and as our physical bodies grew acclimated to our arduous climb through the Great Himalayas, at the same time it seemed my awareness continued to expand. We were perhaps a few days from Namche Bazaar, the mystical Tibetan village that is the rallying point for all expeditions to Everest, when we came to another very special monastery that I had learned about in Kathmandu. This time it was our good fortune that the head lama spoke a little English. Unlike the previous one, this monastery had many monks who lived in adjoining buildings. The head lama invited us to spend the night in the main room with him. This was a much different experience for me as I stayed up into the wee hours engaged in conversation with the lama.

He explained that he was a Tulku Lama, a reincarnated lama. When he was a little boy of 3 years, he was identified by other high lamas as the reincarnation of a famous lama who had passed away a few years earlier. There was an elaborate testing procedure where this 3-year-old had to identify objects that belonged to him in his former life as the head lama of another important monastery. When this boy correctly identified the objects that were his in his past life, as well as identifying some of the older lamas who were giving him the test, he was immediately appointed the head lama of many dozens of monks—all of this at the tender age of three or four years old. That night, he and I spoke of reincarnation and karma and a hundred other things concerning the Tibetan Buddhist teachings, which are

**Just before Scott and I descended down to Taksindu Monastery** for the night. The following day, we descended further down to the river, then the long, hard climb up to Namche Bazaar. Note the deep gouge in the mountain pass caused by thousands of years of foot traffic.

at the heart of this Himalayan culture.

When we left the next morning, he gave me several rice-paper, woodblock prints of various Tibetan buddhas and a very special Tibetan knife, the wooden handle of which is inlaid with various metals. The long, curved blade has stamped into the metal the symbol of the Sun on one side and the Moon on the other. It is still on my bookcase in its yak-leather sheath, along with treasured spiritual books from around the world.

We awoke abruptly at dawn the next morning to Tibetan horns, drums and chanting in the adjoining great-room, more like a hall, where dozens of monks were playing these instruments and chanting. A funeral was in progress. We watched the proceedings for a short while and then headed back onto the trail to start the big push, still many miles away, up to Namche Bazaar, the destination that we had been asking the Sherpas and Tibetans about that we met on the trail these past weeks.

### *Approaching Everest*

There was a sense of exhilaration within as we approached this key point in our journey. We descended the high-mountain pass, again thousands of feet down to the river valley, and then once again started the hard climb up the mountain to Namche Bazaar. Now the towering Himalayas were pressing down upon us seeming to blot out the sky with their vast, huge presence. The valley was so much steeper than the others we had crossed these past three weeks; the thousands of feet we had to climb up to Namche was that much more difficult. Finally, we crested the steep, narrow trail onto the high-mountain shelf, seemingly cut into the side of the mountain by the giant hands of gods.

Here, situated on several concentric step terraces open to the precipitous cliff and cut into the side of the mountain, were situated a dozen or so small structures and the monastery that is the small village of Namche Bazaar. There was also a larger building that we stumbled into where we could sleep and eat for the next few days as we gathered our reserves for the final, extremely difficult push to Everest.

I had been as high as 12,000 feet in the Rockies, but here at Namche, the highest village in the Himalayas, everything was so different, so intense, and so starkly beautiful. The village was literally situated on a ledge carved out of a high-mountain cliff. Just a hundred yards from the rugged, sturdy dwellings arranged in several terraced half circles, one upon another in steps, the cliff dropped off thousands of feet to the raging river below. All around you, so very close that you had the sense that you could just reach out and touch them, were the snow- and ice-covered flanks of the Great Himalayan range towering 10,000 feet and more above.

Occasionally you would hear a distant roar and there, across the valley on the high flanks of the mountain across from us, would be a huge avalanche cascading, roaring down and obliterating everything in its path. Immediately now about us there was the sense that life is very tenuous in such a place. It was a waking dream, completely surreal, to be in such a place.

We spent a few days in Namche Bazaar (at 11,000 feet) acclimatizing to the altitude, resting and preparing ourselves for what lay ahead. We were now required to be very diligent, as every day would bring us higher, and at any time it was possible to get altitude sickness, hypoxia, that would end our journey, and if not acted upon immediately, it could end us. Many who are not used to the effects of the high altitude get very ill very quickly here. Our gradual exposure to higher and higher altitudes over the past 3 weeks helped our bodies acclimatize thus far but the most severe and dangerous portion of our odyssey was before us and extreme caution was the byword.

During the few days that we took at Namche to acclimatize, we would take a few half-day hikes, climbing up the mountain and then back down to Namche, getting my body more used to the higher altitudes. Climbing from 11,000 to above 12,000 on this short hike was difficult even without my heavy backpack that I had left behind for the day. At the end of the day we were exhausted. As stated earlier, in the Himalayas when the Sun sets, it gets dark very quickly and everyone sleeps, and for me it was always a hard, deep sleep. The last night at Namche, I was awakened in the middle of the night by soft chanting. I looked over to the other end of the room about 20 feet away to see a group of Tibetan monks and a presiding Lama standing, chanting over the prostrate body of a little boy. The eerie scene was dimly lit by a few yak-butter lamps that cast a faint, yellow light in the other corner of the room where this ritual played out.

The boy had died in the night. He had a bad cough the previous day and didn't look well. Life is so hard here; most live in a one-room dwelling with a fire that is often vented by an open window. There is no running water or other human comforts that are customary in lower and warmer areas of the world. As a result it seems like there is no middle age—you are either young or old and then you are dead. A few days before we were at the other monastery during the funeral ceremony; now with this boy's passing, it was apparent that death was no stranger to this land. In this intensely beautiful but

**Our first view of Namche Bazaar** (altitude of 11,200 feet) after climbing thousands of feet up the steep trail from the river.

**The Namche Bazaar terraces** upon which the dwellings are built. Usually heated by one, small, open smoldering fire in one corner of the building. Note the precipitous cliff to the side of the plateau.

**The towering mountains across from Namche Bazar.** Avalanches could be seen and heard thundering down from the cloud-covered peaks above.

stark realm of the high Himalayas, I was becoming more and more aware of how delicate the balance between life and death is.

The next morning there was some kind of ceremony near the stupa in the courtyard (for lack of a better word) that was the center-point of Namche Bazaar. This ceremony was attended by many monks and the residents of the village; some were involved in a slow, rhythmic dance wearing garish costumes and masks depicting various Tibetan gods and demons. There was chanting and with the blaring Tibetan horns that were totally discordant, the entire ceremony was eerie. A bit uneasy by what we saw of that ceremony, we set out that morning for the slow, day-long climb above the tree line up to the Tengboche Monastery. Now walking was no longer automatic.

The higher we went, the more we had to think about the slow, measured steps we would take. There were to be no more descents until we were on our way back from our destination, Kala Patar, a hill on the shoulder on the top of the world, located 1500 feet above the 17,000-foot-high Everest base camp, from which we could get amazing pictures of the top of the world.

### *Tengboche Monastery*

Tengboche monastery was an austere, forbidden-looking place, perched on a hilltop at around 13,000 feet. The structure was battered and scoured by the high Himalayan winds that had left their erosion everywhere one looked. There was an ancient stupa nearby made of stone and brick that seemed only a few more years away from turning back into gravel. Old and some newer prayer flags streamed from the stupa and the monastery but were often shredded by the exposed elements. Now at this altitude, we were constantly surrounded by the doleful moaning of the wind that eerily changed its tone as we moved through the great Himalayan Mountains—struggling, climbing higher, and further away from life.

As we climbed up to this mountain shelf that held Tengboche monastery, with a shudder we were able to see the trail that would bring us, after a few days of acclimatization here at Tengboche, to Everest itself. Stretching off into the distance like a mirage across this impossibly rugged landscape was the snow-laden Nupse/Lhotse ridgeline, soaring above 25,000 feet, with the bare, black immensity of Everest jutting above it; as if Everest wanted to make a further statement warning all so foolish as to even consider coming closer about the fatal consequences of error. It was so severe looking, so stark in appearance as to make me shudder; yet still, there was this unrelenting drive to continue onward.

We spent two days at Tengboche acclimatizing and preparing for the huge push up to the Khumbu Glacier and the little pile of ruins that was called Lobeche (over 15,000 feet) where we were to camp the night before we made our final ascent to Kala Patar. Those two nights in Tengboche Monastery and thereafter, there was not much talk between us. The high altitude, the cold, austere sacredness of the monastery, and what we had to individually gather within ourselves for this last part of our hard trek kept us both preoccupied.

We knew that many who attempted to climb Everest took sick on this next leg of our journey and had to quickly be helped back

**Ancient stupa near the Tengboche Monastery** eroded by the never-ending winds. Note the mani walls.

down to lower altitudes or suffer the fatal consequences. We knew that most of those who came this far did so with Sherpa guides and porters. It was just the two of us from the other side of the world that shared a dream to go to the top of the world, which now, after more than three intense weeks of climbing, was only a few days ahead of us. This was also winter here—all climbing expeditions made this trek during the warmer months. If we tripped on the tortured terrain of the vast glacier or became hypoxic, it could get very bad very quickly.

Perhaps it was that long, cold night in the Tengboche Monastery that I lay awake, unable to sleep, with all that was opening before me. I was again the Watcher. I remember laying there looking up at the cold stars that were now so close and realizing that at this point in this lifetime, everything in my life was completely and forever altered. I became completely aware, like a light switch was turned on, with the understanding that now there was nothing that I could not do. It was such an exhilarating feeling and I knew that the next days of this trek, and the days, weeks, months and years that followed, were somehow already mapped out with infinite potential. I knew with an utter certainty at that point on that night that

**Walking up to the Tengboche Monastery** at 12,600-feet altitude. This monastery has been considered profoundly sacred in the Tibetan tradition for centuries.

**The Tengboche Monastery** was destroyed by fire in 1989, in which many precious ancient scrolls and statues were lost.

**View of Mount Everest** peaking above the Nupse/ Lohtse ride from the Tengboche Monastery, showing our actual trail for the next three days.

who I was awakening to exceeded the identity of the name and the life that I was given growing up in this lifetime. The immensity of the potential that I was experiencing reminded me of what I touched on that mountain summit in Colorado.

Starting out at dawn with concentrated effort due to the lack of oxygen, we slowly made our way up the difficult trail that was still readily apparent, past the small Piereche Monastery (14,000 feet) that was closed for the winter.

This monastery was reported to have the scalp of a Yeti in-side. Yetis? Himalayan snow leopards? Tibetan wolfs? Demons? In this land where everything is possible, there was no doubt that there were creatures that we didn't wish to meet looking upon us through-out the long, hard days of our journey. I believe it was while ascend-ing out of Namche toward Tengboche, while we were climbing up a narrow trail carved against the side of the cliff, that above me a huge wolf growled and sprung toward me. In an instant I had my knife out and somehow the wolf magically changed course in midair and landed a few feet away from me and ran off. Neither of us could be-lieve that we really saw that happen.

Throughout this period I frequently had the sense that we were being observed and that there was danger at every step. There was an awareness that something big was about to happen; at the time, I saw it as the fulfillment of a long-held dream, but there was also something that I could not intellectually touch, that I knew was just around the corner, that would be life-changing.

Ever so slowly walking up and up and up this long, rocky trail, seemingly in slow motion, the higher and further we got, the more difficult it was to speak. The high Himalayas began to crowd in upon as did the cold. Eventually even the scrub vegetation above 14,000 feet gave way to bare rock, gravel, and then more and more ice and snow. Even the light of the day was different here—more stark, al-most monochromatic, the sky a deeper, darker blue than I've ever seen. The sound of our footfalls on the trail seemed more distant and then I noticed that when we had to speak, the infrequent comments sounded somehow more distant, there was less air to carry the sound of our voice, or the sound of anything save the eerie, doleful moaning of the wind. We were above 15,000 feet now and most of the Earth's atmosphere was below us; as we pushed on, climbing higher, this effect became more noticeable, more otherworldly.

I recalled another reference about the realm of the high Himalayas, a reference to *Chomolongma* (the Tibetan name for Everest, which translated means the Lord Goddess of the Universe), that we were no longer in the land of the living. I thought to myself how apt a description, for there was nothing but rock and snow and ice, blasted and hard-packed by the unending winds howling down from the top of the world around us.

To underscore this building sense of foreboding, the sound of distant thunder growing closer, then off to the side, way above us, a huge avalanche thundering down the flanks of a nameless great mountain. We watched in amazement as this avalanche ended at the foot of the mountain perhaps a mile from where we stood. Now having to consciously lift one foot and placing it in front of the other with great effort, we continued onward, two more days till we were to reach our goal. Two more days of climbing higher and higher through the most treacherous, blasted terrain I could have ever imagined.

### Khumbu Glacier

We continued pushing on ever more slowly up the Khumbu glacier above 15,000 feet, our eyes watching where we placed our feet on the narrow trail atop the glacier. Straying off this narrow trail less than a few feet wide would guarantee a broken ankle or leg as the glacier was like a wind-swept sea, frozen in motion. There were crevasses a foot deep or more on either side of the glacial trail. Slipping off and breaking something and it would be all over—period, end of story.

Finally almost in a daze of fatigue and lack of oxygen, we approached the stone ruins where we had planned to camp for the

**Our trail from Pierche (altitude over 14,000 feet) up the Khumbu Glacier**. On our return back from Kala Patar, 2 or 3 days later, this was what we traversed lit only by the full moon. It was at the end of this great valley, in the wee hours of the morning when, exhausted and frozen we took shelter in the yak herder's hut, somewhere north of Pierche. It was then that we had that terrifying encounter.

night. The building had no windows or doors but it did afford a break from the relentless, terrible wind. The elevation was somewhere around 16,000 feet. We were both experiencing a touch of hypoxia now, with headaches and dizziness, very spacy as we tried to make some warm tea to prepare our bodies for sleep. I was so spacy that I forgot that I put my all-important sunglasses in the deep pocket of my heavy parka. I forgot about it until I sat upon them and crushed them, knowing with dread that I would have a problem on the morrow climbing up the snow and ice of the glacier to Kala Patar in bright sunlight. Dreading the cold night that was falling quickly upon us we prepared as best we could.

We both had double sleeping bags and this was the night that we had carried them all this way to use. Fully dressed with multiple layers, we crawled in our sleeping bags as soon as the Sun set, for then the bottom fell out of the temperature, it was colder than I ever experienced. I was cold but soon fell into a light sleep. Somewhere in the middle of the night a few hours before dawn, I struggled awake in a dream. I was dreaming about a book I had to read in high-school English class about a guy who was in Alaska and fell into a river and almost froze to death. I remember reading that this guy couldn't feel his feet or hands and just wanted to go to sleep but he forced himself awake, realizing that he was freezing to death. There was a nagging warning that I could just about touch in this dream and then, with great effort, I realized that I was having this dream because I couldn't feel my own hands and feet and I just wanted to go deeply to sleep.

I struggled awake and sat up in the more than bitter cold, grabbed my boot and threw it at my friend several feet away from me, finally getting him to wake up. He was also numb. We got up and started jumping around and then got back into our sleeping bags repeating this until the dawn. At one point I remember spitting and hearing it crack when it hit the ground.

As soon as the Sun crested the mountain, feeling in a daze but still better than we had felt the night before, we set off up the glacier on the trail that was becoming more and more difficult to follow the further along we went. We were to go past Everest base camp at 17,000 feet and then divert onto a trail that in a few miles would ascend another 1,500 feet to the hilltop named Kala Patar. By now the glacier had turned into huge hills of ice and rock that got higher and steeper as we approached base camp. It was ever more difficult to put one foot in front of the other—it required more concentration and mental effort than the previous day because we were so much higher.

The bright Sun reflected off the glacier and the towering snow- and ice-covered Himalayan peaks that surrounded us. It was as if the Gods placed these peaks here as Everest's sentinels—stark white and forbidding against the dark, blue sky as a warning to mortals. The cold wind made a high-pitched, distant keening sound and the periodic avalanches sounded a distant thunder.

Finally, after hours of pushing, we arrived at Everest base

camp. Here a stupa, prayer flags, and several graves of individuals who did not have the protection of the Gods marked this spot quite well. (We were told how it would appear by the expedition supply store in Kathmandu.) The Tibetan name for this place, the base camp of Chomolongma, was Gorak Shep, an ugly word that means dead crow, a most appropriate name, as living was not supposed to happen in this God-forsaken place.

### *Kala Patar*

We decided to leave our heavy backpacks and sleeping bags where we spent the night, making this last, hard day easier. We had planned to spend the night there after descending from Kala Patar, that would make the last hard day of climbing much easier, would make what we were about to do possible. The day seemed to speed by, the Sun glaring off the huge white mountains and the white glacier, the great mountains still towering 10,000 feet and more above us even at and past the base camp at 17,000 feet. Avalanches happened frequently, the sound a distant thunder, the trail of snow kicked up like a long exclamation point heading down the heights around us. I was driven, relentless. The goal was within reach just hours away.

I don't recall stopping to rest save for a brief pause to eat a handful of dried fruit and nuts and to drink some water taken from the glacier melt at a lower altitude days before. We pushed on, driven to get to the summit of Kala Patar. At one point, we took the wrong turn and realized after a few hours that we had likely strayed across the unmarked frontier into Tibet. We managed to backtrack and re-join the trail, continuing our arduous ascent that was now becoming more and more a hand-over-hand climb. Hours went by in this slow ascent and then, finally rounding a curve in the hill, the summit was before us. We had reached our destination next to the top of the world.

Located at 18,500 feet, a shoulder hill of the Nupse/Lhotse Chomolonga massif, it was here that we had learned back in Kath-

**Climbing above the Everest base camp at 17,500 feet.**
Looking back over what we climbed through the past few days.

mandu that we could get the best pictures of the highest mountains in the world. The base camp of Everest lay 1500 feet below us and yet the mountains still towered 10,000 feet above us and all around us. As I was slowly walking to get a better vantage point, what we had dreaded happened. I fell into a crevasse at the top of Kala Patar. I caught myself with my arms and managed to pull myself up and out of the crevasse just as my friend caught up to my position. Just as I pulled myself out, I looked up and the glaring, bright sunlight off the totally white mountains burst into my vision. I went completely, utterly snowblind.

I sat down where I was and told my friend that I couldn't see. He knew that I went snowblind because I had broken my sunglasses the night before. As the minutes turned into a very long time, we just sat there. There was nothing to be said because it was understood that I would not be able to make it down Kala Patar without seeing where I was going. I could hear from a far-off distance the wind moaning and the occasional distant thunder of an avalanche. I felt a great peace about me. Here I was at 18,500 feet on the side of Everest after the hardest 23 days of pushing that I've ever experienced in my life. I was flooded with non-stop memories of the past few years: the events in Israel, my experiences crossing Asia, my almost triumphant return to India (even though it was the first time I had been there in this lifetime), the magic of the Taj Mahal, the beauty of the people, the mystical perfection of Kathmandu, and the amazing experiences these past three-plus weeks, climbing to the top of the world.

There was not one erg of fear or dread; there was just this vast peace as I thanked the Presence, my Father, for allowing me to have all these amazing experiences. I was so grateful to conclude this lifetime here, rather than caught up in what I was living back at the university. In the midst of this gratitude, this deep peace, I became aware that there were other Presences around me. I became aware that these "others" were likely the Masters, who had been in the background of my life for a long time now, and who I had been searching for.

**Climbing up Kala Patar** looking back at what we climbed through this last intense day.

**Ascending the last 1,000 feet to the top of Kala Patar**. Puma Ri is in the background. Note the strain and bleak intensity of my features 24 days into our trek from Kathmandu. The previous night, we almost froze to death at 1,000 feet lower in altitude from where this picture was taken. We left our backpacks and sleeping bags ten miles back so we could do this last, hardest push without that extra weight.

There was, again, some kind of communion that was ongoing that I could only just touch on in the periphery of my understanding. But the Peace and Perfection of the moment was absolute—it was complete. This was it—the final moments of this lifetime. I was ready to let go of this life and consciously go into the experience that awaited me as the night settled in and the temperatures again fell through the floor.

It was in this sense of such peace and perfection and gratitude, with the sense that "others" were with me, that my vision slowly returned. My friend was so relieved as the Sun was beginning to drop behind the western summits, the night and deathly cold comes quickly at 18,500 feet. We carefully made our way down the hardest technical 1500 feet of Kala Patar and approached the small stupa and the graves at Everest base camp just as it got dark.

Amazingly the full moon rose above the eastern summits and blanketed the high Himalayan massifs around us in an otherworldly, silver-white-blue radiance. It was staggeringly beautiful. We had no

**Everest from Kala Patar.**
The last two pictures of Everest were taken from the top of Kala Patar at an altitude of 18,500 feet, immediately before I fell into the crevasse at the top of Kala Patar. Everest is towering above us at 29,028 feet.

flashlights and without the Moon, we would not have been able to navigate the many miles across the narrow ice bridges that were our footpaths on the Khumbu glacier. We walked down and down, mile after mile, so far beyond exhausted but knowing we had to reach our previous night's camping spot for our sleeping bags and warm clothes if we were to survive the night.

Eventually we came to that shelter, and almost without a word, picked up our gear and decided to continue on down the glacier to a yak-herder's stone hut we knew was only another 7 to 10 miles further down the glacier. This hut was closed in and would keep us from the terrible, all-pervasive cold and wind.

How to describe this long night under the full moon climbing down the Khumbu glacier after the events that I experienced on the summit of Kala Patar? It was all but impossible for me to grasp what had happened—what I had experienced and felt upon the victory of obtaining our goal and then falling into the crevasse, freeing myself only to go snowblind for those hours, then experiencing the Peace and that same Presence that I had become more and more aware of over these last years, guiding me from experience to experience.

We were euphoric as we descended lower and our bodies were able to breathe more easily. Our non-stop trekking down the glacier kept us warm despite the deadly cold. The moonlight made the stark flanks of the high Himalayas around us shimmer, seeming to levitate from the very ground. I was very aware that we were watched over, even protected, on this adventure, and looking up at the high mountain cliffs above me, I had the uneasy sense that we were being watched.

### *The Yeti*

After several hours of climbing down, down, down the glacier under the full moon, we saw in the distance, a few miles further on, the yak-herders hut. Miracle upon miracle, there was smoke curling up from the small, open window that served as the chimney in the Himalayas. Soon, our long ordeal drawing to a close, I was knocking on the door and calling to those inside to give us shelter for the short remainder of the night. An elderly Tibetan opened the door and graciously motioned us to enter.

The one-room hut was about 15 feet square and about 5 feet high. There was a fire in one corner and a tiny, square, one-foot-wide window that allowed the smoke to go out of the building, and the heavy timber door. We bowed before the elderly man and his female companion and shedding our heavy backpacks, we sat down heavily against the wall, utterly exhausted—so grateful to be out of the terrible cold, so grateful for everything.

Then, out of nowhere came the most blood-curdling, roaring screech that I have ever heard in my life. My blood turned into ice and my heart stopped. We threw ourselves up against the far wall and grabbed for our knives, terrified as to what would surely come next. Immediately upon hearing the terrible, roaring screech, the old man dove for the door and threw down the heavy beam to lock the door, then ran to close the small window. The old lady jumped into his arms and cried, "Yeti, yeti, yeti!" We were white with dread. The next instant the door banged and shuddered under the repeated roaring screech and hammering of the Yeti trying to get in. We had our knives drawn in front of us, backs against the wall, waiting for the most horrible death that could be imagined to confront us. The four of us looked at each other in dread, not daring to breathe, waiting for the Yeti to burst through the door.

The long seconds of silence turned into a minute, and the minute turned into another minute. We began to breathe again. Did that really happen? The Yeti had to have been following us down the glacier in the moonlight for the past several hours. Somehow we made it to the safety of the hut before the Yeti got close enough to attack. The old man and women were shaking like leaves in a storm. How much more could a person endure? Somehow our exhaustion took hold and we fell asleep with our knives in our hands.

Waking a few hours later to sunlight pouring through the tiny window, I walked out of this shelter with nothing but the high Himalayas and the blue sky all around us. We made our way down the glacier back to Tengboche and then on to Namche where we spent the night prior to heading a few days further south to the high yak pasture that was called Lukla. It was here that the STOL (short take-off and landing) aircraft was to pick us up. We had to wait a few days until the weather cleared enough for the plane to get in, and then in a most amazing experience, after spending the last 26 days climbing through the Himalayas, we flew back to Kathmandu in just over an hour.

Sitting next to the pilot I asked him how he got into aviation. He said, "I always wanted to fly so I found a flight school." It was then that I knew that flying would be part of my future. ଔ

## 10 ~ **Back Home to India**

Arriving back in Kathmandu with only a few rupees in my pocket, I went immediately to the U.S. Embassy and to my great joy, found a wire waiting for me there from my parents. I checked into a hotel, had a hot shower and a nice meal. Later I said goodbye to my friend with whom I had shared the past month. He was flying back to Seattle and the next day, I set out back to India.

I didn't know why at the time but I just had to go to Darjeeling and then on to Sikkim. Walking around Kathmandu the day before I left for India, I found that back in lower elevations, without the weight of my heavy backpack, I could flex the muscles in my legs and without any effort jump into the air. It was quite amazing to be in such good shape. Arranging for the transportation and getting back to India was almost leisurely and comfortable after the pushing of the past month through the Himalayas.

I made my way to a frontier town in northeast India where I could board the tiny train that made the daylong journey through the eastern Himalayas, up to the enchanted town of Darjeeling. The climate here was much different than any place I had ever been. It was mountain-tropical, humid but also refreshing, and the people's features were different. I was close to Burma now and the southeast-Asian features were more prominent than the Indian, Tibetan, or Chinese that I had experienced up to this point.

The tiny train made a long, slow climb up the mountains, crossing many small bridges that spanned huge drops to the rivers below. Eventually in the mid-afternoon, after passing through endless tea plantations decked out on large terraces cut into the sides of the mountains, we pulled into Darjeeling. It wasn't until another several years that I learned why I had to go to Darjeeling—why it had such an allure to me. (Years later I had learned that the Master El Morya, one of the co-founders of the Theosophical Society as well as subsequent activities that were designed to bring the Brotherhood's teachings to the West, had his retreat there in Darjeeling.)

The vibration of this high-mountain town was pristine, the view of the eastern Himalayas all around, with the giant massif of Kanchenjunga (at 28,169 feet) towering over everything. I remember one morning getting up way before dawn to climb to a pagoda temple on a hilltop to the side of Darjeeling to watch the sunrise. It went from dark to light in just a few seconds as Helios touched the top of Kanchenjunga. After spending a few days in Darjeeling, I made a two-day trip up to Sikkim, traveling through the tropical mountain jungles by means of a Land Rover. We had to travel for many hours down a one-lane gravel road that in some places was more dense jungle than road.

Eventually the jungle thinned as we approached the ancient, walled city of Kalimpong. This seemed to consist of one large monastery and was the center for trade in the eastern Himalayan region. As beautiful as this part of the Himalayas was to me, I knew I had to go back south to Benares and Sarnath, where the Buddha had taught his first sermon near the banks of the Ganges.

### Benares/Sarnath

When one arrives in Benares, one has arrived in the holiest city in all of India. This ancient city along the Ganges played a major role in my awakening. I can remember the train arriving from Darjeeling in the mid-afternoon. Even though I was familiar with the teeming crowds of India, I wasn't prepared for the mass of humanity that I experienced in Benares. Walking away from the train station, I was swept along in a flowing river composed of many thousands of people and their rickshaws.

Everything about this place was intense. The energy was electric, the smells so different and conflicting—the ever-present sound of Benares included everything from harmonies to jarring cacophony, from the tinkle of the bells worn on the heads of the elephants that paraded through the tiny streets, carrying the wedding party of the moment, to the chanting of numberless Sadhus that were omnipresent in this place. It was an assault on the senses. The closer I got to the Ganges, the atmosphere became even more charged. (I soon learned that was where the moving river of humanity was headed.) There were more people here in these small, crowded streets than I have experienced anywhere else in India. On both sides of the streets, interspaced with all kinds of shops, were endless temples to every God and Goddess imaginable.

As I made my way further down the street toward the Ganges, I began to notice a more-than-normal amount of people who were ill—some were very ill. Soon these ill people were standing in long lines on both sides of the streets, all seemed to be waiting for something or someone. Everywhere there were the ubiquitous Indian sadhus, priests and holy men, in every type of attire. Everywhere there were beggars. Everywhere there was endless sound, endless smells, endless activity. It was growing dark now but unlike the Himalayas there was no letup in the teeming energy of this place.

Over the past year of my travels, I had increasingly developed a spherical awareness (for lack of a better word) to what was going on around me. Being a stranger in a strange land, especially in crowded cities, it was very prudent to be aware, lest something unfortunate occurs—be it at the hand of another, contaminated food or water, an unsafe building or a failed mechanical something or other. There were countless times when this spherical awareness alerted me that something was amiss and there were countless times that this awareness brought my attention to something very beautiful. Walking down this street that night in Benares, I was totally aware of my surroundings. It was a boiling cauldron of life and it was getting more intense by the moment.

My attention was suddenly drawn to something very unpleasant that was lying on the crowded street before me and I thankfully stepped around it, there were many unpleasant things in such a place.

I progressed further along this immensely crowded, very narrow street lined with ill people on both sides. Some were sitting down in line, some talking to others, some just silent, staring ahead almost as in a trance. Further along the street the ill people were lying down, and then, as I made my way further along this intensely crowded and narrow street, it became obvious that these people who were lying down in line at this point in the road were now dead.

Other people were painting the faces, hands and feet of the new corpses with strange religious symbols. The dream-like quality of this place (and not a pleasant dream at that)—the sights, sounds and smells, the activity, the electricity—just seemed to be getting more intense with every moment. Now and then, a procession of huge elephants, all adorned with bells and symbols and various scarves of myriad rainbow colors, would come sauntering down these narrow, so crowded streets.

At the last possible moment, the hundreds of people in the streets just scurried to get out of the elephants' paths. I became aware that this was some type of marriage ceremony as there were a bride and a groom on the backs of these elephants. It was a more than strange juxtaposition to see a celebration of life on this one narrow street, immediately next to laid-out corpses and hundreds of people who were in their last moments of life. In fact, these people were lining up, while still alive, to be guaranteed their place in the cremation fires at the end of the street on the banks of the Ganges.

Never will I forget standing on the banks of the Ganges that first night in Benares, standing there watching the endless cremation fires and the endless lines of humanity feeding these cremation fires throughout the night. I'll never forget standing there watching a body that only a few hours ago was alive, being placed on a pile of wood, and then before my eyes in a matter of minutes, being turned to ashes.

All night long, until dawn crested over the eastern shore of the Ganges, I stayed in this place meditating on the impermanence of life, watching the ancient, endless ritual that concluded one particular lifetime. Watching the guardians of the cremation fires place body after body onto new funeral biers. Watching the relatives light the fire, watching the guardian take a long staff and after the fires had been burning for some time, cracking the staff down upon the head of the corpse as it burned, shattering the skull, with pieces of stewed brains and bone flying off in all directions, and even a piece of something bouncing off of my face. Then, as the fires consumed the body, watching the guardians rake the ashes into the Ganges. The process would start all over again on the same spot with a new funeral bier being built for the next corpse.

From where I stood that long, endless night, I could see scores and scores of these cremation fires on both sides of the Ganges doing their work, each with the same endless line of humanity feeding them. It was then that I realized so completely that I was much more than this body or this name that I was given 22-23 years earlier. It was then that I realized with absolute certainty that I had been in embodiment many times before. It was here that I began to touch this vastness of my Presence as the Watcher, watching again the life experiences that were occurring around me—the life experiences that, by my free will, I had created, either by action or inaction. Surely I was beginning to awaken.

The Benares area is so very powerful and so very crowded. However, in a remarkable juxtaposition, just a short distance away, is the town of Sarnath, where the Buddha taught his first sermon. There was a great charge of peace here that was quite palpable. There were ancient ruins of monasteries scattered about this town interspaced with beautiful gardens. I ended up staying in this town for a few weeks, meditating upon the experiences of Benares and my year-long journey up to this point, reading books about the Path and meditation that I got from the Theosophical Society headquarters in Benares.

Now looking back on these experiences, I'm aware that my travels took me to specific areas and that at the time, I wasn't aware of their greater importance in the process that was unfolding within me. I was not consciously aware at that point in my life that a Master's presence, by virtue of their communion with their own Divinity, actually anchored the Fire of their Presence into the earth element at the location where the Master was in meditation. I experienced this in several places that I had already visited—from southwest England, Jerusalem, Agra, the Tibetan monasteries that I had stayed at in the Himalayas, in Darjeeling—and now here at Sarnath. Each place was unique and the vibrations completely different, but at each of these locations, there was a subtle charge of Peace that was most tangible. My time at Sarnath was my first direct connection with the Buddha in this lifetime.

Again there was a sense of an appointment that I had to keep, a time schedule that I was on, and it was time for me to leave.

### The Taj Mahal Again

It was another overnight train ride back to Agra and the Taj Mahal. I was at the Taj only a few months earlier but the magnet of this place was so powerful to me. The train approached Agra just at dawn. The mists rising up from the endless plains surrounding Agra diffused the shafts of sunlight. Soon appeared the Yamuna River in the distance and then, like a vision from another world, the gleaming, golden-white splendor of the Taj Mahal through the mists. The towering, ornate dome and minarets caught the golden rays of the Sun that just crested the Eastern horizon. It was shimmering like a great, otherworldly jewel on the banks of the Yamuna River and it took my breath away. Around the Taj is a high, red sandstone fort, perhaps 30 feet tall, with minarets interspaced along the three sides of this fort, the forth side adjoining the Yamuna River.

I made my way to the Taj from the train station, past the many dozens of little campfires that the people who lived on the street started every morning, and walked through the quiet entranceway of the fort, into the landscaped gardens surrounding the Taj Mahal. At this early hour, the Taj was all but deserted. I walked up

**Approaching the Taj Mahal** via train from across the Yamuna River just after dawn.

the steps amazed at the intricate carvings that made the moon marble that comprised every facet of the Taj appear like airy, filigree lace. Inside the great space beneath the huge, ornate dome in the very center of the rotunda was the crypt of Mumtaz, the beloved wife of Shah Jahan. The ornate, moon-marble coffin was surrounded by the most intricate lace filigree curtain composed of the same moon marble just several inches thick, this formed a see through partition around the coffin.

The very atmosphere of this place was so very pregnant with peace; I just stood there in wonder at all that surrounded me. Still, because of the early hour, I was the only person inside the Taj and in the immediate area. (There were some groundskeepers a few hundred yards away by the entrance of the fort.) Standing there that early morning in the golden shafts of sunlight pouring through the magnificent arched windows, I took out the reed flute that I had bought from a poor street vendor in Benares for a few rupees a few weeks back. Several times I had tried to get a sound out of it and failed.

So with a prayer of praise to my Presence for all that was before me, I raised it to my lips and produced the first clear notes that had ever come forth from me in this lifetime. The sound of this simple reed flute reverberated about like a beautiful waterfall in the amazing acoustics of the Taj; it was totally transporting. I started doing simple scales and again, because of the acoustics, the scales tumbled upon each other in the most celestial manner.

For perhaps 20 minutes, I was transported as the music that was flowing through me carried me off in astonishment, in a prayer of praise. The musical scales came forth accompanied by and inter-woven with the celestial reverberations that were produced by the soaring moon marble dome of the Taj Mahal around and above me. Years later, I came to understand that the acoustics that are present in the Taj are unique in the entire world. (Paul Horn, the famous flautist, recorded an album in the Taj in 1968, called "Inside.")

Walking out of the Taj after my very first musical meditation, I was again a different person. Within me, praises to my Presence, to the Divine that was within all, and composing everything all about me, came forth unbidden from my heart. I felt like I was a little boy, without a care in the world, being swept along a great river through the most beautiful places, the most beautiful experiences one could imagine. Again the sense of being guided, almost propelled from one place to the next was so very tangible and seemed to become stronger every day. It was like I had an appointment that I had to keep, and the more that I would turn my focus within, in kind of a waking meditation, the more I sensed this great force that was directing my footsteps. At this point on this quest, I began to smile more and more at the simple beauty and perfection that I began to see just about everywhere.

I followed a road from the Taj toward a small forest-covered hill near the Yamuna River. As I made my way up this hill, there were many simple huts scattered among the trees. The huts were the homes of sadhus—the ubiquitous, wandering Indian holy men that were seemingly everywhere in India. These sadhus were ascetics, usually attired in a simple robe, who lived here on this forested hill overlooking the Taj and the Yamuna River. It seemed that each hut had its own little campfire in front of it where the sadhus would warm themselves from the morning chill and make their chai. Apparently it was well known that the area around the Taj had a pervasive spiritual power associated with it.

## Bombay and Goa

After spending a few days at the Taj, I boarded the morning train for the long multi-day trip to Bombay. As the train began to approach this huge, ancient city, I knew that I would swiftly leave this place even before the train stopped. If possible, it was even more crowded than Delhi but there was a very different quality about this city that I still can't put my finger on. Perhaps in part it was Bombay's location on the Arabian Sea and the fact that it had been a major seafaring port for thousands of years. Perhaps in a different time, I would have chosen to spend a little time here and explore the region, but now, with the mystical experiences and the peace of the Himalayas, Darjeeling, Benares, and the Taj Mahal in my recent past, the dichotomy of the frantic pace of Bombay was just not for me.

I had learned along the way that the coastal town of Goa, some 500 kilometers south of Bombay, was an area where it was possible to live for little money and that it was possible to obtain inexpensive passage to Goa on a freighter from Bombay. I set out from the train station by man-powered rickshaw through the intense, crowded streets of Bombay. The sub-continent of India is home to dozens of different ethnic peoples, each with their own culture, language and dress. Bombay was a stew of all of this and yet, there was a harmony in these masses of humanity. The crowded streets were filled with all kinds of people and rickshaws; the streets were lined with open-air, wall-to-wall shops selling everything that could be imagined from the vast reaches of India and beyond. There were small restaurants, cooking fires, and simple food kiosks set up upon a few wooden crates or a broken-down wagon, creating an exotic haze of aromas that changed every few dozen feet that the rickshaw traveled.

I told the barefooted man pulling the rickshaw that I wanted a hotel near the port. We stopped at a few little hotels that didn't feel right, so I moved on and soon found a clean, very inexpensive hotel. I always gave the rickshaw man double what he asked for in a fare, which was still less than a dollar. After checking in and making sure that my pack was secured, I made my way to the port and soon found that the next freighter leaving for Goa was the following morning. I booked my passage with the freighter company and was told that I would have a cabin for the 500-kilometer, overnight journey along the southwest coast of India to Goa.

For the rest of the day, I explored the streets near the port area of Bombay, again savoring the incredible, amazingly delicious, vegetarian foods that are everywhere in this country. Then later, as the burning Sun slowly settled into the Arabian Sea, I made my way back to the hotel for a few hours' sleep; I had to leave the hotel by dawn the next morning to get to the boarding ramp of the freighter.

I remember sitting in the hotel room that night meditating upon the events of the day, of the past months, so very ready for what the new day would bring with this long, ocean journey along the southwest coast of India. The sense of my "appointment" with whatever I was being guided toward was growing more pronounced and so very exciting. Again I had the sense of great wonder as to what was opening before me as I fell asleep that night in Bombay.

At dawn the next morning, I set out for the docks via rickshaw. My first sight of the ship on which I was to spend 24-plus hours was not very favorable and this was only reinforced as I boarded the gangway, presented my ticket to the ship's officer, and walked on board. I had some familiarity with ships after my time in the Navy, and traveling via ferries in the UK and on the Mediterranean, but I was not prepared for the physical condition of this freighter. It was a rusty old tramp steamer in terrible condition. The deck was cluttered with cargo and when I went inside to check out the cabin where I

**A freighter** similar to the one I booked passage on
from Goa to Bombay.

had a bunk, I took one look and vowed that I would not step inside this ship again. It was filthy and I saw rats scurrying along the darkened passageways, seemingly oblivious to the crewmembers that also walked there.

I went immediately back out the door into the clean, ocean air and made my way to the very bow of the freighter. This area was raised up higher than the rest of the deck and the cargo pallets afforded a bit of privacy and isolation, which was welcome after the crowds of Bombay. I laid out my sleeping bag and backpack; it was here that I stayed throughout this 500-kilometer voyage heading south along the coast of India. Fortunately, I had my supply of dried fruits and nuts and a few bottles of water with me, so there was no need to step foot inside the superstructure of the freighter again.

It was comforting to be able to see the coast of India passing by several miles off the port side of the freighter throughout the journey—as I would not have been very surprised if the ship, obviously on its last legs, had decided to sink during this journey, requiring a long swim to shore. The very wonderful side of this journey, however, was my open-air space on the bow of the freighter—nothing but fresh, warm, ocean air and unlimited views of the coastline.

Many hours later, the stunning colors of sunset set the stage for a beautiful night as the Sun melted into the Arabian Sea.

As the sky darkened and more and more of the numberless stars became visible above me, there was nothing to do save to muse over the events of the past year since I had left America and started this quest. Memories of the frustration and disconnection that was my experience before I left on this quest were from a different lifetime that no longer had any bearing with who I was now. Memories of the past year began to parade before my mind's eye. Was it just several weeks back that I was on the side of Everest, snowblind, preparing to freeze to death as night came? Then jumping forward a short period of time to the warm, magical terraces and people of Darjeeling and the sense of home that I experienced in this region.

Was it just a few weeks ago that I stood on the banks of the Ganges in Benares, all that night long, watching the corpses of human beings turned into ashes in the numberless cremation fires that lined the river? And what of dawn several days ago, watching the Taj Mahal turn golden as the first shafts of Helios crested the eastern sky, and then an hour later, my reed flute making musical praises inside the Taj?

Musing on all of this, then drifting in time and space backwards to the waking dream that propelled me to start this quest back at college. Flashing forward a bit and then I was reliving the events in Jerusalem, in the church of the Holy Sepulcher, along the banks of the Jordan River at dawn talking to my Father and to Jesus by name asking them to "show me" what I was to do—not in the sense of any kind of humble prayer, but more as one in battle, shouting out in urgency to a comrade, "Okay, what now?"

Back to the present, here I am, lying on my back on the bow of this tramp freighter, sailing down the southwestern coast of India, looking up at the star-filled sky. I was aware that the thin, golden string that was pulling me, guiding me from America, from experience to experience, had now become a strong, golden chain. Where was it taking me? What was I being prepared for? Not having any light, save for the limitless canopy of stars above my head, it was the perfect setting for such a long, wonderful meditation. I eventually fell asleep to the gentle rocking of the freighter and the shushing of the bow waves as the ship made its way to Goa.

### Goa

Iwoke at dawn to the slight change in the ship's vibration as the engine slowed. Now the freighter was much closer to shore heading into port. My destination here at Goa was several miles south of town along the coast. I had learned that there was a small village there, composed of bamboo huts, and that a bit further down the coast, one could build a simple hut out of palm fronds and live on the beach, eating locally-grown fruit for next to nothing.

Disembarking the ship and finally, after hiking along the shore for many hours, I came to that village. Then, perhaps another mile further along this most beautiful beach, I came to a somewhat sheltered area that was remarkably beautiful. The palm trees were separated from the sea by about 40 yards of pure, white, very fine beach sand. I sat down near the palm trees and took stock of my new surroundings. After a while, a boy came up to me who spoke a bit of English and offered to help me build a shelter. We cut the palm fronds in half and he showed me how to weave them into large rectangular pieces that, when tied together with individual strips of palm fronds, composed the walls and roof of the shelter. It was a perfect sun- and wind-break. It was here that I would stay for the next few weeks catching my breath and assimilating all that had happened thus far.

A few hundred yards away stood several large canoe-like, open fishing boats pulled up on the beach. Each boat would hold several men and the large nets. At dawn these boats, powered by a small outboard motor and sail, would make their way out to sea and then in the mid-to-late afternoon, they would return dragging their huge fishing nets. The entire village, women, children and men, would come out and then grab hold of the lines that were connected to these fishing nets that were still hundreds of yards out to sea and then pull these huge nets to shore filled with fish. The fish would be loaded into baskets made of these same woven palm fronds and then carried up to the village, there to be distributed to other villages.

The only thing that separated this scene from how it must have been done a hundred or a thousand years earlier was the use of the small outboard motors. Otherwise, the handmade boats, fishing equipment, and clothing were probably very similar.

For the first time in over a year, I was able to completely relax and not have to think or plan what was going to happen next. In this magical place, all of my being grew into harmony with the natural cycles of the day. I woke at dawn with the soft singing of the birds and the sound of the gentle waves and fell asleep shortly after the numberless stars appeared, again with the gentle sound of the waves. I remember the first night, lying on the sand on top of my one long towel that was used as a sheet, which was becoming a bit worn out from being used for this past year. I remember lying there in this shelter listening to the waves softly roll up onto the beach. I remember the deep peace. And then I remember getting bitten and bitten and bitten everywhere. Apparently at night the tiny sand fleas usually enjoyed their dinner, in this instance, it was me.

I can remember as clearly as it was yesterday lying there in just some cut-off shorts (this is the tropics and night temperatures may have been in the 80s). These sand fleas were very busy biting me and this just wasn't going to work. I slipped deeper into meditation upon this discomfort; it was almost a tug-of-war. Do I give way to this annoyance, or do I (whatever this "I" is within me that is so slowly awakening) assert whatever it is that I can assert to make this annoyance go away?

The bitings got more numerous. It seemed that they were all over me and somehow, I was able to go deeper into meditation and the biting began fade a bit and not be so noticeable. Then, as my meditation deepened and my sleep cycle started to settle in, the biting seemed to stop and I fell asleep. The next morning at dawn, I awoke to praises that the sand fleas had decided to leave me alone and walked the few yards to the warm, fragrant, gentle sea for my morning swim. I would swim out a few dozen yards and float on my back, looking up at the lightening sky, meditating on this exhilaration of life that was all around me.

I spent a few weeks in this place, meditating and reading the dozen or so books that I had bought at the Theosophical bookstore in Benares, about the Path, about meditation, and Yogananda's *Autobiography of a Yogi.* I meditated with my simple reed flute and learned to let its harmonies pass through me in praise. After a while, my meditations changed and grew deeper. I had learned to incorporate a certain exercise at the beginning of my meditation period that was becoming more and more effective in quieting the monkey-mind (the non-stop chattering of the outer mind when one wishes it to shut-up).

This exercise consisted of visualizing my loved ones, friends—whomever and whatever—seeing them standing under a glorious waterfall of intense white Light. This white Light was/is the "Presence," the Divine aspect of that individual that always has been and always will be Perfect. I would visualize these individuals opening up, drawing in this glorious waterfall of pure white Light into their body, and seeing it healing, illumining and protecting them. I would see these individuals in this Light smiling more and more as the Light of their Presence did its perfect work. After repeating this exercise for my loved ones and friends there was a change in the vibration that I felt in my mental process. The monkey-mind was stilled. I could just be in this stillness and "coast," for lack of a better word. How to describe this state other than as an awareness of peace without focusing upon being aware of anything.

I didn't know at the time the reason why this exercise worked but I do now. Simply put, it's the law of karma. Whatever one sends forth into the world, be it thought, word or deed, for good or ill, gathers more of that essence and returns to the sender. The more emotion associated with this action, the more powerful its force and therefore, the more powerful its return.

These periods of meditation grew in frequency and duration. I began to experiment with this inner state while walking along the beach at dawn or at sunset. For the past year I had always paused before eating anything to consecrate what I was eating with the Light of my Presence. Now this simple exercise, along with most everything else, took on new depth for me. All of my daily activities, all of my attention, was upon the Path. I read what the Mahatmas (the Great Souls), the Masters, taught through the Theosophical Society, I read about Yogananda's journey and awakening amid the glorious, rich tapestry of mystical India. I pondered dozens of aspect of my early life, my teenage years, my time in the military.

I meditated upon my yearning for this sense of Divine Connection that I had as a little boy that I was now experiencing more and more. I meditated upon my life-long yearning to understand why I always felt so out of place in the culture that I was born into. I flashed back to many, many different periods of my past twenty-two years. I could recall my astonishment of the truth that I felt when I read *The Search for Bridey Murphy* when I was 13 after my Mom gave it to me (Angel that she is)—it was all about reincarnation—the same sense of astonishment of remembering of the Truth when I read Edgar Cayce's *There Is a River* perhaps a year later.

This was the first outer knowledge that I had about the Great Masters and the Path. I remembered teaching people how to feel auras when I was in my middle teens. I flashed back to the mountaintop in the Rockies and the vision that was given to me then and there, about my destiny that I could only vaguely perceive.

All of this and now here in this glorious place of peace in southwest India, sitting in a lotus position on the shore with the gentle, warm, fragrant water lapping against my physical body. Watching Helios slowly settle into the Arabian Sea, again watching the glorious spectacle of sunset, watching the few clouds on the horizon changing colors every few moments as the sky grew darker and the stars began to emerge. I felt that I was in the very beginning of the beginning of the process of awakening to who I really was. With this new and increased sense of awareness, the golden chain was ever-present now, and I knew that soon I would be heading further south but to what, at that moment in my outer consciousness, I had no idea.

## Heading Southeast to Madras

After a few weeks of assimilation in this beautiful place, it was time to move on. My destination, as far as I knew it in the outer, was to travel southeast to Madras to visit the headquarters of the Theosophical Society where the Masters had appeared and given their instruction 60 to 70 years previously and then head down to Ceylon and from there eventually further east to Thailand.

The long, multi-day train rides through this land were enchanting. As I traveled further south into the tropics, India became more lush—the very atmosphere somehow thicker, to the point that you could feel the air against your body. The fragrances of the countryside that the train passed through were often pungent and delightful with the vegetation and the ever-present smoke from wood cooking fires, which were everywhere that there were people. Each dawn and sunset was a special time as the Sun appeared so huge on the horizon through this thick, luxurious, fragrant atmosphere that was south India.

I remember having to wait for an early-morning train somewhere around the town of Bangalore. It was approaching dawn and I had a few hours before the train was to arrive for the long, overnight trip to Madras, so I climbed up this interesting hill to the side of this very rural, remote train station that consisted of a few open air buildings. The top of this hill was only 300–400 feet above the train station and a perfect place to have a morning meditation and watch the sunrise over the hills of south central India.

The sky was getting lighter, the birds and the monkeys in the trees around me becoming more vocal, the eastern horizon now aglow with the golden fire of Helios rising to begin a new day, the mist rising on the sides of the mountains. I stood on the summit of this little hill and in celebration was able to let my reed flute play me.

After a while, caught up in this experience, the sweet tones of the flute mixing in with all of nature that surrounded me, I noticed several people making their way up the hill below me. When I turned back in their direction a short while later, still involved with my early-morning musical celebration, I noticed that this group of several young men was heading in my direction. Soon they stopped a dozen yards or so before me and with their hands upraised in *Namaste* and muttering some mantras, all of them lay prostrate on the ground before me, doing mantras.

I realized then that they thought I was some kind of guru or master and I stopped the music and went over to them, smiling and telling them to stand up. I even tried pulling them to their feet, only to have them bowing with their hands in prayer before their hearts, falling back on their face before me. This just wasn't right, so I said goodbye to them with the customary Namaste, walked back down the hill to the train station, and shortly continued on my way to Madras.

The Theosophical Society headquarters in the Adyar area of Madras was interesting but I didn't feel the charge of peace there that I thought I would. I spent several hours in the large, walled complex, reading in the library and visiting the little chapel that had several standing statues of various masters, including Jesus (I believe). I knew it was time to continue on toward Ceylon. I was on the train the next morning, heading south to the very tip of India. I had heard about a spiritual community that was being built in a little town 100 miles south of Madras, called Pondicherry. I decided to spend a day or two in this town to check it out before I continued south. ❧

# 11 ~ **Pondicherry and Aurobindo**

The land became more and more tropical and beautiful as the train got closer to Pondicherry. When I got off the train, I was instantly aware of a quality in the atmosphere that was most striking. The pastel hues of all the low, open-air buildings that made up the town were quite beautiful. Exotic fragrances mixed with the ever-present wood smoke, the parrots and colorful tropical birds singing in the trees, flowers everywhere and beautiful, smiling people. I knew this was a magical area as I started to wander around the quaint but slightly crowded afternoon streets. As I made my way closer to the sea, as Pondicherry is

**Sri Aurobindo**—This is the picture that was displayed in the foyer of the Ashram courtyard that I initially mistook for a picture of Jesus—the Christ Light radiating from his features.

located on the coast of the Indian Ocean, I sensed that magical quality of peace increasing. Soon I found myself walking up this narrow, cobblestone street with beautiful, pastel open-air buildings on either side. Fragrant tropical flowers were hanging from the trees and from the vines that grew alongside the buildings. Women in brightly colored saris and men in white dhoties were entering into the court-yard before me.

I had no idea what I was doing (in my outer consciousness) but I got in line with these people and walked into the courtyard. At the entryway of this beautiful courtyard in the open foyer after you entered in from the street, was an amazing photograph of Jesus. At least I recognized it as Jesus, and then I realized it was a photo and not a painted picture. It dawned upon me then that it was an Indian version of one who had obtained great mastery as had Jesus.

The peace here was extraordinary. I walked through the foyer into a beautiful courtyard, to fragrant flowers and tropical trees and singing birds and many people sitting in meditation before a large, rectangular, raised marble dais covered with hundreds of flowers laid out in a design in the very center of the courtyard. I walked toward the outer perimeter of the dozens of people meditating here, near the outer wall so as not to intrude. I took off my backpack, laid it on the ground, and sat down in a lotus position, as was everyone else and instantly slipped into a very deep meditation. It was early-to-mid afternoon when I sat down in meditation. Now as I slowly returned to my body, it was late afternoon and I knew that something extraordinary had just happened. I got up in a daze, grabbed my backpack and very slowly walked out of the courtyard, so aware of this intensely electric peace that was around me. Walking down the street a few hundred yards, I checked into a beautiful small, open-air hotel. I knew that I'd be staying here for a while.

The Aurobindo Ashram period of this story is difficult to write about for multiple reasons, for this was the time and the place of my "appointment." Looking back on this now, there was a foreshadowing of this period. This is what I had been prepared for by all the experiences that made up this past year and then, as I was realizing more and more, by all those experiences that had made up this lifetime and probably many others.

With a charming and immaculate hotel room as my base, I learned about my surroundings. The Aurobindo Ashram was the central point of the town in so many ways. It seemed that everything else just radiated out from there, in one way or another. The ashram complex was only a block or two from the sea. In the other direction was the town's commercial district that consisted of a few streets lined on both sides with one- or two-story buildings with open-air shops that shuttered down in the early evening and opened again in the morning. Interspaced between the shops were the ubiquitous temples, each one dedicated to a different god or goddess of the dozens and dozens of deities of India.

The roads were all gravel then, with the exception of the area immediately around the ashram complex, which was paved with cobblestones. The masses of India were here, too. There was constant movement on the streets all the time that did slow down a bit around noon for the "siesta" period. We were now close to the equator and the heat of noon was intense—everyone tried to get out of the sun. Even in this heat the cooking fires simmered all day and night. Every item imaginable, and then some, was being sold by the street vendors who set up their wares on the side of the road on a few crates. The more established businesses, like clothing stores and small restaurants, were in these open-air shops that lined both sides of the streets. To my absolute delight, there was a street vendor roasting delicious, local cashews, just a block from my hotel room.

My hotel room was typical of South India, the wobbly ceiling fan in my room turning just fast enough to move the air. I would stand on a chair and tug at the fan with my hands to make sure it wasn't going to come down on me while I was sleeping. (On a few occasions over the past several months in South Asia, I had changed my room because the ceiling fan was so dangerous.) The hotel as usual for the tropics was designed for maximum air circulation. There was an open window to the street and a large door that was left open most of the day to the inner hotel courtyard, filled with tropical flowers and plants, where some other hotel guests prepared their chapatis over an open fire and made yogurt for their morning, noon, and evening meals.

Everyone smiled here; even the innkeeper was also unusually friendly. I wondered at this until one day, when paying my bill, I noticed that upon his desk were pictures of Aurobindo and the Mother, Sri Aurobindo's soul mate, who at that time was in her late 80s.

**The inner courtyard of the Aurobindo Ashram**—where I would spend many hours in meditation. Throughout the day, dozens of ashram members would be in meditation here.

**Closeup of the Samadhi**—Aurobindo's tomb detailing the intricate designs made with fragrant flowers that would be freshened throughout the day.

My morning would start just at the crack of dawn. I made my way to the courtyard for a cool-water shower and then as the parrots started their praises, I was sipping my first coffee at the local restaurant, sometimes even savoring a *Masala Dosi* for breakfast, along with my coffee. Other times I would have just a pastry or a type of cool oatmeal/pudding. Then I would be back at the ashram by 7 a.m. when the gates opened for morning meditation.

Approaching the ashram early in the morning was a delight to the senses—the ever-present morning mists, the sound of the tropical birds and monkeys beginning their day, the fragrance of the flowers mixed with the background hint of wood smoke. Walking into the ashram this early, there would be only a few people sitting in meditation before Aurobindo's samadhi (tomb), the raised, polished, marble dais in the center of the ashram courtyard. (He had made his transition to higher planes in 1950.)

The raised dais was rectangular, perhaps 3 by 6 by 12 feet, the top of which was entirely covered with an ever-changing array of floral designs (yantras, pictorial mantras) made by the most beautiful fragrant flowers that grew abundantly on the ashram grounds. Above the samadhi was a beautiful hand-painted silk awning that was changed throughout the day. Each one had a different yantra painted on it. There was a hint of incense amidst the fragrance of the flowers. It was so very easy to just relax in the lotus position and enter deep meditation.

I continued to expand the technique that I first began to practice in Israel and began to refine in the Himalayas and then later in Sarnath and Goa. Somehow in this place, the exercise of holding my loved ones and friends in the Light became richer, there was more detail, and this accompanied by a vast, silent peace. In the early days at the ashram, I was at first somewhat surprised at the amount of time I spent in meditation—usually a few hours at dawn, followed by an hour or so at noon, followed by a few more hours at dusk.

Sri Aurobindo was educated in Oxford and was a prolific, much followed writer in Calcutta during India's Independence movement. He was known as "the pen of the Indian revolution," and Gandhi's counterpart. At the height of the tension between India and England, Aurobindo was thrown in jail for his writing that, according to the British, was fuelling the rebellion. At that time Aurobindo was the editor of the newspaper for the city of Calcutta, the largest city in northeastern India. During Aurobindo's stay in jail, he had a very special visitor—Krishna, the Christ-like God of the Hindu faith, appeared to him and began to give him instruction.

When Aurobindo was released from jail, his entire life-focus had changed. He traveled to the south of India, to Pondicherry and began meditating. Soon a group gathered around him that grew and grew, thus began the Aurobindo Ashram. He was a prolific writer and his spiritual works consisting of a score of volumes occupy a space of honor in the foyer of every Indian embassy in the world. Aurobindo's birthday is the anniversary of India's Independence, August 15th.

All of these volumes were written around the theme of Aurobindo's Integral Yoga—meaning that all of life should and can be lived in union with the Divine. I was captivated with his writing and by the peace and fire opening to my mind's eye that I experienced following the cadences of his words. I realized that much of the premises outlined in his writing had been a longstanding framework of my life.

After several days of this cycle, I was approached by an elderly gentleman upon the conclusion of my morning meditation. Walking away from Aurobindo's samadhi where other people were still in meditation, he said in very clear English with the rich pronunciation characteristic of India that I was "supposed" to be a member of the ashram. We sat on one of the benches in the beautiful courtyard and he explained to me that over the past several days, I had come to the attention of the ashram elders, and that it was obvious to them that I was supposed to be part of the inner ashram community, not the outer one. He identified himself as Santosh Chakravarti and told me that if I accepted, I would be assisting him for a few hours each day in arranging for the distribution of Aurobindo's books to the Indian embassies around the world. I would be given an apartment, a bicycle, and a meal pass to the ashram dining room.

Later, I discovered that my dear mentor, Santosh was formerly a Justice of the Supreme Court of India. Many of the people who now lived in the ashram and its extended community had came from high positions in India.

I spent many hours over many weeks engaged with Santosh in conversation about life and the Path. My heart wells up in such love for this beautiful man, and for our heart ties that go back many lifetimes. That same morning, Santosh asked me to walk with him to the Aurobindo Ashram library. It was a block away from the main ashram building heading toward the sea. We approached a large, walled compound and passing through the always-open, ornate gate, we stepped into a beautiful, tropical courtyard. In the middle of the courtyard stood a large, two-story, columned building with the interior of the library opening onto open-air verandas on both the first and second floor.

From the second-floor verandas, you could see over the courtyard walls, through the tropical trees and vines, to the Indian Ocean beyond. When I wasn't meditating or working at the ashram, I would sit here in this beautiful and peaceful place and read Aurobindo's masterpiece, *The Synthesis of Yoga*. It was so easy to slip into a meditative reverie watching and listening to the colorful parrots and the monkeys in the trees surrounding the library, the sea breeze and the ceiling fans making the tropical heat not so noticeable. A few times a week in the early evening, a small group of musicians would perform sacred, classical Indian music in the courtyard. Was the sitar and tabla made for this place, or was this place made for them? I had never before experienced the celebration of Life in its infinitely glorious multiplicity and perfection as I did here at the Aurobindo Ashram.

Despite the four-to-five hours of the day in formal meditation by the samadhi, it was here in the early days at the ashram that I realized that I was actually in a constant state of meditation. Even when driving my bicycle from my apartment to the ashram at dawn, or working in the ashram office with Santoshda, or doing anything, I was in the place of the Watcher. That sense of the Presence that I first came to understand in Israel was now a very tangible, constant, physical pressure in my awareness. When I would close my eyes for a moment, the sweet pressure of the Presence would just carry me away. This sense of the Presence allowed me to delve deeply into *The Synthesis of Yoga*, a compendium of how the goal of the human experience is first to remember and then once again, through conscious practice, to become more and more Divine.

### An Inner Perspective

Over the course of this narrative, I've tried to describe those instances when the barrier between the physical and the spiritual worlds thinned for me—when there were those experiences prompted by my physical location and my inner process at that moment that transcended the physical, overwhelmed the physical incarnate consciousness. (Now, as I write this 39 years later, at 3 am on my notebook computer, with the peepers, the rushing brooks, and the waning half-moon keeping me company, I'm struggling for the wording to convey what is about to occur.)

It has always been the intent of this accounting to provide a historical and scientific framework for others who, at some point in their lives, might be interested in how a boy, and then a young man, began the process of awakening in this lifetime—of how the accumulation of those experiences and the knowledge gleaned therein set a series of events into action that have allowed for repeated, dramatic occurrences of Divine intervention.

This Divine intervention—not just a mystical subjective experience but also a most tangible shield of protection and acceleration becomes a Reality when invoked and afforded to oneself, one's children, one's family, and to countless others who have embraced the Path. Grandiose as these words sound, they still fail miserably to convey the astounding immensity of the Presence of God, I AM, Individualized as You and I. I have attempted to describe the process by which we all, through the cycles of incarnation and reincarnation, eventually remember our Divine source, develop mastery over these outer worlds, and claim our Divine birthright—just as Jesus and so many others have done over Earth's long history.

I have tried to recount the experiences and inner processes that I lived, growing up in this lifetime that have led me to this point in this narrative. I have sought in these pages to paint a picture with words of the deep frustration, emptiness, and the feeling of out-of-placeness that I felt in my early years, which led to my yearning to make sense of it all. That combined with those early mystical experiences propelled me into this quest. Over the first year of this long journey throughout Europe, the Middle East, and Asia, many pieces of the puzzle became more and more obvious as the days, weeks and long months unfolded. Through the non-stop yearning of my heart, I began to perceive perhaps a portion of the big picture.

Now, here I was, on the other side of the world, more than a year after I left that old life at the university in the United States behind. So much had happened in my outer experience and in my inner experience. Now, here I was, on the verge of something big, assimilating all that had gone on, but now assimilating it as the Watcher. I was very aware that the part of me watching this experience was ancient—more than the name that I grew up with, more than my old outer personality and all that I had associated with it. In fact, this Watcher identity that was synonymous with the constant state of meditation that I was in so superseded my former personality that I realized that what I had been before was all but unrecognizable to me. My former life was like an old collection of childhood things that had long outlived their usefulness or enjoyment.

Within this backdrop, the exquisitely rich days at the ashram unfolded before me. Every morning at dawn, my day would begin on the second-floor balcony of my room, doing pushups and visualizing the sun pouring through my circulatory system. I would stand facing the Sun and continue visualizing the fire of the sun pouring through my circulatory system until my breath came back to normal. My early-morning bike-ride through the misty, quiet streets of Pondi-cherry, the cooking fires rekindled by the waking street, the little restaurant for coffee, and then to the ashram fully engaged for my long morning meditation.

Recounting this now reminds me of a portion of a beautiful affirmation written by Mark L. Prophet, "All the days proceed in order from the current of Thy Power, flowing forward like a river, rising upward like a tower."

I had shared earlier that in India it was possible to see and experience things that just couldn't happen in the West. This was be-cause, for ten thousand years and longer, the entire population of this vast region of the world had a very different way of looking at life. Every day was a holy day in honor of one aspect of the Divine manifest as one God or Goddess or another, one Master or another. Every day had deep, spiritual significance, because everyone knew that the things that one did throughout the course of a day created karma; and it was far better to create good karma than bad karma and karma is what determined the circumstances of one's life, one's reincarnation.

This allowed for a culturally and spiritually rich multiplicity of expression to arise throughout southern Asia that was far, far different than the materialistically oriented culture of the West.

### What Is This?

Without getting into the mechanics of the various planes of life that lie just beyond the vibration of the physical, suffice it to say that the barriers to these worlds that exist in the West due to the excessively materialistic culture are very much thinned in the East because of the thousands of years of their intrinsically spiritual cul-ture. This acceptance and lifestyle allows for all manner of experi-ences, which would be deemed supernatural and impossible in the West, to be not so impossible in the East.

With this as a brief explanation, at noon one day, I was walking down one of the main streets in Pondicherry, fifteen minutes from the ashram. The gravel road was crowded as usual with hundreds of people milling about the stores and temples and food kiosks that lined both sides of the road. Suddenly about a hundred yards up the road, I heard people yelling and then screaming. I saw people start running; soon more and more people were running down the street in my direction in an effort to get quickly away from whatever was so alarming, the street began clearing out. I was very alert; I had never seen this behavior and just stood there, watching to see what was happening. The sense of alarm grew as the shops and temples that lined both sides of the street quickly closed their shutters and doors. The people running by me to get off the street were frightened; I could see nothing alarming looking up the street where the commotion began.

Then, perhaps 75 yards away, I saw one obviously very old woman stumbling down the street coming in my direction. At first I thought that she was also trying to flee from whatever but as I saw her approach (she was about 50 yards away now) the few screaming people left on the street took off running as she got closer to them. It seemed like she was trying to grab at them before they took off running. I couldn't understand what was so terrifying about one elderly woman. I stood there watching her approach and noticed that now I was the only person on the street. All the stores and temples were shuttered up—what had been a very crowded, market street a few moments before was now deserted and closed up.

As she got closer to me, she had this curious walking movement that took her in kind of a half circle, sauntering, lurching forward, I assumed she was very ill and/or mentally out of it. Soon she was about 25 yards away and obviously coming toward me gesturing and screaming. She was old, perhaps ancient, and had a ragged sari on that left one breast exposed. It seemed at first that she had long hair draped over her shoulder, coming down to her breast. She got a bit closer and started moving more quickly toward me, gesturing with her hands, her eyes were wild and she was screaming. It was then that I realized that what I thought was her hair was also a writhing mass of snakes or huge worms that were writhing, and worse, it seemed that they penetrated through her shoulder and breast.

This was way out of my experience and this was a very dark, very negative vibration. I was not going to have anything else to do with it. I stood there in shock until she got about 10 yards from me, the unbelievable horror of the scene almost spellbinding, then as she lurched toward me I turned and ran too.

Death, horrible disease and disfigurement were not infrequent sights in India once you got away from the main cities. I had seen much of this over the past several months but what I had experienced this day was something else. The only explanation that I was able to get from my friends at the ashram about what I had experienced was that, while there were many beautiful, positive, mystical traditions in India, that there were also some dark ones, and that this unfortunate person had some connection with that. It surely was a scene out of the lower astral plane that in the West, people understand as hell. Looking back on this event now, I only wish that I had more mastery at that time that I might have helped that woman. Bless her and all who suffer so.

There was only one other incident during this period in which I encountered something that was so startlingly jarring. I was sitting in the second floor of the Aurobindo library one afternoon, completely at peace, reading *The Synthesis of Yoga*, enveloped in the pressure of the Light of my Presence. As I was meditating on the concepts that Aurobindo was writing about in these pages, someone sat down across the table from me where I was reading. I looked up to see this beautiful, smiling woman looking right back at me. I realized instantly that she was the subject of a very sexual dream that I had the previous night. Her smile indicated that she was aware of this also. In astonishment, I broke eye contact for a second and looked back at my book and when I looked back at her, she was gone.

I quickly looked around where I was in the library. There was no way she could have moved more than a foot in the second my eyes were diverted. I was more than amazed, for I would have loved to speak to her. Santosh told me later that day upon learning of this that she was probably a *rakshasi*, a beautiful demon-like being from the inner worlds, and warned me to take care lest I be distracted from the Path. She never showed up again either in my dreams or in the physical.

My months at the ashram were, for the most part, introspective, the lifestyle there conducive to meditation and study. One day, Santosh brought me to meet a "master" who lived at the ashram and was a disciple of Aurobindo and the Mother. I remember walking into this man's small room and noting that an entire wall was covered with many dozens of pictures of Aurobindo and the Mother.

This man had a large following of disciples in northern India who revered him and did everything for him, as is the customary way that gurus are treated in India. When this man learned about Aurobindo, he and many of his disciples traveled hundreds of miles to meet Aurobindo. He asked Aurobindo what he should do and Aurobindo told him that he needed a dish washer in the ashram. This man, who was the revered master to many and had everything done for him for many years, now became the ashram dishwasher and here he stayed for the remainder of his life practicing Aurobindo's Integral Yoga—living the principle that simply every aspect of the human experience must become again Divine. Through much meditation, everything one does, everything one thinks, everything one feels, everything one experiences occurs by and through and in one's Divine Presence.

### The Aurobindo Ashram and Acceleration

Around this magical backdrop of my days in the ashram, my meditations, my understanding of Aurobindo's work, and of my life grew deeper. Again, "All the days proceed in order from the current of Thy Power, flowing forward like a river, rising upward like a tower...." One particular warm evening, I decided that I would have my evening meditation on the beach a few blocks from the ashram.

The sea was very tranquil and it was a touch cooler here with the light sea breeze. It was with anticipation that I sat in the warm sand in the comfortable lotus position and started the familiar process of inner preparation for my meditation. The sound of the gentle waves on the shore, the fragrance of the sea breeze, combined with the tropical vegetation was heady and soothing—just perfect.

I was approaching my 23rd birthday and I was aware of the acceleration that this cycle always brings. During a segment of my inner preparation for meditation, I would muse with an unspeakable gratitude to my Father, my Presence, for the blessings and opportunities that were afforded me through this lifetime that has now brought me to this place—both the physical location and the inner understanding of what was opening before me.

Still, to this day almost four decades later, I do not know how to paint an adequate picture of what occurred in this prayer and meditation session. Over my years in meditation, I frequently summon the memory of this event that was forever branded into my awareness that evening on the beach in Pondicherry. Again, I share here what I am about to share in the hopes that it might bridge some common ground with others who will read these words and take comfort, that someone else has had similar experiences and they need not be afraid.

Through this long journey I had become more aware that there is a most holy, sacred science to Life, to every aspect of life, the engine of which is one's free-will actions in this lifetime or previous lifetimes. The overall concept of karma is at least partially understood by many but there are so many subtleties involved—indeed such a vast history, a tapestry of events that make up, compose, the great symphony of one's current experience. It is only via the intercession, the volition, of one's own Presence and concurrently of the Great Ascended Masters that one begins to see even the tiniest portion of this. So it is with the process of meditation, as one with motive increasingly pure seeks to re-establish, to remember, their connection with their Divine Source. The actions, the phases, the depths of this remembering, this meditation, as with everything else, is dictated by the laws of one's karma.

I relaxed into the warm sand, the soft breeze, the sound of the tranquil sea on the beach a few feet away, the sweet peace of the Presence always a palpable, physical pressure throughout my awareness now. I closed my eyes amidst this perfection to begin the inner exercise that up to now had produced the deepest peace. Then came some kind of explosion of Light and I was literally riding an immense lightning bolt holding on for dear life, accelerating and accelerating as a rocket does, breaking free of Earth's gravity on its way into orbit.

I had absolutely no idea what was happening, other than that it was beyond all I could do to just hold on. I was in this vast immensity of the most intense Light and Power and Everything. I was moving so quickly and it felt like my entire being was an empty, tiny sphere in this vast Allness of Light and Power. Through a tiny pinprick opening in the tiny vacuum sphere that was me, such an overwhelming Allness and Power poured through into me that I felt I was literally going to explode. In fact, I was exploding and I was scared.

To this day almost four decades later, I cringe in sadness that I did not understand and did not have the faith at that time to proceed with what was occurring. Holding on for dear life, the Light and Power streaming forth into me through this tiny pinprick opening so vast, exploding and exploding, I said, "Father, I'm not ready for this" again and again. Then, because of the Great Law, I was released from this immense current and sank back into my physical temple, sitting once again on the beach that evening in Pondicherry, and I was crying with the deepest regret that I have ever known. I was crying because I stopped that sacred process, by my fear. I did not have the understanding to allow that process to continue.

So many times I've wondered what would have happened if I had only had the faith to let go in this great current, this immense lightning bolt. So many times I've mused over this, wondering if only I had some outer understanding of what was happening, what more could have happened. If only the faith that took me around the world to this place had been strong enough to know that whatever was going to happen here, it was the plan of my Presence. How was it that I faced a slow, freezing to death on the side of Everest several months back with equanimity and yet, here in this paradise, I'm rattled to the core in meditation by this summons from my Presence? So many times I've wondered how different this life would have been if I had only been stronger, if I had only known in my outer consciousness, what could have occurred.

Years later, I learned that the Kundalini Fire on its initial ascent is explosive. Could it have been this? This was so far beyond the sense of cosmic consciousness that I was blessed with in Colorado's Rocky Mountains a few years back in that other lifetime. Sitting on the beach back in my body, the stars beginning to appear. My body shaking like a leaf, I tried to sort all of this out, still feeling the deep regret but at the same time a vast sense of expansion, of holy wonder, of peace. Still, in spite of my frailty in not being able to continue with that experience at that moment, I knew that never, ever again would I ask to be let go.

It may have been that evening or another around that time that when I returned to my physical consciousness, there was a man kneeling in the sand, hands raised in prayer before me. I said no, no, no, shaking my head smiling at him trying to convince him that I'm just like he, certainly no master or guru. He pointed to a small Maltese cross that I was wearing around my neck that I had purchased in Darjeeling or Benares as proof of his actions. I stood up and bowed before him in Namaste, smiled and walked away.

Throughout the past year, especially since the experience in Jerusalem and Israel, I often had these one-way conversations with Jesus; I would muse on the different facets of his mastery. So many times I said to him, show me how to do this. That connection grew stronger as did the Golden Chain from my Presence. One day when walking through a little open-air bazaar, this small Maltese cross caught my eye. It was made of a silver, rose-colored metal that I had never seen before. I purchased it for a few rupees and decided to wear it as a reminder of what I was about. After this event, I took it off realizing that, although this connection with Jesus was stronger

than ever, I was not to wear it any longer. This Maltese cross still re-
sides in a place of honor upon one of the altars in my home.

I've tried to convey here the sense of the momentum, the
magic, and the perfection that was so abundant in the Aurobindo
ashram environment. There were so many little incidents that occurred during this period that I've omitted from this narrative but the
one continuous theme that filled all of the hours of all of my days
was that none of this was a chance happening of blind fate. This was
all ordained by my Presence that every day, even the most mundane
tasks, were an exercise of bringing the Divine into the physical. The
science of this was so simple, yet so difficult; I was almost breathless
in wonder trying to follow and slowly understanding the cadences
of the Master's teachings.

One morning upon waking, I remembered being in a classroom with others and Aurobindo teaching us. He was standing at the
head of a typical classroom explaining something and writing on the
blackboard. This wasn't a dream experience; I knew that I was participating in a very real experience on an inner plane of life while my
physical body slept.

Years later I would come to understand this experience more
clearly. My outer consciousness was becoming more accustomed to
the subtle energies of life and through this, I was able to retain memory of the experience in the Master's retreat, receiving instruction
with several other students.

## Special Days

There was a sense of celebration in the air this morning throughout Pondicherry, for today was the day of the Mother's *Darshan*
(a Sanskrit word meaning "auspicious viewing, the beholding of a
deity or one of great attainment"). As the morning progressed hundreds and hundreds of people gathered on the cobblestone road in
front of the main ashram building; as noon approached it was shoulder to shoulder. Santosh told me that the Mother (Aurobindo's Twin

Flame), who at that time was very old and frail, would step out onto her 2nd floor balcony and give a blessing to all. This was a very quiet but expectant crowd and as the time approached and the balcony door opened there was a deep hush that settled over the many hundreds gathered there looking up.

I had never experienced anything like this before; it seemed that the entire town of Pondicherry, young and old had gathered here for the Mother's blessing. The only sound now was of the ever-present birds singing in the trees lining the road. The curtains in the balcony doorway moved and the Mother stepped out supported by her two attendants. As she raised her hand in blessing, such a vast veil and pressure of intense peace descended upon all gathered there. Time itself seemed to collapse in the great weight of this peace. This interlude in the silence, without boundaries, immeasurable—it seemed that the very cognitive aspect of myself just ceased to exist.

There was nothing anywhere to perceive but this great, great peace that always was. The sense of the Watcher within was gone; even the birds stopped their singing. At some point she turned and walked back inside through the curtains, the intense weight of this experience lifted, and slowly the crowd began to dissipate.

To this day almost four decades later, I don't even know how to describe this, save to say that the Mother, at that time in her incarnation, was an unascended Master of great attainment in her own right, wielding such Divine Love, Wisdom and Power that she was able to bring about this vast blessing to all gathered there and beyond.

The above account of the Mother's Darshan blessing, of itself, paints a picture of a cultural occurrence so different from what is the experience of most in the West. Simply put here, imagine how people who lived in the West would conduct themselves if they knew that not one but many who approached the attainment of Jesus were incarnate, living among them. When you factor this in with a culture-wide acceptance of the laws of reincarnation and karma, of one's accountability for thought, word and deed, you begin to see the cornerstone belief structure that is so very rich in opportunities for self-understanding and fulfillment in India that is not present in the dogma of the West.

There exists here a comprehensive science of the framework of an individual's life—how free-will decisions and actions mold and shape each individual's experience in that specific lifetime and subsequent lifetimes. There is a culture-wide aspiration to follow the living examples of the Mahatmas (Sanskrit for "Great Souls or Masters"), so that each individual may progress in each lifetime to become more of the Divine. All this is a treasure trove of ten thousand years of examples that western Christian mystics have only just touched upon.

## *The Birthday Appointment—*
## *The Completion of a Cycle*

It is interesting to me that on this day in 2012, I finally write down what I have shared so many times over the past decades that occurred on May 25, 1973. Throughout the writing of this narrative I have sought to consciously remain centered within the sphere of the charge and pressure of the Light of my Presence so that what is written might be an accurate accounting of those events that transpired over the years. What follows is certainly written in this manner.

The summer solstice was less than a month away on this beautiful but steamy morning on my 23rd birthday here in Pondicherry. This May day started out just as all of my days began here over the past three-plus months—an early morning bike-ride through the cool streets to the ashram for my long meditation. However on this day I had planned to take a long bike ride up the gravel, coastal road perhaps a dozen miles or so to the location of what would come to be known as Auroville. It was here that Aurobindo and the Mother chose for the location of their community that would be founded on the principles of Aurobindo's Integral Yoga. (Simply put, Aurobindo taught that all of life is Divine and when you strive to live as the Divine in of all life's matters, you increasingly become that.)

At that time in 1973, there was already some mention of this place in different esoteric circles. I had read that it was to be a sister community to Findhorn, the famous spiritual community in Scotland. In fact, I had decided to visit Pondicherry just for the sake of seeing what Auroville was all about; I knew nothing about Aurobindo or his ashram. Auroville, though it was not yet built, was to be constructed on a very powerful location that apparently others, outside of Aurobindo's sphere of influence, also concurred with. There were supposed to be powerful ley lines that connected this location to Findhorn in Scotland, to a region in Peru—Lake Titicaca, the focus of the Mother Light for the Earth—and other sacred power centers of the Earth.

I got directions on how to get to Auroville from Santosh after my morning meditation. Carrying only my water bottle, I set out mid-morning, hoping to get there before the intense, tropical heat of mid-day turned everything into a sauna. The gravel road was a beautiful, easy bike ride as it wound its way along the coast. It was extremely rural, off the beaten track, and once outside of the town limits, there were less and less people evident.

Finally after an hour's ride, I came to the side road that ascended up a little hill overlooking the Indian Ocean. The summit of this hill opened up into a plain and where the road stopped stood a huge cashew apple tree that I immediately went under to get out of the sweltering tropical sun. Here I was on the exact location where some years in the future the Auroville community was to be built. Now it was just a very remote tropical hill overlooking the Indian Ocean—there wasn't any sign of humanity for many miles around. I had seen drawings of the spherical *Matrimandir*, the center focus of Auroville that was to be built on this very location.

However now, the only structure that existed here was a very simple bamboo hut. This structure was about nine feet in diameter and was obviously built as a place to rest out of the intense tropical sun. There was a wooden bench in the middle of the hut so gratefully

I walked inside and sat down on this simple bench. Taking a long drink from my water bottle, I crossed my legs into the lotus position gazing out through the opening, across the sweltering plain in front of the hut, and out to the Indian Ocean in the distance. I was so grateful; it was the perfect place to be at that moment in my life.

Here I was at high noon on my 23rd birthday on the other side of the world from where I had entered into this incarnation. Now, at this point in my journey, it was approaching a year and a half since I had left the United States on this quest. I was so aware of the Grace, the golden chain that had guided me. Sometimes it seemed to have actually pulled me from experience to experience, both in the physical and on the inner, through this long cycle. I was so profoundly grateful for all that had happened in my life, which had led me to this point of clarity. I was so grateful for all the amazing experiences that had happened to bring me to this point of awareness. It was in this state of revelry and the deepest love and gratitude to my Presence for All that is this life that I settled into my noon meditation.

The energy of this place was most obvious. I had shared earlier that the peace around the ashram was like a physical pressure; here there was an electric quality to the peace and this took me very deep into meditation. At some point in this meditation, my attention was brought back to my surroundings. I became aware of a slight movement in my extended aura; it was as if someone was approaching the hut from a few dozen yards away. I slowly opened my eyes expecting to see someone, but there was no one there. I closed my eyes and quickly went very deep within, back into this great ocean of electric peace. Shortly thereafter, there was again a movement in my aura and a sense that I was the "focus" of someone's interest.

There was an alertness to this sense as if I was required to take note or do something, and it quickly pulled me from deep meditation. I opened my eyes and again no one was standing in front of me in the opening of the hut—just the cashew apple tree and the beautiful ocean beyond. Still with this sense of alertness in my aura I closed my eyes and slipped back into deep meditation. Then there was an urgent movement in my aura and my eyes shot open, this time there was a sense of danger present. Still in the lotus position as I had been for at least an hour, all of my senses were 100% focused upon this unseen impending threat—but there was nothing before me. Still in this super-alert, meditative state with my eyes wide open, I again felt the movement in my aura and the sense of alarm. Now there was a direction to this sense; it was above me.

Slightly inclining my head above and to the right, I saw it. Draped across the wooden pole that spanned the hut supporting the thatched roof was a very large king cobra. It was over seven feet long and his middle was as thick as my thigh. Most of his body was coiled around the pole, with three feet of him leading up to his magnificent head, the distinctive hood of the king cobra was fully opened, his tongue darting out, swaying before me, suspended from the pole in a big U, so that his head was upright less than three feet from my face. Still in the greatest peace of my meditation, I was astonished at his beauty.

My eyes locked on his sparkling, hypnotic eyes and his fully-opened hood with the intricate designs upon it like the sacred yantras that the women would draw in the sand before their huts every morning at dawn. Except in his case, this yantra and the swaying of this magnificent head is a warning to the king cobras victims of what is soon to come. The hood is opened when the king cobra is most alert, just before the king of snakes strikes its prey with his deadly, long, poisonous fangs.

It seemed that time stopped as I gazed in wonder at this beautiful creature swaying before me. There was a great sense of royalty about him and I was astonished at his beauty. There was not the slightest doubt that, in a tenth of a second, he would strike me and I would die here on this sacred spot at high noon on my 23rd birthday. I smiled within at this thought, for I knew that the slightest movement, even the flicker of my eyes not looking directly into his eyes would bring instantly his strike and that would be that. While taking in the diamond designs of his long body while never moving my eyes from his I was aware of the passage in Herman Hesse's "Siddhartha," where Gautama Buddha was sitting in meditation by a river

**Satellite picture of Auroville (2013)**—This view of Auroville is very much different from the remote hilltop that it was in May of 1973. Then, the only thing there was that small bamboo hut that I sat in to get out of the sun. Now the golden spherical structure in the middle of the geometric lines is the *Matrimandir*, which sits on the exact location where the bamboo hut once stood in which I had my birthday encounter.

when a king cobra approached. Through the Buddha's great attainment the cobra went on his way without killing the Buddha. Smiling, I remarked to myself within that "I'm no buddha..." and the outcome of this encounter will be very much different. I smiled again thinking of the newspaper article that would appear in my hometown papers, "Local man killed by king cobra at high noon during meditation on his 23rd birthday while living in India...." I would be happy with that obituary, I thought with a peaceful, inner smile.

Still not moving, not blinking, in the deepest, wakeful, peaceful meditation I ever experienced in this lifetime, I marveled at the perfection of this, my final moment in this lifetime, expecting at any moment his strike. I was the Watcher now, totally unconcerned with the outcome of this experience, aware of the majesty, the beauty of these final moments, knowing that all was proceeding according to my Father's Great Plan for this lifetime. This endless moment was pristine, it could not be more perfect—I was in holy awe at what was unfolding.

After seemingly a very long time in meditation, with these thoughts parading before me, while fixed upon his swaying head and burning eyes, I had that thought "well if you're not going to take me now, I'm not going to wait around here all day until you change your mind..." Very, very slowly I uncupped my hands that were across my knees in the lotus position and very, very slowly slid them onto the wooden bench. In the deepest peace, my eyes never leaving his, I began to transfer my weight onto my hands and very, very slowly uncrossed my legs and lowered them to the ground. In the deepest peace, very, very slowly, I started to slide off the bench. My eyes locked on his swaying head and sparkling eyes, his tongue darting out. As I slid away from him, he uncoiled more of his body and started to come closer to me. I continued to slide off the bench with the king cobra approaching closer until I was upon my back on the ground, my eyes still locked on his eyes, his hood fully open. He was still coming closer.

Now he was moving from the beam that was above me to the bench that I was sitting upon. On my back gazing up at him, I crawled out of the hut, and then I was outside, now further away from the king cobra than before. I stood up and looked at him coiled upon the bench I had been meditating upon, his head swaying upright a few feet above his body looking at me. In astonishment that I was still alive, I said, "Thank you, Father." I thanked the king cobra and walked away. Everything was different now, somehow complete, and I knew that I would soon be leaving to begin the next chapter of this lifetime.

Today, 39 years and a few weeks after this event occurred, I looked up this location on Google Earth and was astonished at the satellite image that zoomed onto the screen. The most amazing patterns, like a huge very ornate crop circle with that spherical Matrimandir located right in the center of the elaborate pattern—exactly where my encounter with the king cobra had occurred.

This cycle was now complete. The golden chain that was pulling me from event to event had now shifted into a new direction and I knew it was time to go back to the United States. I knew that I had a lifetime of work ahead of me in assimilating, applying, and expanding all that I now was—all that had transpired. I knew that there were further appointments that I had to keep and that they lay back in the United States. Now almost a month later, I had prepared myself for the departure from this inner life that I had been living for so long now. Saying goodbye for now to my dear mentor, Santosh, feeling such a deep love and seeing the tears in his eyes, we knew that we would not see each other again in this life.

I remember sitting on the train in an alert meditation, which was my constant state of awareness then, and watching the pressure of the tremendous Peace of the ashram shift as the train traveled further away from Pondicherry. It was quite interesting when, at a certain distance from Pondicherry, perhaps 10 miles or so, I suddenly felt another shift and instead of this intense, so very tangible pressure of the peace and the light seemingly pressing down from the outside into my being, it suddenly shifted and this pressure that I had come to know as the Light and Peace of my Presence was now very much exerting this pressure from within out—not from without in as it had been.

There was an instant realization in this—that henceforth anywhere and everywhere I was, I would always be within my Presence. In this deep state of gratitude, meditation and awareness, I began the long journey across the length of India to Delhi and then, instead of traveling overland through Asia, the long route that I took to get here, a jet took me back to the world that I had left 17 months before.

CR

# 12 ~ **Integrating Back into America**

Now the hard part. I knew that I was supposed to be back in America and that it was time to begin to employ what I had learned over the past year and a half into life here in the United States. I knew that I had future appointments to keep. I knew it was going to be difficult but I didn't realize just how difficult. The culture shock that I experienced upon my return to the home that I grew up in was surreal. I took a bus from Boston to Springfield and walked several miles from the bus station to the house and knocked on the front door. My brothers and my mother didn't recognize me at first as even my physical features had changed.

Family and friends asked when meeting me again what had happened. They knew somewhat of my travels, but something had occurred with me that they couldn't understand. The person they knew before I left was gone, never to return again. I tried to explain using this analogy: The East is like an intellectual genius with a handicapped physical body, while the West is like a super-athlete that was mentally challenged—there needed to be a blending of the two perspectives of life. To me then, it seemed an all but-impossible task, but then, this is what I had to do.

I soon made my way back to Amherst, the college town that I had lived in, and was able to move into a house in a very rural area with some college friends. Meditation was my solace, by grace I was able to summon the peace of my Presence and use this as a cornerstone of strength and direction. This allowed me to navigate through this new world in which I was now living, making sense out of what was before me, and what I was supposed to do with it. I started back up at the university a few months later to get the GI Bill funding coming in, and at the same time, I began the process of exploring what was involved in getting my pilot's license. This was something I had wanted to do since that return flight from Lukla, several days south of Everest.

Those first years back in this country were difficult years. How to integrate what I had experienced in the East with college life in the mid-1970s? This was the era of Watergate and the Nixon impeachment, followed by the energy crisis and fuel shortages. As I sought to find direction in my life, the early-morning meditation ritual became my touchstone, my reality check, for the day. Seeking to align myself with the will of my Presence, I pushed myself forward into those activities that were required to make a living in this culture. Against this backdrop of my experience, college seemed superfluous, but on the other hand, aviation was exciting and seemed a much better fit for my time and limited financial resources.

Life continued to unfold. Some time later, my flight instructor told me about a man that he had met that was a famous author and scientist. He said that I reminded him of this man and he gave me a book called *Voices of Spirit* by Charles Hapgood. It was his accounting of work done with a trance medium, Elwood Babbitt.

Charles Hapgood was quite well known in scientific circles and had several books published, one of which, *The Path of the Poles*, had a forward by Albert Einstein. Hapgood and Einstein collaborated on some aspects of Hapgood's work on the movement of the Earth's poles. This groundbreaking work that Charles Hapgood brought forth was decades later proven by new scientific discoveries.

There were concepts in *Voices of Spirit* with which I was very familiar and upon learning that Charles Hapgood lived in the area, I determined that I would seek him out. I found out where he lived, drove to his rural home, and knocked on the door. The door burst open and a large, old man stood before me. He had white hair and bright, blue eyes and stood a few inches taller than my 6-foot frame; however, neither of us were really looking at each other. Our attention was upon the few-foot space between us. We were both astonished; between us was a whirlwind of Light, and more remarkable, we could both see it and feel it.

I didn't even have time to introduce myself for he blurted out, "Who are you, man...?" and grabbed me pulling me into his home. We sat down in his living room, just staring at each other, realizing that we had always been very close friends. There was half a century separating us in age and he was probably half-a-century heavier and a few inches taller, but we were very close. Charles interrogated me quite thoroughly that afternoon and thus was resumed a long, close friendship.

He told me that he was going to do an experiment with me and his friend, Elwood Babbitt, who was the focus of his current work. Charles told me that he was going to arrange for a "reading" for me with Elwood in which Elwood would go into a trance and that a "control" would then take over Elwood's sleeping body and proceed to give me a "life reading." Charles told me that Elwood was considered by many, including the people at the Edgar Cayce Institute (the A.R.E. in Virginia Beach), as the most accurate trance medium since Edgar Cayce, 40 years earlier.

Edgar Cayce's book had played a role in my initial awakening, when I was thirteen or fourteen. With this understanding of what Elwood did, I was very interested in going along with Charles' experiment which, simply stated, was that I was not to tell Elwood anything about my life experiences. Charles wanted to hear what the trance reading would reveal.

A week or so later was the appointment for the reading, I came to Charles' home and was introduced to Elwood Babbitt. Elwood was probably in his late 50s then, twice as old as I was. We talked briefly while Charles set up the professional tape recorder to record the session. Elwood smiled and sat back in a rocking chair and said, "Excuse me while I get out of my body..." I smiled back at him in anticipation of what was to come. Elwood closed his eyes and started deep breathing.

Within a few moments, I felt the energy shift in the room and I saw another face, composed mostly of dim light, superimposed over Elwood's face. This being's eyes were open, looking at me. I had returned to the United States eighteen months previously and was ready for anything. I was completely focused on the experience that was before me, watching the energy about me, and watching "Dr. Fisher," the spirit-person who was giving me this reading through Elwood's physical body.

He proceeded to tell me things that no one else knew about me, such as that the reason I had "removed myself from this world" and gone on the "quest" was to rekindle the memories that I had from previous lifetimes in these places that had a direct connection for the mission of this current lifetime. He told me that I was there in Jerusalem when Jesus was there, and that I had lived in the monasteries in the Himalayas and was associated with the Masters there. That this has always been my work throughout numerous lifetimes and that I was in training now to bring forth all of this again in this lifetime for the great changes that would be coming with the new century, then twenty-five years in the future.

Charles and Elwood became my close friends and Charles ended up living with me off and on over the next seven years until his transition. In those early years, as I struggled to integrate the East with the West, he was a mentor and my older brother on the Path.

## A Reminder of the Purpose of This Work

Lest the reader become tired of this story, I break into the chrono-logical flow of this lifetime's experiences to state once again that the objective of this exercise has been to provide the historical facts and the choices that were made over the years, and to describe the sacred sciences involved that enabled the repeated intercession of Archangel Michael and the Ascended Masters, not only in my life, but also in that of my family and dear friends. I have sought to detail these experiences interspaced with the sacred sciences, as I understand them now, which allowed all of this to come forth.

My ardent prayer is that what is shared here might assist others in the unfolding of their lives' sacred intent, in the remembering of their Divine Source, and in the bringing forth of the subsequent beauty and protection to their life and that of their family.

## The Peace of Vermont

The years continued to unfold. I became a professional pilot and began a relationship with a woman who eventually became the mother of my daughter. We moved around a lot, always going to a more rural location. At this time, I pondered about either buying a piece of land and building a homestead or moving to the South Pacific and flying charters around the islands. Every time I flew over southern Vermont on a charter or during flight instruction with a student, I was aware of a quality of peace to the rolling mountains and rivers below me.

I took a few day-trips driving up into southern Vermont and was very aware that there was something special here and I started looking for land. After a few months of visiting several parcels with realtors and walking over hundreds of acres, I was directed to an older gentleman who had a lumber business and owned a lot of land in south-central Vermont.

The second piece of land that he showed me was stunningly beautiful, with brooks and waterfalls falling into deep swimming holes. It was just Heaven. It was a 100-acre parcel and way more land than I was looking for, but I knew then and there that I had to be the caretaker of this land and somehow I'd be able to purchase it. In the background of my excitement I knew that because of the gradual drop of the larger of the two brooks that ran through the land, I'd be able to build a hydroelectric system to generate power for the homestead that I would be building.

## Building and Attunement

As I proceed with this next chapter of the narrative, where major (at least for me) building projects were undertaken, it's important to state that every day, no matter what was on my plate, whether flying or building something or just relaxing, that first and foremost, I had my morning meditation and consecrated all to my Presence. This action was part of my daily ritual—that the day might unfold perfectly and that I might be reminded that, "everywhere I Am, Father, I Am in Thee."

In fact, as my family and closest friends know, every time I've built something, I would always pause first and make attunement with my Presence, so that I would be able to "see" how the building project was to unfold. Oftentimes, in the early years, I had not the slightest clue as to how I was going to do something, save reading a brief article in a magazine or a book. There was no instant Internet in those days, where one could get detailed instructions, including videos, on anything.

Also as I built the house, the hydroelectric system, and then the barn, and everything since, I would frequently write down mantras/prayers and the sacred *Om*, and the date and perhaps a few words, on the boards as I nailed them up. While I wrote the mantras, I would pause in the middle of a construction activity, even leaving my friends or family just dangling, waiting for my direction or for me to continue to do something, and I would enter that inner state of attunement with my Presence.

Pausing thus, I would become mindful of the flow of Light and Peace. I would then write the mantra on whatever board was nearby to anchor the Presence back into the physical. I would make this attunement with everything I was doing, including working on clearing trees, landscaping the land, and designing the ponds and gardens that now surround the house. I would share this activity with my family, my children, that they might know the multiple benefits of such a practice.

For me, this process of attunement started consciously in my early twenties. Perhaps it was when I got out of the military and knew that I had to do something I didn't know how to do—like live my life in a place that didn't make sense to me. This sense of pausing to make attunement grew and grew until it became a cornerstone of my life, of my daily approach to anything new, or even rudimentary, daily work activities. This action began to take on an entirely new dimension when I left upon the quest, and then it accelerated greatly in Israel in my early meditations on the meaning of it all, and Jesus' teachings in the Aquarian Gospel.

My understanding of this process came to new levels as I began to understand the concept of Karma Yoga, the Union with the Divine through work and through every aspect of one's life. I remember being told while in the Himalayas that every building, every pagoda temple, every monastery is built with one obvious flaw, as a reminder to all that only the Buddha is Perfect. Whenever I entered a new land, a new country, a new city or town that I was visiting or traveling through, this sense of making the attunement first would re-polarize me back into the current of my Presence, and set the tone for what I was about to experience in this new location, this new activity or experience.

Now, from the "coign of vantage" of my sixty-second year in this incarnation, and as a student of the Path for many decades, there is much science to this act of making attunement that I will endeavor to share here as we move into the next phase of this narrative. Somewhere Jesus is quoted as saying that, "where your heart is, there is your treasure." This is really an action of the great Law of Karma, much more than the convention that, "if you do something bad it will come back and bite you," etc.

## *The Great Laws that Govern Everything*

In order to understand these Great Laws that govern just about everything some groundwork must be laid here. What follows is not new information, but a synthesis of what the Great Masters have taught for millennia. While the world's great religions were based on the life and teachings of these Great Masters (Jesus, Buddha, Krishna, Moses, Zarathustra, etc.), in many instances, those teaching have been obscured by many centuries of dogma.

Because of the approach of the new age of enlightenment over the past 140 years, the Great Masters who comprise the Brotherhood of Light have worked with individuals and sponsored organizations to compile and publish these Great Teachings for the quickening of humanity. Prior to this, these teachings were only available to those initiates of the mystery schools who reached a certain level of attainment and could travel to the Masters' Retreats in their spiritual bodies.

Some of the more well-known sources of these teachings, each with Messengers who brought forth the teaching of the Ascended Masters for their time, have come from the work of the Theosophical Society (1880s–1900s), The I Am Activity (1930s), The Bridge to Freedom (1940s), The Summit Lighthouse (1960s–1980s), and now, the next step in the Brotherhood's work The Temple of The Presence, the dispensation for which was given in 1995.

## The Teachings of the Masters

Long, long ago, the Fall from Grace occurred. This was not Adam and Eve getting expelled from the Garden of Eden (although Genesis is describing this Fall in a symbolic way). This was the free-will choice of humanity over a long period of time through many incarnations to allow their attention to focus more upon the material, physical world and increasingly less upon their Divine Source that is individualized as each one's unique I Am Presence. The stories of a great flood that appear and re-appear in most ancient cultures (Noah's Ark, Atlantis, Lemuria, and Gilgamesh) are vague cultural remembrances of the records of the aftermath of the Fall that took place over tens of thousands of years.

Various accounts of the Fall and previous civilizations have been passed down through the Great Masters over the past 120 years. Most people are familiar with Atlantis, whose final destruction (according to these esoteric sources) occurred approximately 15,000 years ago. The remnants (survivors and high priests) of the Atlantian culture built the great megalithic structures scattered around the world—the pyramids and the immense stone structures in South America that are so intricate and huge that current technology cannot duplicate them. However, there are indications that there was another great culture that was chronologically much closer to the actual period of the Fall; this was Lemuria or Mu. There is much more written about humanity's early civilizations, in relation to the Fall, that is contained in numerous Theosophical writings, and in Saint Germain's I Am Books. (For further reference, there is a list of recommended reading the end of this book.)

In this next phase of the story where even more dramatic events occur it is helpful to convey an overview of the basic foundations and principles of these Great Laws, these sacred sciences —for this is how what happened to me occurred.

The physical incarnation of each subsequent lifetime is but the learning process, by which each one (the Individualization of our unique Divine Source, I Am) is projected into this most outer physical world in each incarnation. Thus in each lifetime, the individual acquires more experience, more mastery, through the understanding of and living according to the Great Laws of Life.

Eventually, through right action, limiting karmic patterns are worked through as the individual unfolds, perhaps expands is a better word, into new Opportunity and greater levels of Wholeness, by which one's life becomes more full, rich, more harmonious and loving. Through this awakening process, one develops the mastery that is their unique keynote gift, which is theirs alone to give to Life. This is one's sacred *Dharma* (one's Divine Plan or reason for being) that each one brings to the great symphony of Creation.

The Individualized I Am Presence projects an emanation or ray, down the Crystal Cord and anchors it in the Threefold Flame of the Heart (the Divine Spark of Love, Wisdom and Power, containing the triune nature of our Divinity). It descends through the various planes of life, magnetizing the substance of those planes around it, so that the Divine, as the I Am individualized, can express in these worlds through its four lower bodies: the Memory, where the so-called soul abides between incarnations, the Mental, the Emotional and finally, into the Physical world. This Threefold Flame is the spark of life that is ignited at conception in the physical plane.

Prior to the Fall of Man, in full outer awareness of the Individualized I Am Presence within, incarnated Sons and Daughters of God were not confined to the limitations we have now. Anything and everything one wished for was immediately precipitated from the Universal Sea of Life (the Divine Substance from which all Creation comes forth at the behest of the I Am Presence).

The Crystal Cord that conveys and sustains the Threefold Flame, by which the Individualization of the I Am Presence creates these outer vehicles (again the memory, mental, emotional, and physical bodies of man), was much larger prior to the Fall than what it is for modern man currently—a thin, gossamer thread for most. This allowed for more transmission of the Allness of one's Presence into the outer worlds. (Unfortunately, this Love, Wisdom, and Power of God's Substance was abused by the incarnate ones' free will and the Laws of Karma and Mercy dictated the crystal cord be reduced.)

A case in point: what Jesus accomplished in his victorious incarnation 2000 years ago was brought forth in part by Jesus' greatly expanded Crystal Cord and Threefold Flame, so that the full power of his Father, his I Am Presence, might come forth to do that Perfect Work. Jesus' own words describe this process in the parable that he was required to use in that era. "To him that has, more shall be given; to him that has not, it shall be taken away." As one advances on the Path, the Crystal Cord that sustains and maintains the Threefold Flame in the physical world expands, empowering the individual to be more of the Divine in action here below—again, just as Jesus demonstrated.

The size of the Crystal Cord and the Threefold Flame is determined by one's previous actions and is directly related to one's experiences in this lifetime. The karmic record of the free-will choices of the use of God's Sacred Substance, through thought, feeling, word and deed, mandates the circumstances of rebirth in every incarnation, and directly determines the opportunity (or, unfortunately, the lack thereof) that extend throughout one's lifetime.

The sacred purpose of this process is the means by which each Individual I Am Presence acquires more experience, gains more mastery, and becomes more of the Divine in embodiment through each successive lifetime. Through this process of the unfolding of one's Divine Keynote, each one forges and then gives back to life that special Work, that special Gift, that special Service to Life, that only that specific Individualization of the I Am Presence can bring forth throughout all of Creation. This is how the Individualized I Am Presence forges and contributes its unique Keynote to the great, ever-expanding symphony of Creation.

This is how the Great *I AM That I AM* is ever creating, ever enabling, more of the Divine to express, for the sake of Love and through Love, throughout the infinite, timeless tracts of Perfection and Majesty of all Creation. The culmination of this long process of physical incarnations is what Jesus came to demonstrate 2000 years ago in his great public ministry and example—the reunion with One's Divine Source, the I Am Presence, which he demonstrated in his public Ascension.

So with the above framework established, the act of pausing before any activity to remember, to re-establish, the flow of light and peace from one's Presence, is a karma-producing act, as is everything one does in life. However, in this instance it is "good karma," contributing to the reversing of the long, slow process of the Fall, instead of continuing on in *Samsara* (as mentioned earlier, a very appropriate Sanskrit word meaning the outer world of illusion in which most of humanity lives, seemingly oblivious for the most part to the great Law of Karma). In this state of *Samsara*, humanity are much like puppets that are controlled by the strings of past events and decisions—the effects that each individual sets in motion in their current and previous lifetimes.

This tapestry of the outpicturing of karma works on the scale of persons, of groups, and even on large cultural levels so that the same groups and dynamics of people come forth again and again, lifetime after lifetime, to balance the negative karma that they created. They also come forth, hopefully, to create positive karmic actions that bless life leading to the gradual awakening and remembrance of each one's Divine Source. Thus comes the Golden Age through this process of the conscious awakening of humanity.

Each action—be it thought, feeling, word or deed—that one allows oneself to participate in either reinforces positive, neutral or negative momentums. Because all actions emanate out from their creator according to the emotional power in which they were allowed to occur, they gather more of that energy from the Universe and it returns to the sender multiplied.

Unfortunately, for the greater part of humanity, especially now in our fast-paced and unconscious culture, this sacred process might as well be a fairy tale, or some advanced quantum-physics mumbo jumbo. It is not understood—but the fruits of these actions are most certainly understood when they impact the quality of one's health, one's disposition, one's happiness, or one's comfort in life and on a planetary scale.

### Back into the Physical Plane

Now with the preceding groundwork laid out I jump back into the physical plane and into the chronological order of the story.

On August 17, 1977, I bought the land in Vermont and the next day the former owner began building the road and the beautiful stone-and-steel bridge that were part of the sale requirements and negotiations. By early September, I began clearing the trees on an enchanted area set up on a hill with views to the south. This spot had such a sense of peace and a magical fragrance that permeated the area every time I walked through it. I would sit here in meditation and time would stand still, lulled by the gentle rushing of the brooks and the breeze through the trees.

After researching the design for passive-solar houses, I drew out the plans for what this home would look like. I hired a friend for a few months who was a builder to teach me how to build and together we started building this home in late September. With the help of friends and family members, and huge work parties on the weekends—very wonderful and productive times—the construction process unfolded quickly. On these weekends my parents would set up a grill and cook for the crew that sometimes numbered a dozen or more; it was literally a working party of family and close friends. With this kind of support, we were able to move into this house in early January of 1978.

The very first room that I finished was the meditation tower. This 3rd floor tower room has a balcony overlooking the mountains to the south and it was here that every day began and ended for me. (Until many years later when I built other sacred spaces in this house and on this land.) There was no utility power here, so I had a gas-powered generator that charged a battery bank for electricity, a wood stove for heat, and a big, old truck with a plow to keep the ¾-mile driveway plowed that winter. (This in itself was quite a chore since we got a lot more snow in those early years here than we do now.)

In the summer of '78, after lots of research, I began building the high-head hydroelectric system to power the homestead (as described earlier in this book). Without getting into a lot of technical detail here, I did the measurements of the drop and the flow of the brook that would determine the size of the hydroelectric system. I arranged for the building of the steel turbine that housed the Pelton Wheel (an aluminum wheel with cups around the edge that the jets of water hit, that turned the axel and the generator). At the same time, I began work on building a small 30-inch high dam across the brook that would feed the water into the penstock, the 6-inch pipeline that ran 1000 feet downstream and over this run dropped 100 feet in elevation, creating a huge amount of power.

My house was far from finished but I was also very tired of running the generator to charge the battery bank, so building the hydroelectric system became a top priority. The entire construction process was grueling. I designed the dam to be minimally obtrusive to the flow and look of the brook (at 30 inches high, it looked like just another waterfall, and you had to look closely at it to see that it was made of concrete). The long pipeline was an ordeal. I wanted it buried in the forest so that it would not take away from the stunning beauty of this clear, mountain brook. This resulted in the hand-clearing of a twenty-foot-wide by thousand-foot-long path through the forest along the side of the brook with my chain saw, cutting up and piling all the trees so that a small crawler-tractor backhoe could pass through to dig the trench to bury the pipeline.

In this process, of course, we hit ledge rock, so we had to frequently blast the ledge out. This meant dragging down big compressors to power the pneumatic drills that drilled into the ledge to make holes for the dynamite. Finally after a summer's hard work, the dam and pipeline were built, and the turbine house was in place at the bottom of the pipeline.

It was a very magical moment when I first opened up the gate vales that fed water into the turbine and watched it spin up to speed and start generating power. We had two-way radios so that my engineer friend who was up at the house a half-mile away could monitor the electrical output and make adjustments to the battery charging system. It was a very crude but very effective system that was my only source of power for over 15 years.

There is an old saying that you never own a house—the house owns you. It is more true when you've got a chunk of land. There are always 101 things that need attending to. I remember well the expression on my parents, siblings, and friends faces when they came to visit (really to work) those first few years and saw the scope of work ahead, of carving out mountain forest to make a home. Every day began and sometimes ended in the meditation tower, it was here that I got my marching orders for the day, that the impetus, the drive came forth for me. Day by day, week-by-week, month-by-month, and year-by-year, a Heaven-on-Earth world was created. The incredibly beautiful brooks, waterfalls and swimming holes always flowing, sometimes raging with their clear, sparkling, super-oxygenated water set the tone for the unfolding of this homestead and what was to occur here.

After the hydroelectric system was built, the next project was the building of a large barn. The posts and beams for the framing were recycled from an old barn and the boards used for sheathing came from trees felled on this land that I had milled. Now we had a place to store equipment and keep the snow off the vehicles in the winter. Bit by bit, I cleared back the forest away from the house and began to see the potential that was waiting to be brought forth. In 1982, prior to the arrival of my daughter, I cleared several acres and built a large pond so my daughter would have another place to play and learn how to swim. I didn't realize at that time how pivotal the creation of that pond would become in the years that followed.  ଔ

# 13 ~ **A Different Direction**

This narrative moves in a different direction now. I have sought to paint a picture of a boy's yearning to understand the world in which he lived—an unfolding drive so powerful that it crushed all complacency and the creature comforts of friends and home, which drove him to the far corners of the Earth on a search for the thread of meaning to it all. I have tried to touch here the striving, the acceleration, the continued unfolding, and the incomprehensible wonder of the dawning remembrance of the Divine I Am Presence within that was experienced throughout the quest and since.

I touched briefly on how terribly difficult it was to come back to the West and to figure out how to live the life I now knew—as a stranger in a strange land. "A fish out of water" is apropos, but then, as I was learning through my immersion in the Teachings of the Great Masters, the entire point of the exercise of incarnation was and is to become the Teachings. To transmute the patina of the consciousness of the Fall from Grace; to balance the layers of karma from hundreds of lifetimes that obscure the radiance, the very memory, and therefore the empowerment of the Divine I Am within.

I described how the solution to this conundrum for me was to find a piece of land on which I could build a consecrated life, a veritable shelter from the storm of *Samsara*. I have always been a very strong physical person. I knew that I would need strong and constant reminders of the glory of God all about me if I was going to be able to pull it off and not get sucked back into the depths of materiality. The creation of this homestead afforded that lifeline. After all, aside from the beauty of nature all around me, everywhere I now look, there is something that has been built with sacred mantras inscribed upon it. So even if I forget, I'm reminded by the charge of Peace of that record.

We have moved quickly through the years of professional aviation and of the initial engineering and building of the homestead—all of which came forth in the atmosphere described earlier in the framework of my daily meditations and ongoing immersion in the Teachings of the Great Masters. By now you have seen how the disparate pieces and dreams of such a life have come together in the physical plane, producing an environment conducive to the gradual unfolding detailed herein.

## The Brotherhood in America

It was somewhere in the late 1970s to early '80s that while in a bookstore in Brattleboro, Vermont, a book seemed to jump off the shelf into my hand. The cover art was captivating—some kind of sacred ceremony inside an Egyptian pyramid, and the title, *Dossier on the Ascension*, by Serapis Bey, was most intriguing. I was immediately aware of a particular vibration to this book that was similar to Aurobindo's books. I recall being almost excited as I started to read it, to discover something with this vibration originating in America. The book was about the great Ascended Masters, Serapis Bey being one of them, and their activities in working with humanity, especially those who are in the process of consciously walking the Path.

There was a different quality to this material from the Great Masters. It was fresh, it was current, it wasn't written in the flavor of the Theosophical material from a century earlier. I was aware of the pressure of the Light flowing from my Presence as I read. I realized that the words conveyed another action that I was able to perceive within me—it was almost like a second dialogue going on while I was reading. There was a sense of joy, of peace, and of connection. I later called the bookstore and asked if they had any other titles from the same author and publisher (The Summit Lighthouse).

There were some very powerful affirmations in these books that when reading them, and better still when speaking them out loud, produced a greater acceleration. I incorporated these into my daily meditations and I was astonished with the results. Something was happening here that was on a par with what had happened in the ashram in India several years earlier. There was electricity; there was a new impetus. More so, what I was reading felt extremely familiar to me—like I already knew all of this material, like I already knew of these Masters. I bought another book that the store had, this one, *Studies of the Human Aura*, and I knew big changes were coming. There was an affirmation in this book written by the Ascended Master Kuthumi (who I learned was Saint Francis of Assisi in a previous life, as well as the Shah Jahan, builder of the Taj Mahal) that moved me to the core. I include this and others in this narrative because as the reader puts their free-will attention upon these words, for the reasons described earlier, there will be a quickening that, once begins, never ends. Here is Kuthumi's *I Am Light*:

I AM light, glowing light,
Radiating light, intensified light.
God consumes my darkness,
Transmuting it into light.

This day I AM a focus of the Central Sun.
Flowing through me is a crystal river,
A living fountain of light
That can never be qualified
By human thought and feeling.
I AM an outpost of the divine.
Such darkness as has used me is swallowed up
By the mighty river of light which I AM.

I AM, I AM, I AM light;
I live, I live, I live in light.
I AM light's fullest dimension;
I AM light's purest intention.
I AM light, light, light
Flooding the world everywhere I move,
Blessing, strengthening, and conveying
The purpose of the kingdom of heaven.

As I read these words, the charge of Light within them was so very tangible, it propelled me into meditation. From that moment, the reciting of these affirmations became the focal point in my meditation in which I was able to more fully let go—in which the shuttle of love from my heart to my Father for all the blessings in this life seemed most complete. In the midst of this upwelling love, there was often a charge, a rush of electricity (for lack of a better word), emanating from my crown or my heart area that fanned out to envelop my physical body that I came to associate with the descent of the Light from my Presence. This would occur immediately after I felt my heart burst forth in boundless love and gratitude to my Father.

These two titles from The Summit Lighthouse contained several of these affirmations (decrees). All of them produced a subtle, inner action that was most conducive to my meditations when recited within. Something was definitely going on here that was quite extraordinary. I read and reread these books, drinking in the Master's words and the "thoughtforms" that they painted before my mind's eye.

## The Science of the Spoken Word

Throughout history's earliest cultures, sound has been an integral part of spiritual expression. Even the roots of the Judeo/Christian religions have used the recital of spoken prayer and rhythmic chants as a fundamental aspect of their exercises. Throughout the East and the West, all ancient cultures have used chants in their religious application.

When a person begins the process of awakening from the long sleep of the ages—when a person, by life's experiences, begins to sense that there is much more to life that the paltry fare served up by the culture in which they live—the quickening begins. By and by, such a person begins a search, a quest, to find out the meaning of it all. Sooner or later, depending on the purity of their aspiration and the intensity of their yearning, they will make contact with an outer arm of the Great Brotherhood of Light. As one progresses upon the

Path of Awakening, it becomes more and more obvious that there is never such a thing as an accident or coincidence. All occurs according to the great, immutable Laws of Life, which include seemingly "chance encounters" with other people, experiences, etc., that provoke life-changing events.

When such a person makes contact with the great Ascended Masters, one of the principle exercises that the Masters encourage in order to assist the awakening one is the understanding and implementation of the Science of the Spoken Word. Indeed, an entire encyclopedia would fail to describe in the fullest the process here involved, because it is the principle activity, the engine, of all of Creation. But here I will attempt to give a simplified overview of the process.

First, it must be understood by the aspirant that every thought, word and deed that comes forth from the consciousness of any individual is a free-will, creative act that does produce karmic ramifications in the individual's life. This is a very difficult concept for most in the West to understand. They have never been taught that they create their reality by the thoughts, feelings, words and actions that they allow to come forth from within themselves. They've never been taught that even private thoughts and feelings are a creative force—and as such are karmic acts—going out and attracting like energies, whether sublime and of the Light, or negative, chaotic and dissipating.

The reason why this is so is because we are and of God, in the process of awakening, of remembering, our own Divine Identity. Obviously this process is the process of Life and as such, it takes many, many lifetimes to master. The great saints and founders of all the world's great religions are those who have, through many lifetimes, forged their own Christ identity and reunited with their Great God Presence, I Am, and as such, have become the fullness that Jesus, Buddha, Mother Mary, Kuan Yin, and many others have demonstrated throughout recorded history and beyond. This is the birthright, the Divine destiny, of every Son and Daughter of God evolving upon this planet.

It's because of this latent Divine Identity within each of us that the Science of the Spoken Word is all that it is. As a person enters into this exercise with the dawning understanding that they are the focus of their own I Am Presence, individualized in Action in these lower worlds, then these words that compose the dynamic decree that are at first read quietly (painting pictures in the mind and feelings), then spoken out loud, do go forth into the world as creative acts. As such, they are karmic acts that produce and attract those experiences of like fruit to the person—attracting circumstances of like vibration—thus further adding to one's momentum of awakening.

In addition to this, because these decrees are inspired by great Ascended Masters, every time one of them is read, thought about, or spoken, there is a connection with that Master, who may multiply the power of that decree, making the activity of giving these decrees even more powerful. (In Sanskrit, this science is known as *tratek*.) Through this cumulative exercise, a purification of the consciousness takes place, bringing forth increasing levels of perfection in every aspect of one's life.

It is the sacred labor of the Ascended Masters (and there are countless numbers of them) to assist humanity in this Great Awakening. Giving these dynamic decrees throughout the day contributes tremendously to the expanding, awakening consciousness of each person's Christ Presence, bringing forth harmony, perfection and protection to the individual engaged in this exercise and, according to God's Will, to those loved ones included in the person's invocations.

Expanding further on this concept: the difference that separates spoken prayers/decrees/chants as given in the Ascended Master teachings and further clarified by The Temple of The Presence, compared to the religious prayers and practices of the West, is that with the former, the individual is in the process of awakening to their own indwelling Divinity; whereas, in the latter, they may be without this fuller understanding. As one becomes more aware that they are awakening to their own I Am Presence through this sacred exercise, the pure aspirations of the heart expand. A momentum is developed and the sacred thoughtforms that are depicted in these calls are visualized more strongly; they are propelled more quickly into physical manifestation.

Thus the awakening one is "pulled up by his own bootstraps." It is because of this sacred process that so many aspirants experience so quickly such tremendous clarity, healing, divine purpose and the joys that accompany this free-will act of illumination.

Lastly on this subject, please be forewarned that some kind of change is always experienced as an individual begins to awaken in this process. After all, for many lifetimes, the limitation of *Samsara* has been the standard fare for most embodied souls. Now it's like taking a shower or bath in Sacred Fire for the first time.

Each time that you engage in this practice, more and more of the karmic substance that has accrued over the ages is cleaned away from one's being. You begin to see clearly, to act clearly, and to love more clearly, by and through and in the Light of your own I Am Presence. The eventual end-point of this is the great Mastery that Jesus and so many others have demonstrated over the long epochs of Earth's history.

As I shared in the beginning of this section, this is a very brief overview of The Science of the Spoken Word. A much more thorough understanding can be gleaned from the book of the same title, published by The Summit Lighthouse, or by listening to any one of numerous discourses and dictations released by The Temple of The Presence on this subject. Furthermore, this entire work is meant to serve as a general introduction to the Brotherhood of Light and the Great Laws that govern everything. For those who thirst for a greater understanding and experience of what is only lightly touched upon here, integrating the material released via the Brotherhood's work in the past one hundred years, most currently through The Temple of The Presence, is the work of a lifetime.

## A Comparison

Now I wish to use an analogy for the reader to consider. If someone not used to exercise were required to run or swim a mile without any previous training, they wouldn't get very far. The same concept would hold true if a highly educated person were to be placed in a foreign land where they didn't understand the language. So it is with many who are yet completely caught up in the material world, who have not allowed their mind and heart to ponder the mysteries of Life. However, as touched upon earlier, this condition will not last forever. Somewhere, sometime, in this lifetime or a future one, life's circumstances will propel such a one to begin to wake up and seek to understand, to remember, what they once knew but have forgotten. It is always hoped that this awakening will be prompted by the inner yearnings of the heart, rather than by the hard hammer-blows of tragedy, due to returning negative karma, be it personal, group or planetary.

The above analogies are used so you might consider that, like all things in the physical world, training is required to obtain mastery. The books that are referenced here represent the outer thrust of the great Brotherhood of Light to kindle the fire of humanity's Divine Memory. Specifically the concepts and thoughtforms conveyed in these affirmations, mantras and decrees, all of which were inspired by the great Masters (Beloved Jesus included), are designed for the quickening and purification of the lower bodies (physical, mental, emotional and memory) that are the four vehicles through which our Divine Presence is intended to expresses itself (and gain self-mastery) throughout each lifetime.

What differentiates these affirmations and decrees (we shall refer to them as calls) from the Christian concept of prayer is that these are given with the understanding that the I Am is really the Individualized Presence of God within us that is giving this decree, these fiats to all of Life.

This is the same *I AM That I AM* that brought forth and sustains all Creation. The more that one begins to grasp this concept, the more powerful these calls become. The more powerful they become, the more purification and transmutation of old, sluggish, karmic records occurs, as the patina of lifetimes of misqualified karma is burnt away in the Sacred Fire thus invoked.

The more these records are transmuted, the more the indwelling Light of the Threefold Flame shines forth and enables the outer consciousness, and all aspects of one's life, to come increasingly into alignment with the Will of one's Presence. There is buoyancy, a clarity, and a strength that lends itself to every facet of one's life.

The dross of the physical becomes more refined and one begins to feel and perhaps to see the action that occurs as the calls and meditations are engaged in. One begins to remember, to have the inner experiences that continue to unfold with the purification and application of the Path. By and by as the purification and acceleration continue and as one's waking consciousness is drawn again and again to the Divine within, the words that Jesus said take on a new meaning. "What I have done, you will do even greater...." The process described here is the mechanics of the Sacred Science that comes forth when one is so engaged.

The wonderful expansion and depth of my meditations continued as I began to understand more and more what was happening when I gave those affirmations. I would sit in the Silence for some time in meditation, following the visualizations that I had learned in India to quiet the mind. At a certain point in this process, when I could feel the love for my Father welling up in my heart, I engaged in those calls. It grew into something akin to excitement as I approached that state within.

### The Master's Touch

I begin to share the following account with some concern that it may not always be appropriate to share such personal, sacred experiences. However, the point of this entire work is to provide an accounting of the outer and inner journey that I traveled and the remarkable events that transpired, so that others might avail themselves of the same assistance, not only for themselves, but for their loved ones and the world.

The encounters with the Great Masters that you are about to read are not unique to me, for I have met many others over the decades that have had similar, transcendent experiences with the Great Masters and their own I Am Presence. What is so important to note here is that this is ongoing today. This is not limited to events from decades or centuries ago. This is available to all. The only requirement being, as Jesus said, "... the pure in Heart."

One precious day, I approached the high point of my meditation in the tower, this being the first room I completed in my home that was designed and only used for prayer and meditation. I was just about to recite in my heart Kuthumi's *I Am Light* decree. Something wonderful happened. I felt the rushes of electric joy as described earlier, then in a flash, my entire being started vibrating at a very high frequency and the Master was standing before me and said, "Say it with me now, Gene."

I recited this blessed decree with the Master. My entire being was charged and vibrating with such an intensity of Light. I was aware of several other Masters in a circle around me, also engaged in this action. My eyes were wide open, the Master before me completely visible but, for lack of a better description of what I saw, the Master was composed of differing graduations of Light.

I never took my eyes from the Master's eyes, but in my peripheral vision I was aware of the other Masters standing in a circle around me. When the decree was concluded it was like the light slowly decreased and the Master was gone, even though my body continued to vibrate for a long period of time afterwards. I was completely overcome with emotion and gratitude and unworthiness. I just lay on the floor of the meditation tower trying to absorb, to process, what had just happened. In all the mystical experience that had happened over the years, some of which are related in this narrative, I never had the fully conscious experience of a Master standing before me until that moment.

After a few hours, I was reeling in the energy and excitement of the event and it was then, through abject ignorance and density on my part, that I made a mistake.

I drove over to a dear friend's home and shared the experience. Immediately I felt the charge of the event lessen. I realized that I had made a huge mistake. If I was able to listen clearly within, I would have known that I was to keep that event private. It wasn't until years later that I learned the motto of the Brotherhood of Light, "To Know, To Dare, To Do, and To Be Silent." So, this is a word to the wise to all those who will read these words. As the quickening and acceleration takes place in your lives, share it with no one so that the sacred alchemy might unfold and do its perfect work, without your ego, or the egos of those you share the experience with, dissipating the charge.

The teachings of the Brotherhood continued to accelerate within me as I made my way through life. I would often give these calls while flying charters or giving flight instruction above the northeastern United States. One of the beautiful aspects of being a professional pilot is that, after the intense concentration and activity of the preflight, the takeoff, and the establishing of the en route segment of the flight, there are long periods of time when the workload eases up and it's a joy to watch cities, towns, and the countryside pass by beneath your wings. It was during these periods that I would often give these calls, seeing the Light envelop all that was beneath me.

(It was years later that I realized that, when flying or being in the mountains, one's application of the sacred fire is more powerful because the weight of human, discordant thought and feeling is much more prevalent near lower elevations, and in and around cities.)

## *Divine Intercession Again*

A few years later I felt the approach of my daughter's birth, and I wanted her to have beautiful wide-open spaces to play and learn about life in. Before she was born, I clear-cut several acres of land adjacent to the house and barn, and started building a pond. Pausing to discern the potential that was here, I opened a large section of land that had previously been a dense, marshy forest, transforming it into landscaped, open areas cradling the large acre-wide pond.

It was another large building project that family and friends could not understand. What had been a marshy, heavily forested area at first turned into several muddy acres of debris where heavy equipment removed large trees and stumps. After several weeks, the debris was cleared up, leaving a large, rolling muddy field. Then the heavy equipment began the excavation, and weeks later, there was an immense muddy hole in the middle of the muddy field. It was hardly beautiful but I could more easily see the potential that would come forth. The hole filled with water from a dozen underground springs that were uncovered and from a tiny stream that I directed into it. I then began to shape and landscape the open area around the pond with my tractor.

While engaged in this work one day, I was driving my large tractor along the bank of the pond when suddenly, as if a giant had kicked it, the tractor was rolling over on top of me into the pond. I have very quick reflexes. (You have to if you wish to survive as a flight instructor when your students try to kill you.) Instantly I knew that I had to jump off the seat or else the tractor would pin me underwater as it rolled over. (Not a nice way to go.) But no sooner had I launched myself off the seat when my shoulder and then all of me was underwater, with this huge John Deere tractor with loader and

**The excavation** of the acre surface area pond that is 18' deep.

**Looking directly across the pond** to the area that the large
John Deere 420 Tractor rolled over on top of me.

rake, rolled over on top of me.

In the next instant, there was an explosion of Light and I was standing on a large rock that was placed right in the center of the heart-shaped pond. I was standing on this rock with my hands upraised in prayer, my entire body vibrating at such a high frequency, akin to what had happened in the Master's presence a few years earlier. Totally detached, in a full and very powerful voice, I heard myself saying, "Thank you, Father; thank you, Father; thank you, Father."

My voice echoed out across the full pond, across the tall, forest trees that surround the pond and seemingly across the mountains in the distance. My body was shimmering, glowing, and vibrating so intensely. (I remember that I thought I had been struck by lightning from the white Light that was everywhere around me.)

In the deep peace, from the Watcher perspective I knew so well, I looked out to where my tractor was, about forty yards away. Only the very top of the vertical exhaust muffler was sticking out above the water. (The top of the muffler was over seven feet high.) The tractor had rolled completely over at least two times and was completely submerged in six feet of water standing upright on the bottom of the shallow end of the pond.

In wonder, I looked at my hands and noted that they were glowing with white Light. With my entire body still vibrating at such a high frequency, I started to understand the full impact of what had transpired. I had been moved from underneath the tractor. A Lightning Bolt of God's Grace had struck, moving me from being pinned and squashed at the bottom of the pond underneath the several-thousand-pound tractor as it rolled over and over. I had been transported in this great flash of Light to this rock, forty yards away, located at the very center of the heart shaped pond, standing upright in prayer and thanksgiving—without consciously knowing how I got there. I was completely overwhelmed and profoundly humbled by this near-death encounter, this extension of Divine Grace that had just saved my life.

I remember walking across the field, perhaps floating across the field, to my home a hundred yards away and walking into my home. My daughter, just a baby, her mother didn't even comment upon my soaking wet clothes; she just said something akin to, "My God, you are glowing white light...."

An acquaintance with heavy equipment was able to pull my tractor out of the pond. He made a comment that, "it wasn't your time to go." My dear friend Elwood Babbitt (the clairvoyant trance medium referred to earlier in this narrative) simply said with a smile that, "They moved you." Again I had the sense of an appointment that I had to keep, but it seemed very far off. I was very aware that I was being protected for something that I had to do.

### Beloved Mother Mary

As previously stated here, over the past few years, I had read several books written and published by The Summit Lighthouse, containing the teachings of the Ascended Masters. One day, I received a flyer in the mail stating that there was going to be a seminar in Washington, D.C. Having read their books and incorporated the wonderful, powerful calls into my daily meditation practice, I was very interested to get to know more about this organization.

I flew a small plane down to Washington arriving at the hotel just in time for the first evening session. Walking into the Hilton conference area that was the venue for the seminar, I was aware of a definite current of spiritual electricity in the air. There were a few hundred people there listening to a woman speak about the Masters. She was impassioned and articulate and I quickly got caught up in the flow of what she was expressing.

The teachings were simple and at the same time profound. It was the same type of material that I have become familiar with over the past decades in various books describing the work of the Great Masters of the Brotherhood of Light. There was a palpable excitement in the air and the energy kept building and building. I recall, at one point in this opening session, wondering why they had different color spotlights on her while she was speaking, and then I realized that it wasn't colored spotlights at all, but aspects of her aura that I was seeing.

I had never seen auras before like this—but I was seeing this now and it was fascinating. The energy kept going higher and higher, the Messenger (as she was referred to), Elizabeth Clare Prophet, was now talking about Mother Mary and her discourse was interspersed with the most beautiful songs and these wonderful, powerful, rhythmic calls that everyone in the auditorium would join in with. Obviously, unlike me, most of the people attending were very familiar with what was happening here.

I was in new territory now—this was outside of my experience. I was aware of the energy and the charge of Light building and thought to myself that something has to give. The pressure of the Light and Love kept welling up inside me. It was intense and getting more so. I was about thirty feet from the platform where the Messenger was located when she finished her discourse and some very beautiful music started playing. There was a solemn expectancy in the air. Through the playing of this beautiful music the energy in the room shifted dramatically and became actually more intense.

The Messenger, sitting on a chair on the platform before me, closed her eyes and the pressure of the Light, pouring forth like a great waterfall, increased. Then, for lack of a better description, there was a soft explosion of Light where the Messenger was located and I literally felt pressed back into my seat by the force of this. When my eyes could focus again, there on the platform was a crystalline sphere of pure golden fire perhaps twelve feet in diameter. Within this sphere was a smaller sphere of the most intense sky blue and inside this sphere, Mother Mary herself was looking right into my eyes, right into my heart. She had long, blonde hair and her eyes were the crystalline blue of the sky. I had never seen anything so beautiful, so perfect.

The love that I experienced, blazing forth from Mother Mary, was completely overwhelming. Tears were streaming down my face and I started talking with her from within, completely unbidden prayers were coming forth from my heart. And then she started speaking directly to me, answering my prayers, and I cried and cried in the most complete love that I had ever known.

This interlude of such profound Grace seemed to go on for eternity. Throughout this non-stop communication, which I had absolutely no control of as it arose completely unbidden from my deepest heart, was as if I was in a hurricane of the most intense Love—and within this Love was all of God. My entire being was blasted asunder by the force of this great love, from within out, from without in.

After what truly seemed an eternity, Mother Mary bowed her head, her hands held before her heart in prayer and the twelve-foot-diameter sphere of golden fire started to decrease in size and intensity. And then Mother Mary was gone. There in her place was the Messenger sitting there with her head bowed and her hands together in prayer, just as were Mother Mary's a few moments earlier.

I was simply overwhelmed. I had no wish to move. I don't know if I could have moved my body. For thirty minutes or longer, I sat there in stunned meditation, with tears flowing, my body still vibrating at such a high frequency from what I had experienced in Mother Mary's Presence. By now, most of the people in the room had left and the staff was preparing to close up the venue for the night. A few people looked at me and smiled and said, "First dictation?" I could only nod my head.

I had learned some years later that the first dictation (address by the Master directly through the Messenger) at which one is present holds the Key to one's Divine Plan. I don't remember an erg of what Mother Mary said to us that night, but I do know that it is written in Sacred Fire in the deepest recesses of my being. I do know that this blessed Grace set the tone for the remainder of this incarnation and reminded me what I had come to do.

To this day, almost three decades later, the sacredness of this experience with Mother Mary that was afforded to me and to the others present overwhelms me to my very core. It was similar in magnitude, but so very different, than what had happened to me on the beach that evening in Pondicherry, when I felt that I went into the Great Central Sun. That was immense and Impersonal—this experience with Mother Mary was immense and so intensely personal.

Who was I to be so blessed? How could I even begin to understand, let alone integrate, the immensity of what had just happened to me? This was not in the high Himalayas or at the Aurobindo Ashram on the other side of the world, but right here in Washington, D.C. in a Hilton Hotel conference room.

Then and now, as these words are written, through the hard demeanor of a very physical lifetime, I can just barely perceive with my consciousness the absolute purity of the charge and instructions that were conveyed to me during that experience and it humbles me to the very core. I was given this strong physical temple. I was given these lifetime experiences for a most definite reason, and I was still (then in my thirty-fourth year) in training and preparation for this work that I was being called to do—the problem being that in my outer consciousness, I still had no idea of what I was supposed to do differently, save to continue with my daily meditation practice and the study and integration of the Master's Teachings, and to share it with all as best I could.

It was around that period, perhaps a year or two before, that I began giving public presentations on the Teachings of the Masters of East and West at local venues in the area and surrounding communities, taking out small ads in the local newspapers and putting up posters announcing these free presentations. During this time we also began hosting meditation retreats here on this sacred land. The new acre-wide pond changed in a year from a muddy construction site to a beautifully landscaped mecca covered with wildflowers and rolling lawns, reflecting the peaceful beauty of the Green Mountains that surrounded us.

The exact place where my tractor had rolled over upon me a few years earlier was now where many gathered weekly in prayer and meditation, giving the calls of the Ascended Masters and talking about the Path. There was a sense among all of us who gathered here that we were doing a service to life, assisting the Great Masters with their sacred work. There was such a peace and joy among all of us as we gathered here, giving these dynamic calls for our loved ones and the world, and then after the calls, going into silent meditation—sitting there by the pond, listening to the breeze rustle through the tall pines, the birds singing, absorbing the return of the actions we had just created and sent forth into the world via our calls.

We were aware as we paused that we were reflecting the beauty of what we could then perceive of our I Am Presence, even as the pond reflected the beauty of the blue sky and the Green Mountains of Vermont around us. This happened here, week after week, and was my daily practice (even then) for many years.

An interesting footnote: Consider the tractor accident and intercession that occurred on this spot a few years before. Now consider the service that we were so blessed to render with the calls and meditations that have occurred on this very spot all these long years now. Consider the karmic relationship between the two events. Was it the future events that were known by my Presence and the Great Masters that allowed for the Divine Intercession that again saved my life when the tractor rolled over on top of me? Or was it that Divine Grace was extended that allowed for that place to become a holy, charged and sacred spot that, in the near future, would become a place of prayer, praise and meditation for many? Was it both?

Adding to this footnote: Back then in 1984, I shared with several that were gathered together by the pond that I just had the flash, the sense, that someday we would host a formal service with the Messenger of the Great Brotherhood of Light right here. It took a few decades, but that is exactly what happened, not once, but several times with the new Messengers of The Temple of The Presence (the Ascended Master activity that came after The Summit Lighthouse).

### *The Summit Lighthouse*

My involvement with The Summit Lighthouse now took on a new dimension. Aside from the overwhelming impact of what happened with Mother Mary, the other people that attended this event in Washington, D.C. were different—everyone had a smile and a sparkle in their eye. There was tangible buoyancy present here. I met for the first time in this lifetime some dear, special friends with whom a sacred work would transpire in future decades. I had never been with so many people who shared the same inner knowing as I did of the reality of the Great Masters and of the Path.

All here seemed highly motivated (in the highest sense of the word). All here were well along the way in extricating themselves from the trappings of *Samsara* and *Maya*. These are similar Sanskrit words, often used interchangeably, referring to the outer world and to the seemingly endless karmic cycles of rebirth, describing "the various worldly activities that occupy ordinary human beings, the various sufferings thereof, or the unsettled and agitated mind through which reality is perceived." [Wikipedia]

At that time, The Summit Lighthouse was a large organization with many thousands of members scattered around the world. All were aspiring students of the Masters and hundreds would gather regularly at large events held in different cities around the United States. The focal point of each public presentation, as with the one that I had attended in Washington, D.C., was the sacred teachings and empowerments of the Great Brotherhood of Light (the collective body comprised of all the Great Ones of all time). By empowerments, I mean the actual conveyance by the Master in conjunction with one's I Am Presence of immense currents of physically tangible, spiritual fire. The purpose of this is for the acceleration and purification of the lower bodies that we might increasingly integrate and increasingly remember more and more, who we really are—our I Am Presence in action.

The amount of spiritual fire generated in these gatherings,

when hundreds were physically present and engaged in the calls, was exhilarating and amazing to participate in. This exercise built a forcefield that, along with the assistance of the Ascended Masters, created an opening by which the Master might step through the veil and, through the spiritual mechanics of the Messenger's initiations, give a formal address and a great charge of Light to all present.

The Messenger of the Brotherhood was a concept that was new to me. Far, far different from the "channels" that are ubiquitous in so-called New Age circles, a true Messenger of the Brotherhood is a different order of magnitude and cannot even be compared in the same breath. Obviously she had to be very far along on the Path to be a vehicle by which the Great Ones could step through the veil and pour forth their blessings and instruction, conveying such an electric, fiery current of Love, Wisdom, and Power to such large groups of people. To say that it was completely exhilarating is a great understatement.

Each individual participant experienced something different depending on the state of their own attunement and inner preparation prior to and during the event. Some actually saw the Ascended Master who was addressing the assembly; some saw groups of Angels or other Masters on the platform near the Messenger. Others were simply caught up in their own communion with their Presence, oblivious to all but the Master's words and the transmission of the Sacred Fire.

These were amazing events. Had I known about The Summit Lighthouse in my teens, I would have traveled to California in an instant to delve into this and Heaven only knows how this life would have changed. Still, I was here now and I had many hard-won experiences on the Path before my association with The Summit Lighthouse began. I knew enough now to understand that nothing was an accident, that I had to go through what I went through, in training, in preparation for what I was experiencing now.

At that time there were perhaps a dozen or more books published by The Summit Lighthouse about the Ascended Masters and the Brotherhood. There were also dozens of cassette albums that were recordings of the sessions with the Messenger delivered over entire multi-day conclaves, attended by hundreds of people and covering a wide range of esoteric subjects. The Messenger's instruction was usually followed by a Dictation from the Ascended Master as the focal point, the amazing crescendo of every session. These sessions were also published and sent out to subscribers around the world as Pearls of Wisdom. These chronicled at that time the 20-plus-year history of The Summit Lighthouse.

### *The 1985 Easter Conclave at Camelot*

After my experience in Washington, D.C., I decided that I would attend the Easter Conclave at The Summit Lighthouse location in the hills near Malibu, California. Arriving at the conclave I was very aware of being with hundreds of others who shared my love for these teachings. It was a charged atmosphere. Every day we attended one or two sessions with the Messenger and each one seemed to build upon the previous. There was the expectant hush in the assembly as the Messenger came to the platform, everyone knowing that the Masters were present and that they might begin their address at any moment.

On Friday afternoon, I was participating in the decrees and affirmations in preparation for the session prior to the arrival of the Messenger. I can remember the joy and the electricity building and I remember feeling such a strong sense of gratitude that I was here in this place at this exact moment.

The Messenger arrived and immediately stated that we were all asked to recite their new rosary to Archangel Michael. The Messenger then led everyone in this powerful decree/affirmation matrix that came to be known as Archangel Michael's Rosary. I was flooded with joy and gratitude. I knew at that moment, in the very beginning of this forty-minute matrix, that henceforward I would be giving this rosary every single day in addition to my daily meditation practice. The rosary continued that afternoon in the Holy Grail (their main chapel) and the electricity increased. Immediately upon the conclusion of the rosary, Archangel Michael came.

After all these years and Dictations from the Masters that I've been blessed to have been present for, it's still not possible to convey the immensity of these experiences when the Master steps forth. Archangel Michael gave instruction about why he asked for this rosary and its importance. I saw a pillar of indigo-blue fire where the Messenger was standing during Lord Michael's dictation, stretching to the top of the Holy Grail, perhaps thirty feet high. I felt such joy and gratitude for this moment with Archangel Michael, for this new rosary—somehow I knew at that moment that things were now better.

### Inner Preparation

The Easter Conclave concluded on Sunday and I made my way back home to Vermont shortly thereafter. Every day, with purpose, I entered into Archangel Michael's Rosary. It wasn't even a question of whether I would take the additional forty minutes, added to my already long, daily meditations and decree matrix. It simply was part of my life. (For the next several years, I never missed a day of participating in Archangel Michael's Rosary.)

Upon my return to Vermont, I resumed giving public presentations on the Teachings of the Masters. I would rent a venue that could hold a few dozen people and I would poster the area where the presentation would be held and take out a newspaper ad or an article to publicize it. I also arranged for the airing of a series of videos programs that The Summit Lighthouse had produced for cable-TV broadcast, in which I had to provide an introduction in order for these to qualify as containing locally originated content. Soon there were several people who would join me in the decrees and meditations on a weekly basis, usually at our place, outside by the beautiful pond if the weather was nice, or inside at a makeshift altar room if it was cold or rainy. Archangel Michael's Rosary continued to expand in my life.

The days, weeks and months unfolded. I was flying several times a week, playing with my daughter, and spending time with my father, watching him deal with his upcoming end-of-life transition in peace. One October day, I was giving flight instruction to a student and got a call on the radio from the airport stating that I had to call home immediately. I landed and made the call and knew that my father was close to passing. I drove the hour-long drive to my family's home making calls for him, that his transition would be smooth and that the Angels would escort him to the great Retreats of the Masters. I was perhaps thirty minutes away from my parents' home, driving along a beautiful country road with falling leaves and bright sunshine. It was a beautiful afternoon and suddenly, my Dad was sitting next to me in the car, smiling with such an amazingly beautiful, loving smile.

He looked like he was just as old as I was (mid-thirties) and he was so happy and excited. There was so much love that passed between us and I was so very happy for him that he was now free from his old physical body that had become a prison for him these past months. There was a huge burst of love between us as we looked into each other's eyes and then—he was gone. I was by myself in my car with tears of joy and such love for my Dad. I continued driving home.

When I got there a few of my younger brothers were standing in the driveway crying. My Dad had died about thirty minutes earlier. Exactly at the time that he came to visit me in my car to say goodbye, for now, with all of that amazing love. I shared this account with my Mom and siblings but it was hard for them to fathom it. Now, as I write this twenty-seven years later, there are tears and I am flooded again with my Dad's love in a magnitude that I've not experienced since that day.

My Dad was a war hero. He was considered, as was his father and grandfather before him, to be a town father. He was loved and respected by so many. With my being the oldest of six, we had butted heads several times while I was growing up; but the memories of getting up early to go fishing with him, and then when he came to see me when I was in the military, and how he helped me with cash when I needed it, are joys for me to look back upon.

Throughout all of these events, I never missed my morning meditations and calls, and I never missed giving Archangel Michael's Rosary. ◌

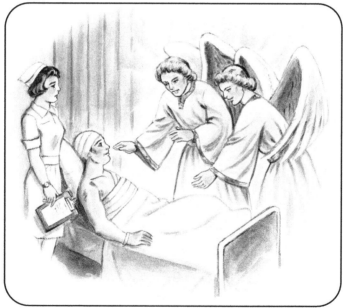

*A children's version of Gene's miracle story* was printed in
*"Angels, Your Friends and Helpers,"* (2009, <u>RoseLightBooks.com</u>)
by Nancy Kolze, illustrated by Alvera Kubal. The first picture above depicts
the moment just before the crash when Archangel Michael appeared and
commanded me to prepare. |The second illustrates the angels' visitation at
my hospital bed and their intercession in my healing through the night.

# 14 ~ **Archangel Michael**

A s I write this, it is December 3rd, 2011, at 7:00 pm. The unfolding timeline of this narrative has caught up with the anniversary of Archangel Michael's great intercession in my life. After all these years, the impetus has been provided to begin writing and this has continued to this day and will continue until this accounting has been concluded and published.

Now, as I write about all the events that surrounded Archangel Michael's intervention, which happened twenty-six years ago today, I don't recall ever before feeling the pressure of the Light so intensely as I have these past few days in conjunction with this anniversary. Surely this is another indication that the writing of this story must come forth now.

My father made his transition in mid-October of 1985 after a terrible 3-year ordeal. In the weeks that followed, I initially thought my preoccupation with transition was due to my father's passing; however, as fall progressed, I started having premonitions that I would have a big appointment coming up that was going to take me out of this lifetime. The premonitions got more insistent. Every day in morning meditation I had a sense that something big was coming. I mentioned this to my daughter Azure's mother and had conversations with her about what needed to happen when I was gone.

Then, on the morning of December 3rd, 1985, the sense of my "appointment with destiny" was so very concrete that I can feel it even now, 26 years later. I remember saying something to this effect to Azure's mother on my way out the door for the airport. I got about a mile from home and had the sense of something intense happening, something so huge that I thought that I'd better go back home and get my heavy, warm parka in case the plane crashed in the mountains of Maine that afternoon. It was a cold, December day and I had two students who were going to come with me on this instructional flight to Maine.

Aside from my morning meditation and prayers that begin every day for many decades now, anytime I drive anywhere, I would always do some calls for the world, my family, etc. I did this same exercise as I began the hour-long drive to the airport. I was driving on U.S. Interstate 91 heading south, just outside of Greenfield, Massachusetts, about fifteen minutes from the airport, thinking about flight planning with my students. I was traveling about 70 mph in my VW Jetta. Suddenly there was an explosion of electrifying Light. It was not enough to blind me but it sure got my full attention. A sphere of Sacred Fire appeared, maybe one or two feet in diameter, immediately in front and to the side of me, not blocking my view of the road, but in front of where the radio is in the car.

This Sphere of Fire was Lord Michael. I don't know how I knew that at the time—I just knew it. He commanded me to give his decree, immediately:

Lord Michael before, Lord Michael behind,
Lord Michael to the right, Lord Michael to the left,
Lord Michael above, Lord Michael below,
Lord Michael, Lord Michael wherever I go!

I AM his Love protecting here!
I AM his Love protecting here!
I AM his Love protecting here!

I was dazed and astonished, to put it mildly. Although I was very blessed to have had several experiences over my lifetime, never one such as this, never one so Urgent, never Commanded to act as I was at that moment.

Everything was in an altered state around me. I slowed the car down to perhaps 50 mph and everything seemed to proceed in super-slow motion while I did the decree I was commanded to do. There was not even a thought of, "Did I really experience what I just experienced?" The altered state, the Fire of his Command so Intense, my giving his call so powerful. I came up on a curve to the right and pulled over as far as I could to the rock cliffs, as if expecting it to happen at that place. I was giving the decree. Just as I started to clear the curve, a car in the opposite direction lost control and shot across the dividing line in the highway, across most of my lane, and hit me head on. At the very last second before impact, I can recall recognizing this event; it was completely familiar, like it had already happened to me.

I was in the void, a white blackness—a black whiteness, hearing a very powerful, beautiful male voice doing the decree that I was commanded to do. I remember saying (expletive deleted), "____, I'm dead." Moments later, I was commanded, "join me, Gene" and I said/thought first something like (expletive deleted again), "____, I'm really dead." I joined in as I was commanded to do, in whatever passes for a voice or a conveyance of thought in that place. After a period of time doing that decree, I had the sense that I was somehow traveling quickly (down?) and then, presto, I was back in my body in my car, still doing the decree with Lord Michael.

I was then given the command or the impression that I had to get out of the car quickly, perhaps because it could have caught fire. Still doing the decree with whatever voice/thought that I was using through this experience, I tried to get out of the driver's door, but it wasn't there anymore. The head-on impact at 80+ mph pushed the engine, steering wheel and the door into the driver's seat. Somehow I was able to climb out of the passenger door with my hands; I found that my legs didn't work at all.

I remember it being very hard to breathe, somehow pulling myself out of the car onto the road, still doing the decree with Archangel Michael, and with only my hands, pulling myself over to the guardrail. It was very hard to breathe and as I tried to breathe, there was a gurgling sound and big red bubbles of blood coming out of my mouth with every difficult breath. Still I was doing the decree.

I was pulling myself up on the guardrail to try to breathe easier, gurgling blood bubbles, doing the decree in great peace, and then suddenly, it was like doing a backflip from a diving board.

I was out of my body and I was falling or flying upward in this white tunnel. I was moving very quickly away from the Earth, still doing the decree with Michael, in absolute peace. I didn't have the sense of not being able to breathe anymore and there was no pain. I was moving very quickly, decreeing. The intense peace was everywhere.

Then another Master Presence is next to me; I could not make out any details of his features, I just knew that there were now two. I was commanded, "Violet Fire now, Gene!" so I started doing a Violet Fire decree with this Master (whom I believe was Saint Germain). Immediately a cool, electric fire around and through what was me, and the sense of moving very quickly away from the Earth stopped. Joining in the Violet Fire decree, the sense of electricity, of coolness and peace.

And then I was descending, slowly at first and then faster and faster. Doing the Violet Fire decree, seeing this world grow from a star, getting bigger and bigger and then, presto, I pop back into my physical body and I'm staring into the eyes of a medic. He says "OK, this one's stable. Let's get going." And they put me into the ambulance on the stretcher. In the process of being moved, I see the other stretcher with the driver who lost control and hit me. He was dead and I recognized him in a flash, although I've never met him in this lifetime.

I was in and out of consciousness. In the Intensive Care Unit (ICU), they said my back was broken, my chest and ribs were broken, hand broken, and heart damaged and misfiring from the fatal 80+ mph head-on impact. I remember returning to consciousness and seeing my brothers with tears in their eyes. (They had to drive an hour to get there.) I remember it being said that I might not make it through the night. I knew I had to summon the energy, the drive, to do this ritual with Lord Michael that I had been doing every day for seven months now—Archangel Michael's Rosary. I remember how hard it was to stay conscious during the giving of the rosary in the ICU of the hospital. I remember almost finishing it when I passed out again.

I came back to consciousness in the middle of the night, hearing two nurses who were watching over me in the ICU, talking about out-of-body experiences. I remember a rush, a charge of Light, and somehow in words that were not mine, I proceeded to tell these two nurses about the Light of the Heart and the Path. They were shocked. Then, I asked them if they could see the two Masters or Angels that were standing next to my bed. I could see their radiance, their auras, but I couldn't move my body to look at them. I remember the nurses both started crying, thinking that I was soon to die, and then I passed out again.

I awoke sometime later with a doctor yelling at the nurse, something like, "This machine isn't working, quick, get another one." There was great commotion and after a while, I was hooked up to the new machine and the doctor said, "A few hours ago this guy was ready to die and now he has the heartbeat of a 21-year-old athlete." The next morning in x-ray, they said that somehow, they had made a mistake the previous day; my back wasn't broken, just several compressed disks. I was aware then that the two Masters/Angels who attended to me the previous night did their perfect work.

Through the next week, many people from the hospital would come into my hospital room to look at me, to talk about what had happened. Word had gotten out throughout the hospital that something major had occurred and Archangel Michael was involved. Every day while in the hospital, I continued my daily morning ritual of meditation and decrees, and the rosary to Archangel Michael.

I remember my brother coming into the hospital room a few days after the accident. He told me that he went to my wrecked car to get my personal belongings out of it. While there, he met a policeman who was concluding the investigation. As the officer looked into the wrecked vehicle, on the driver's seat he found a white cassette tape that had my blood splattered on it. This cassette tape was so obvious by its color and the fact that everything else in the car was wrecked. The officer picked it up, noting the title: Archangel Michael's Rosary. The cassette tape contained the prayers and mantras to Archangel Michael that I had made part of my daily meditation practice for the past several months. The officer told my brother, "I guess Archangel Michael was really with your brother." Archangel Michael had left his calling card.

A week later, as my brothers came to drive me home, I remember how everything looked new, everything looked different. I could hardly move, but I was buoyed by such a charge, almost an electricity of Grace and Purpose.

## After Lord Michael's Intervention

As I shared above, after Lord Michael's intercession, everything was different. How could it be otherwise? While I was still in the hospital, people I didn't know would stop by my room to say hi. Word had spread quickly that something amazing had happened. Though I was home in a week, it was a month before I could do much of anything. I wasn't able to pick up a half-gallon of milk for a month. Still, my physical healed quickly. Every day my meditations and Michael's Rosary had a new and special impetus, a charge, to them.

Within a few months I had resumed the public presentations on the Masters and the Path that I was doing prior to the accident, and I most surely included the instances of Lord Michael's intercession. Obviously this experience was a very tangible outpicturing of what is possible when one engages oneself with all aspects of the Path. These presentations would last about an hour and would include a very basic overview of the Masters and the Path, with the design of the Brotherhood of Light to awaken humanity to life's sacred purpose, as outlined throughout this narrative.

At a point in these public presentations, I would lead those in attendance in an exercise so they would be able to experience the

Science of the Spoken Word for themselves. I conveyed Master Morya's instructions that if the aspirant gave the "Heart, Head, and Hand" decree matrix every day for two weeks, (it took only about ten to fifteen minutes to do this exercise) that they would see such an increase of Light in their life that they would know the power of the Path for themselves. I would ask the participants to take what I called a reality check, to note their inner vibration prior to the start of this exercise and to be aware of the thoughtforms that were painted in their mind's eye as they gave this decree matrix. Then, when concluded, we would go into a brief silent meditation, so they might feel the return current of their action—the peace generated by this exercise. It was always the high point of the presentation.

Several months later, I decided to write up what had happened to me, sending it to the Messenger Elizabeth Prophet, that she might, in turn, share with the thousands of members of The Summit Lighthouse. Within a few weeks of mailing that accounting I received a call from Summit Lighthouse staff saying that the Messenger had read my story during a Sunday service and gave a teaching on it. This was followed by a Dictation from Lord Michael in which he further commented upon what happened to me by name and why the intercession occurred.

I was told that this service with the Messenger and Lord Michael and the Master Kuthumi (referenced earlier in this work) was going to be sent out around the world to the extended Summit Lighthouse community as an example of the power of Lord Michael's Rosary.

### *Moving On from The Summit Lighthouse*

A few years later, when I returned to The Summit Lighthouse in California for a conference, I was troubled by certain behaviors that I experienced in the group decrees. That conference took on a political bent and the vibration had become very different for me. The purity and the power of what I had experienced in my first interactions with The Summit Lighthouse seemed to me to be greatly diminished. It was to be my last visit there.

The Summit Lighthouse really deserves more than the brief mention written here. This organization, by some accounting, was the fourth outer activity in the western world focused on the dissemination of The Brotherhood's teachings since 1875. It had established such a broad reach that it included tens of thousands of seekers in their outer membership, with teaching centers in many large cities across America and around the world. Mark L. Prophet (the founder) and then some years later, his wife, Elizabeth, were trained Messengers for the Brotherhood in this activity.

When Mark made his transition in the early 70s, Elizabeth took over the running of the organization. She carried the work forward for many years and then suffered a decline in her health, eventually stepping down and leaving the organization to carry on with its own leadership, but no new Messenger. The work of the Summit Lighthouse has helped to awaken many thousands around the world, and still does. Its early materials on the Masters' Teachings remains a great Treasury of Light.

## What Is a Messenger of The Brotherhood?

Until one actually experiences this, it's all but impossible to fathom. By now many who have been interested in the spiritual path have encountered channels and psychics of all sorts, who are claiming to be overshadowed by this or that master, etc. This has become so common in esoteric circles that it seems that there is a master on every corner. From my earliest experiences in searching for truth, I had no interest for these things whatsoever. It seemed to me that even the written words about such a person or activity had a vibration to them that felt off. I decided that I had infinitely more important things to do than to allow my attention to dwell on any of that.

In India and in the Himalayas I had seen many who were in some kind of trance, doing this or that. It made no difference—it just wasn't for me. The teacher or master that I was interested in finding didn't have to go into a trance to channel a master. Their outer life had to be a demonstration of that mastery. My only role model in those early years was what I knew the real Jesus had to be. I say "real" because I wasn't even then buying what organized Christianity had to say about Jesus. It wasn't until Israel and what had occurred there that I began to learn the truth of what Jesus did and taught.

So when I encountered the concept of Messenger of the Great Brotherhood of Light, I was intrigued. Aside from having such profound experiences in meditation while reading those early books from The Summit Lighthouse, such as *Dossier on the Ascension* and *Studies of the Human Aura*, I was aware that something different had to be occurring for a book to contain such a high vibration. In those early years, everything I read and later heard from The Summit Lighthouse felt so familiar to me.

When I felt my body accelerating during meditation and during the giving of the calls, I was absolutely certain that there was Truth there. My first experience with the Messenger in Washington, D.C., when I so vividly saw her aura and then had the life-changing, blessed experience with Mother Mary, crystallized what a Messenger was to my outer consciousness.

Simply put, a Messenger for the Brotherhood is one who has been trained for many lifetimes to make of their life a chalice through which the purity of God's Love, Wisdom and Power might pour forth and express in this outer physical world—this expression always being by the Will of that one's Individualized I Am Presence. Messengers come forth when a certain work is to be done, when the Great Brotherhood of Light wishes to formally introduce spirals of illumined instructions and empowerments to a group of individuals who have also been trained through many lifetimes to receive and then embody that instruction. All of this for the Great Awakening of Humanity.

During these formal services, the anointed Messenger conveys the Ascended Master's instruction and the charge of spiritual fire to those in attendance whose conscious preparation for the service (with group decrees, affirmations, prayers and song) helped to establish the forcefield. This forcefield enables the Great Ascended Masters to bring forth the instruction and the corresponding release of tangible Sacred Fire as a World Action, deemed appropriate by the Brotherhood at that time.

The mechanics of a true Messenger, which I have attempted to describe above, are all but impossible to convey or to understand unless one knows how to perceive with their heart. That is why I've stated that this is best experienced in person, because then, according to the Will of one's Presence, it's either time to have this understanding now, or one's Presence has some other business to attend to first. Lastly on this topic, many who have been on the Path for some time, whose hearts are open, and who have some level of subtle perception that is always expanded in the presence of the Master, may have inner or outer experiences in the Light, including seeing the Master addressing the gathering. It is always better not to discuss such experiences with others because of the blessed (and private) alchemy and acceleration unfolding in the aspirant's world.

When one shares their inner experiences with others, the charge of light is often dissipated. There can be an opening for subtle ego thoughts (one's own and another's) that would contaminate the purity of the experience. It can also convey a sense of unworthiness or the indignation of "why not me?" in the consciousness of someone who hears of such experiences. Again the Brotherhood's motto: "To Know, To Dare, To Do, and to Keep Silent," is one's best course of action. ᴄᴋ

# 15 ~ Continuing on the Path

The next several mini-chapters in this accounting are included here (though the descriptions are brief) because they delineate the subsequent major events in this life, further demonstrating how a lifetime's experience was molded and came forth when the first priority of every day was seeking alignment with my Presence.

The years unfolded. Still I had a sense of an appointment to keep. Every day began in meditation, affirmations and praise. Although I was no longer directly involved with The Summit Lighthouse, much of the material that had been published over the decades was such a rich tapestry, continuing to fuel many on the Path. Several of us still gathered to engage in group meditations and affirmations, but I had stopped doing the public presentations.

## *Roop*

In 1989, I attended a sitar concert at a local college and was astonished at the Light that I experienced in this music. I stayed after the event to speak with this man who obviously was from India and instantly we recognized each other from the past. Instantly we remembered a close bond. My friend and brother on the Path, Roop Verma, is an extraordinarily gifted teacher, musician and composer. As a young man in India, he had studied under the great spiritual teachers of his time. Roop's training in sacred music of Nada Yoga comes directly from Ravi Shankar and Ali Akbar Khan, as he studied, traveled and perfored with them extensively.

Listening to Roop's music was much more than listening to the wonderful musical traditions of India. There was a tangible spiritual charge to the music that I could feel interacting and moving within. Roop shared that his music was Nada Yoga, the ancient Vedic science of sound.

I learned that aside from the concerts that he performed, he also conducted sacred-music meditation retreats, usually a two-day event, with many sessions in which Roop performed ancient sacred ragas. These are musical formulas passed down through countless centuries that were designed and composed by the Masters for the purification and acceleration of the chakras and the subtle bodies. Based on what I had experienced in one 45-minute concert, I knew that a continued immersion in this would be wonderful. I decided to facilitate a retreat with Roop, found a venue in Brattleboro and spread the word to my existing network of friends.

Roop provided a brief overview of the process to the group and then we sounded the sacred OM, something that had been part of my meditations for decades. Each session seemed to last for perhaps 15 minutes but an hour had passed; the music not only wove a spell but many could actually feel it interacting with the different chakras. When Roop concluded a particular raga, the Silence was deafening, amazing.

The music was now vibrating everywhere within and without even though Roop had concluded and was sitting in meditation with all of us. There was a definite sense that the Great Ones were present, overshadowing this unique meditation. Each session performed a clearing and an acceleration that prepared the way for the subsequent session. By the end of the day, all were in a much-altered space. Throughout these sessions, there was a profound sense of joy that was contained in the acceleration. It was a remarkable experience.

I told Roop that I had been conducting group meditations at my place for over a decade and told him that it would be a wonderful place to hold a summer Sacred Music Meditation Retreat. At first, he was concerned that doing it outside, by the beautiful, landscaped pond amidst the mountain forest, would be too difficult for the instrument (humidity and temperature affect the sounds) and he was also concerned about the comfort of those attending. However, after

**Roop and Tracy Verma** during the annual Sacred Music Meditation Retreat under the white canopy next to the large pond previously pictured, 30 yards from where the tractor flipped over into the pond all those years before.

the first session, surrounded by the beauty and the supporting spiritual energy that has always blessed this sacred land, all concerns dissolved. The first retreat with Roop on this land accelerated beyond what any had imagined. For twenty-three years now, the high point of our summer has been hosting these blessed Sacred Music Meditation Retreats here, introducing many to this wonderful, ancient tradition. People who had little experience in meditation, or none at all, found themselves caught up in this profound peace and exhilaration and were able to let go. Over the decades there have been many physical and emotional healings here during these sessions.

Roop and I and our families became very close over the years. This gentle man's life is truly a blessing to so many who have attended his remarkable Nada Yoga meditation retreats or attended his concerts in small or large venues around the world. He is an internationally respected sitarist, composer, and accomplished teacher of Indian Classical and Sacred music. Roop has taught at major universities and has played high-profile concerts in prestigious concert halls in Europe, North and South America, and India. You can listen to this sacred music and obtain CDs from his website: Roop Verma.com.

## *Aquaculture*

Turning 40 and very tired of making a living flying around, I took the week off over my birthday and meditated by the pond, knowing it was time to figure out another way to make a living. I needed to find something that would keep me close to home so I could be around my daughter as she grew up. I also felt that my son was approaching (even though I was single at the time—I had gone through the divorce with my daughter's mother years before). On my birthday, looking down into the water, I saw several fish swimming around. There was a flash of inspiration and I immediately wondered what kind of market there was for fish in Vermont.

I started researching this and saw that there was an untapped market with all the local restaurants that supported the Vermont tourist industry. I then began planning out an aquaculture facility that would allow me to make a living from this sacred land.

In addition to the beautiful mountains, the abundance of water was most obvious to everyone who visited. You had to cross our bridge over a stunningly beautiful large mountain brook that immediately below the bridge had waterfalls and crystal-clear swimming holes. (It was on this brook that I had built the hydroelectric plant 13 years earlier.) Proceeding up the driveway to the house another few thousand feet, you could hear the waterfalls from both brooks and when you arrived at the house, to the side was a beautiful pond. Everything was just charged with life, so creating an aquaculture facility seemed very plausible in such an environment.

The next years saw the building of the aquaculture facility and business; suffice to say this was a huge project with lots of science, engineering and way too much work. This was touched upon earlier, so I will not digress into this now (but will continue with how it all concluded shortly), save to say again that all the days began in the same manner as they always have, with prayer and meditation and praises.

### *Joanne*

It was during the Sacred Music Meditation retreat cycle in 1993 that Roop and I were sitting out by the pond meditating one early morning a few days prior to the start of the retreat when Roop asked me "where is the lady that is supposed to be here with you now?" At that moment I had a flash of vision and I told him that I could "see her approaching and that she was with our son." I distinctly saw two forms together and I knew that one was to be our son. It was quite an interesting experience.

The weeks unfolded, the building of the aquaculture business infrastructure was intense but most of the work was now completed and money was coming in. Periodic meditations throughout the day were required for me to keep it all together. Late one August afternoon, a few months after the retreat, I was sitting on the dock drying off in the sun after a swim, slipping in and out of meditation. I clearly heard within that I had to go into Brattleboro right then and there. I was tired after the long day's work but the experience that I just had was so very clear. I had that sense that I was to meet someone special.

I drove the thirty minutes into town and immediately went into the Common Ground, one of the oldest vegetarian restaurants in the country, one of my favorite places. I immediately did a circuit of the restaurant as if I was on a mission, scanning who was about, to see if I recognized anyone. At the conclusion of my circuit of the restaurant I was dazzled by the bright blue stars of this lady's eyes. Mesmerized, I proceeded to walk right into the wall. Smiling sheepishly I spoke to her and asked where she was from. When she said Long Island, I said too bad, and we laughed and walked out of the restaurant; she and her friend Val went one way and I the other.

We walked around the block in opposite directions and as I had hoped, we bumped into each other and I asked them if they wanted to have a glass of wine and talk. They agreed and we got involved in a very beautiful, spiritual discussion for an hour or so. When it was time to leave, I gave Joanne my business card and I told her that, "if you are afraid of fire, you don't want to call me." We hugged goodbye and the energy between us was just beautifully intense.

Over the next days she was completely in my awareness. I kicked myself for not getting her contact info and throughout the next several days in meditation, I asked my Father that she contact me, as she had my card. Finally a week later, I got a short letter from her and immediately sent her flowers. The next day we spoke on the phone for perhaps an hour. After several such phone calls, Joanne drove up to visit the following Labor Day weekend. On her first night here, I suggested to her that she make the calls to be taken to the Master's Retreat while her body slept, that she might have some interesting experiences.

The next morning I went into the guest room to see if she was awake yet. One look at her luminous eyes and I knew that she had an interesting experience while she slept. Joanne was very courageous coming from Long Island, New York, to the wilderness of Vermont following her heart. She shared that at some point during the night she awoke and looked to the foot of the bed. There she saw a huge, oscillating, geometric form of Light, over 7 feet tall. (Years later when she saw a color picture of an electron, she said that was the closest thing to what she had seen at the foot of the bed years before.)

She related to me that she had absolutely no fear at the moment but couldn't remember anything else about it, really, just the magnitude of the oscillating figure of Light and Peace. She remembers that she didn't even think to ask any questions. She just remembers falling back to sleep quickly and feeling enveloped in Peace. In years to come we would often reflect that perhaps it was our son in his Light Body who had visited. Whoever it was though came with a clear purpose to accelerate all that was to come in the months and years ahead.

Her scheduled two-day visit turned into a week. By the time she returned home to Long Island her friends knew the minute they saw her that something major had occurred and that she would be moving up to Vermont. By the end of October I had helped her move out of her apartment up to Vermont. A year later, Jesse was born.

Joanne had a considerable spiritual background already established for many years at this point, but her heart immediately leapt with Joy when I introduced her to the Teachings of the Ascended Masters. She instantaneously recognized the Teachings as Truth—in her heart—and never questioned this response for a moment. She quickly began integrating all the material I had collected over the decades. She incorporated the calls into her daily practice, and together we watched life unfold.

### *Trial by Fire*

In the summer of 1996, I got word from the state of Vermont that my aquaculture facility had been contaminated and had to be closed down. A large international company had committed federal fraud, altering federal inspection reports, and had knowingly sold us fry (baby fish) that were diseased. The very first thing that I did after getting this information and sharing it with Jo was to go out and meditate by the pond. I knew that this was the direct and immense answer to the prayer that had been daily in my heart for years now— to find a way out of this labor-intensive business.

I knew in meditation that afternoon that the only way that I would be victorious in this great ordeal before me was by going deeply into meditation every day and staying completely centered in the current of Light throughout the day. I knew that I had to engage attorneys and fight a legal battle against the multi-million dollar company that destroyed our business. We were told to destroy all of our fish and to dismantle and disinfect the entire aquaculture facility—the business was over.

The cold financial reality was everywhere; there would be no money coming in. Huge monthly bills wouldn't get paid. My daughter was 13, my son 2, and I had a huge mortgage for the business, secured by our home and land. Soon the state and federal government started the foreclosure process on our home and land.

And literally here is the saving grace to this ordeal, here is the key to victory that I knew then in a flash was absolute and undeniable. Perhaps just a week before I got the phone call from the state, I picked up Saint Germain's *Unveiled Mysteries* for the second time in fifteen years and immediately started accelerating, as I read this special book that was written in the 1920s, Saint Germain's instruction about the absolute power of the I Am Presence took on a new and immediate purpose in my life. Now, facing this unimaginable turn of events and the possibility of losing our home and land, I steeled myself and forced my emotional body to be at peace. I knew that we would be victorious one way or another.

Breathing Saint Germain's decree many, many times throughout the day, "I Am the Only Presence Acting Here," with Joanne doing the same, we went forward into this intense, two-year legal ordeal. As stated in the beginning of this story we were finally victorious with a large settlement that allowed us to get out of debt and start a new business. ∝

# 16 ~ The Temple of The Presence

We were into the second year of our trial by fire having fired two different sets of attorneys when I got a phone call from a dear friend who lived a few hours north of us in Vermont. Genevieve and Henry called me to share what they thought was "exciting" news. Henry told me that there were "new Messengers" and that they were coming to Vermont to put on a weekend seminar for the Ascended Masters and wanted me very much to come up and meet them. I thanked them for thinking of me and shared with them that I was very involved in my decades-long spiritual practice and had absolutely no interest in any new Messengers. My friends were so persistent I finally acquiesced and took the two-hour drive to Montpelier to meet these new Messengers.

I walked into the stone church that my friends had rented for the weekend event. Gen and Henry along with another couple were very busy cleaning the main room in the small church that was to be used for the seminar. They introduced me to the other couple, Carolyn and Monroe. The four of them thanked me for taking the drive up to meet them and asked me if I would participate in a little service to help anchor the Light for the seminar that was to begin the following day.

Carolyn stood before a makeshift altar just several feet from where Genevieve, Henry, Monroe and I were sitting. It was with a subtle excitement that I joined in a few of the old Summit Lighthouse decrees and then as best as I can describe it, the Light increased and then in a shimmering golden Light where Carolyn was standing, Gautama Buddha was before me. I cannot remember all that he said but what I do remember is this; he said, "The Fire that burns in my heart I pass to you and my Fire will arc from your heart to those whom I wish to touch."

All I can say here is that I was flooded with the intense electric Peace and Love that radiated from the Buddha. I was more than astonished; I was euphoric. After the service Carolyn and Monroe asked me to come over to their hotel so we could talk. They shared with me that The Temple of The Presence was the Brotherhood of Light's new dispensation and that they had been chosen to be the new Messengers, to set the record straight on many facets of the Teachings, including the primacy of the individualized I Am Presence, which, coincidently (if you believe in coincidences), at that time, I was again reading Saint Germain's "I Am" books that focus upon this very subject.

We spoke perhaps for an hour and then I had the long two-hour drive back home. While on this long drive, I thought how truly perfect was the name of the Brotherhood's new dispensation—The Temple of The Presence—for I had always known that the Temple of The Presence was within each person's heart. I was vibrating at such a high frequency from the Buddha's blessing that it seemed that I was floating; the ride home went very quickly. I immediately shared what had happened with Joanne and the next day I contacted two other dear friends from our former group and conveyed what I had experienced with Carolyn and Monroe and the Buddha.

In the space of twenty-four hours the Temple had doubled the number of people who were interested to see just what the New Dispensation was all about. Before I move on with this narrative, I will state that it has been my great blessing to have shared, at least to some extent, Gautama Buddha's charge to me from that first night with many over the past fifteen years and I share that sacred charge anew with you, here in this writing, right now.

### Archangel Michael's First Release

It was during that first seminar in Vermont that Archangel Michael came for the first time through The Temple of The Presence. I had stayed home with Jesse (he was four years old and into everything) so that Joanne could attend the weekend seminar as this was her first experience with a live dictation from the Ascended Masters in this lifetime. I got a message from Carolyn that I needed to attend the Sunday service and that Carolyn's daughters would take care of Jesse. I was supposed to be present for Archangel Michael's first appearance with the Temple.

There were perhaps 15–20 people present in Henry and Gen's sanctuary building, which was still under construction. It was more similar to an unfinished large barn with a beautiful window looking out to expansive views of the mountains. We were situated in a semi-circle with Carolyn at the center of the circle before the large window. Henry was given the cue by Carolyn and he started the keynote musical meditation that Carolyn told him to play. The energy was just electric and so powerful; the keynote built and built as the Sacred Fire increased. Suddenly Archangel Michael was superimposed over Carolyn's standing form. At the height of the musical keynote meditation Archangel Michael turned and faced the four directions with his right hand raised summoning his Legions.

The top of the barn dissolved and in its place was a great amphitheater with row after row of intensely fierce standing angels who were arriving in obedience to Archangel Michael's summoning. The passion, the resolve on their faces so Intense, absolutely nothing could stand in their way as they answered Lord Michael's call. Archangel Michael then said that each of us present was given a legion of his Angels to command. That we were required to command them each and every morning as they would be waiting for their orders to go forth around the Earth to attend to whatever situation we felt needed their action.

I remember that we were asked to stand so that his Angels would remember and identify the keynote vibration of our Presence so that they would be in attendance during our morning meditations and calls. The recording of this dictation from Archangel Michael can be obtained from The Temple of The Presence.

I spoke briefly of my first encounters with Gautama Buddha and now with Archangel Michael. How do I even begin to convey here what it was like when Jesus first came, standing there with his arms outraised in power and blessing, seeing him through the mist of tears streaming down my face, tears of joy and such overwhelming love and gratitude to be here in this exact moment to experience the intense fire of his love and empowerment. Then again what of Saint Germain... I felt I didn't know him until he first came to the Temple in his Violet Fire cloak, his great passion and dry humor wrung our hearts out and filled us with the fervor of Freedom for the great Victory of life. His mission—to bring forth the Great Golden Age and all of us would follow him anywhere. How do you begin to convey the immensity of all of this to those who have never experienced it?

## The Early Days

In those early days of the Temple in Vermont, there were only a handful of us to assist Carolyn and Monroe and Henry and Genevieve in the immense sacred work that was before them. Those who have only been part of the Temple for several years now may not have heard of Henry and Genevieve but they are included here in this early accounting because of the tremendous hard work and sacrifice that they above all others, save Carolyn and Monroe brought to the Temple in those very early days.

Truly none could embody the sense of selfless service to life more than Henry and Genevieve did in not only hosting each Temple Sunday service and quarterly conference for over three-and-a-half years, but also in being the major financial support for the Temple for those years. As a close friend who witnessed the all that they gave, It was a humbling experience witnessing their complete dedication to this work.

There was so much organizational work to do and so few to do it; still as more were drawn to the Temple, more and more volunteered their time as they could to assist. The Temple was located in very remote north central Vermont. This meant that while a pristine beautiful area, there was not the infrastructure of a large city nearby to provide employment for people who wished to render part time service as they could. Most who came to the Temple services in those early days had to drive a minimum of two to four hours one way.

There were several of us who were galvanized to the unspeakable love and the fire of the services who gave what we could of our time, all of us having families, careers and lives to live. We would spend as much time as we could in Chelsea, Vermont (the Temple's location) helping and then we did what work we could for the Temple when we returned to our homes. It went on like this for three-and-a-half years, slowly growing as more and more of us shared our experience with the others.

Those long weekends in Chelsea when several of us were gathered together trying to assist were quite magical. There was such a sense that we were all in this together, there was so much joy and it was obvious that we had all been together before (in the Retreats while our physical bodies slept or previous lifetimes). Joanne's gift was on the organizational side so she assisted Genevieve and Carolyn; I was able to communicate the special fire of the Temple to others so I communicated with many people whom I had never met on behalf of the Temple.

Oftentimes I was able to share my experiences with former members of The Summit Lighthouse who were well versed in the teachings of the Ascended Masters, but with the decline of The Summit Lighthouse were unaware of the Temple. Joanne and I subsequently were very involved in giving public presentations introducing many to the Temple in Vermont, New Hampshire, and Toronto. Henry and I were the ones to move in and out all audio equipment that was required for each service, when we traveled to New York, to Montana, Boston, New Hampshire and Toronto with Carolyn and Monroe for introductory Temple services.

Prior to the Temple's move to Tucson, I spent a few days with my brother (who lived in Tucson) and Carolyn and Monroe driving around exploring the outskirts of Tucson and the southern mountains. During those few days, my brother arranged for the physical venue of the Temple's first service in Tucson at a Tibetan meditation center that my brother Brian was associated with. Of course the dictation, the first of many to come in Tucson, was from Gautama Buddha.

## Differences between The Temple and The Summit Lighthouse

In those early days many old and new friends whom I had contacted were quickly galvanized by the purity, the love, and the charge of fire that was their experience, as they made their conscious connection with their I Am Presence during the Discourses and Dictations of the Temple.

What was the process that differentiated the Temple from The Summit Lighthouse? It was the absolute reliance on each one's I Am Presence first and foremost, rather than the reliance on the Messenger. It was the forging of the remembrance that one's I Am Presence has always been there—loving, guiding, and unfolding us, as much as our outer consciousness, our free will would allow. It was the foundation laid by Saint Germain's instruction in the I Am books of the 1920s and 1930s that when one calls forth the perfection of the I Am Presence, all lesser states of consciousness that create one's experience begin to dissolve, and perfection comes forth in greater and greater measure. All according to the great law of karma that whatever one puts their attention upon, they bring forth into their world. And when one's attention is fixed upon the Presence, it's literally pulling oneself up by one's own bootstraps.

Another marked difference between the Temple and the former activity that the Brotherhood had brought forth was that there was such a sense of joy, love and purity permeating every facet of the services. The Messengers would frequently say in those early years that they were students of the Masters, just like us. They were on fire with the Love of God and this was just the work that they had to do. Carolyn shared that they would still hold these services even if no one else chose to attend any of them, because of the world action that went forth, as this immense Light was anchored in the physical during each service. Those of us called to be present in those very early days were all but overwhelmed with the aspects of this action that we experienced again and again.

An astonishing facet of the The Temple of The Presence was music. Many of us were introduced to new levels of musical perfection for lack of a better word. Though I was very familiar with the traditions of Indian sacred music through my dear brother Roop Verma's work, the musical keynotes that Carolyn and Monroe surrounded each service with were truly transcendent. Because of Carolyn's musical background and her own attunement, the most beautiful, celestial compositions were played prior to the beginning of each service. Carolyn told us in those early days that the Master would tell her to obtain a specific recording that was to be played as the keynote meditation piece, immediately before and at the conclusion of each address by the Master. Carolyn further stated that the Master would identify which specific recordings (including the date and location of the recording) that contained the purest charge of Sacred Fire that the Master wished to use in the release. It was during these keynote meditation pieces that the release of the spiritual fire grew and grew right through the Master's dictation.

There was a very tangible physical pressure of the Light that ebbed and flowed during these services, oftentimes in great intensity. There was such a tangible joy, a buoyant love and electricity that was so physically palpable, that all who entered into the doors of The Temple of The Presence could readily touch. At the conclusion of the Master's dictation most in attendance would sit in meditation, not willing to move. Desiring instead to absorb the intensity of the Sacred Fire, savoring the refined exaltation that was left in the atmosphere as the Master withdrew their Presence, and the extraordinary musical keynote meditation played as the backdrop of the experience.

In each and every service this was repeated in so many different variations; each service building upon the previous one in grandeur and depth as these profound experiences lifted us higher and higher. Eventually we understood that the purification process one experienced during each service allowed for a greater assimilation of the Sacred Fire, which in turn allowed for more of the Sacred Fire to be assimilated during the next service. So it continues to this day.

Most remarkable was the physical change that I noticed, that everyone noticed in the outer appearance and personality of others, of ourselves as more and more the dross of the outer world was consumed during these weekly Sunday services and then the quarterly 5- and 12-day conclaves. Oftentimes, as one became more and more infused with the pure Sacred Fire of our I Am Presence, all one could do was just cry because the Love, the Remembrance, the Gratitude was so intense. For myself, I felt in those early days and still to this day, like a little boy held safely and completely loved in the arms of my Father and my Mother. At other times, I felt, no, I was the awakening one, a great warrior feeling the immense Love, Wisdom, and Power of my Presence flooding through these bodies with a sacred purpose that I can only dimly perceive, too fantastic to dare to even dream of.

The Temple of The Presence was referred to as the New Dispensation; it was a new paradigm for me and for everyone, the impetus of the Great Golden Age of Saint Germain. If it wasn't for the very physical pressure of the Light and the transcendent beautiful experiences that many had, it might have been possible not to believe that the Great Ascended Masters were actually standing before us, showering us with the most intense Love and Light and Instruction that was so simple yet so profound.

If one, if many didn't experience again and again the greatest of thrills at the approach of the Master during the keynote musical meditation, throughout the service; then on some occasions a mixture of sadness and sometimes relief that the Master's address was concluded because the intensity of the Fire that the Master and one's Presence released was extremely uncomfortable to be exposed to— then it might have been possible not to believe what was before us.

If one, if many didn't experience again and again the incomprehensible joy and love in the visceral understanding and empowerment of the absolute reality and immediacy of one's own individual I Am Presence, the emerging understanding and responsibility of the wielding of this great power just as Jesus did, as all the Ascended Masters do—then it might be possible not to believe what was before us.

If one, if many didn't actually see or perceive these Great Masters standing before us in such resplendent living Sacred Fire during these blessed services, instructing, empowering us in the Christic Virtues, and the precepts of the Dawning Golden Age of Saint Germain—then it might be possible not to believe what was before us.

If all of this and so much more didn't happen again and again every Sunday service, the fortnight period of every quarterly Conclave (the 12-day period around the solstices and equinoxes) and those services held on Thanksgiving, Christmas and other periods through the year for over 15 years now, with each service surpassing the previous service in Glory—then it might be possible not to believe what was before us.

What happened in those early days when services were attended by less than can be counted on the fingers of two hands, still happens today with hundreds participating in person and via the live streaming broadcast of these blessed services as they go forth free of charge around the world.

In addition to all the above, over the years, more and more of the most beautiful, dynamic people were magnetized to the Temple. There was always a sense that you were home with one's family when you gathered for a service or a 12-day conclave, the sense of being with others who had a similar determination as yourself; a sense that you were all in this together, was joyous. So often that I've lost count, the strong impression when meeting someone for the first time at the Temple, was that you knew each other from before. It was really so apparent that you're just reconnecting again in this lifetime, at this place for this unfolding work, that all had been prepared, for many lifetimes.

When Saint Germain first came for several consecutive days at one of the early 12-day Conference/Acropolis Sophia cycles he gave forth the instruction, the blueprint, for how the Temple was to expand. He stated that there were many who had been trained for many lifetimes to play a part in this activity that would recognize the Temple, would be galvanized by the Sacred Fire. That these ones would come to Temple services, have their chalices filled, and then take what they've experienced and received out into the world to share with others as their hearts empowered and guided them to act. He stated (something to the effect that) for various reasons, these individuals were best suited to convey the Fire of the New Dispensation to those in distant places who would not be able to physically attend.

It seemed all of us were warriors, comrades in arms—arms of Light. All of us had our troops to whom we were to convey the charge that we received again and again in our own devotions. Thus comes the Great Golden Age. ☙

# 17 ~ **Everything Counts**

Chronologically I've now reached the point where the Temple enters the picture, this narrative shifts gears. For a very long time now I've known that I had to somehow organize all of what happened in this lifetime into a cohesive story that would be a record for others of the remarkable adventures, experiences, blessings, and intercessions that have so shaped every facet of this life. That these hard won events perhaps might make it easier for others, and if not for others, then at least my two children and those directly related to this life would have this record of how it all came about, that they could use and pass along as they wished.

In this narrative I've detailed a lifetime's experience where my Presence and my outer conscious awareness of the Brotherhood and the Master's teachings progressively unfolded and molded this lifetime. This directly outplayed in the nature of the experiences that my karma dictated and opportunity afforded. I have omitted much of the mundane ordinary experiences that most have in the process of a lifetime, but I have sought to convey the inner motivation and the actual events, without an erg of literary license, that were milestones for me along the way; each event setting the standard, the tone for what was to follow.

Still I felt that I never had an option, after the first tastes of the Brotherhood's Teachings, even in old diluted accounts from more than a century previous, there was a thrill, a touch of wonder, of hope that there was something very real out there, that would make sense of it all. For me acquiring, experiencing this scientific understanding and then conveying it to others has been the driving aspiration of this lifetime.

Now that this story is all laid out and you have a basic understanding of the sacred sciences involved herein, it's time to drive home the point, to clearly state, for the record, why all of this happened and what it could mean to you.

Simply and bluntly put, our true nature is Divine and is ours for the taking; perhaps better said, it is ours for the remembering. The sacred purpose of each life is to remember, and by remembering to become, moment by moment, day after day, year after year, our very own I Am Presence, the individualized Presence of God that we have always been, in action in every facet of our outer lives. Because of our many lifetimes and all that we have been a part of, this process of awakening and striving to outpicture the Golden Precepts of the Path is, unfortunately for most, a long one. This is because the karmic limitations that we have created by our free-will choices have to be overcome, have to be balanced, through acts of selfless love.

However, the good news is this: the very fact that you're reading this now is a certain indication that you're already well along on this Path, even though it may seem new to you at this moment. Oftentimes one's Presence holds back on revealing past attainment from conscious memory in order to develop other aspects of one's nature. It usually takes lifetimes of considerable striving to be at the point on the Path where one can begin to hear the soft promptings of the heart that grows stronger and stronger as karma is purified, and love for the pure sake of loving increases.

### Visualizing the Great I Am

So now again, at this point in the story, follow me in this meditation: In the very heart of our being is anchored the sacred focus of our Individualized I Am Presence—The Threefold Flame of Love, Wisdom and Power. This is projected from our Presence via the Crystal Cord at the beginning of each lifetime and contains the impetus, the wherewithal to bring about the special mission that is the plan for that lifetime that will contribute to the unfolding mastery of the Divine within. We, each one, have a beautiful, glorious keynote of love that is unique in all creation. This keynote is our special talent, our sacred labor, and our most precious gift to life, forged and expanded in love through all of our lifetimes. This is our contribution to the great, ongoing symphony of creation.

Throughout the long epochs of time and space, through countless lifetimes, we have striven in love to achieve this mastery, to perfect our keynote offering that is the very core of our being. This we lay on the steps of the high altar of our own I Am Presence. As this process unfolds, each one begins to create more and more of this Divine perfection in their affairs, adding to the glorious splendor of all life. This is the process that the Great Ones of all time have demonstrated, forging the fullness of their own individualized Divinity and in turn, creating more of God's Life to experience. It is in this manner that the Great *I AM That I AM* creates more of God to love.

I don't believe that words exist that can adequately convey the sense of wonder that one experiences when standing in the dawning awakening of their Presence, wielding the power of the creative fiats contained in the decrees and affirmations that the Great Masters have released over the past hundred years, especially with the advent of the Temple.

How can one describe, save by doing it, the action of these great fiats streaming forth from the Upraised Chalice of one's conscious awareness? Each one understanding that these calls are emanating from one's I Am Presence, blazing forth through one's free-will, conscious choice, to be again the instrument of your I Am Presence in this outer world. Knowing with utter certainty that what you have decreed must come forth, because you are a Son or a Daughter of God—and this is your birthright, to create, to wield, the self-same Love, Wisdom and Power that Jesus and so many others have wielded over Earth's long history.

## *Looking Back and Looking Forward*

At the beginning of this accounting, I stated that nothing gets one's attention like one's imminent demise. How about several such instances? (Some wonder if I finally got the message.) At this point in the story, you now know somewhat of the drive that I've always been blessed with—the very physical, scientifically oriented life that I've lead, and you've read about my little tolerance of the palliative mediocrity that is abundant in this culture. You can imagine my astonishment, when driving my car to the airport preparing for a long, cross-country flight to Maine with two students, to have Archangel Michael appear in my car before me in a sphere of fire, commanding me to do a decree that less than a minute later resulted in the Grace required for the continuation of this lifetime. How to describe the intense electrical fire radiating from the sphere of his Presence at that moment?

How to describe what it felt like to do the decree that I was commanded to do? How to describe the events unfolding in super-slow motion when the other car crossed over the center line and hit me head-on at a combined speed approaching 80+ mph? How to describe being out of my body, quickly falling away from this world and then the two Masters commanding me to do the Violet Fire Decree that instantly charged my being with a cool, effervescent fire and stopped my transit to the other side, allowing for the continuation of this lifetime. And what was the plan for me to accomplish in this lifetime? How to convey this and all the other instances where the Great Ones interceded in this lifetime?

Just one of these instances like the one detailed above could be rationalized off with something like, "it must not have been your time yet," but when you add all of them together, when you understand the overall motivation propelling this lifetime forward, when you add to them all the amazing transcendent experiences, it's obvious I was kept around to accomplish a certain task. It's also obvious that the spiritual disciplines detailed in this accounting assisted in providing the wherewithal by which all of this could take place. Put more directly, there is a greater protection and more opportunity afforded those who are committed to the Path.

When one encounters the charge of Peace, the Light, that has accrued here on this sacred land that I have called home over the years, anchored here by decades of praises, prayers and meditations, the spiritual retreats, the several formal services of the Temple of The Presence that were hosted here, and the record of this vibration etched in the physical plane, it makes a very tangible statement. So much so that others, even those who are not consciously on the Path, have commented on it.

When your children having grown up in such an environment, grow up in harmony, and are admired by others for their character and their determination to make a difference, it's obvious that something is working. When your children growing up and as young adults convey to you their own inner experiences with the Light, you thank God for the Path. You thank God that you've been able to convey this to your children, because you know that they will always be guided and protected by Archangel Michael and the Great Masters. You pray to God that somehow all children might be thus taught from an early age lest they make the mistakes that I made early on, and that so many others do, because they don't know any better.

My Mom used to say, "The proof is in the pudding." Looking at the big picture here, from a scientific, objective perspective, most would have to say that the pudding, while perhaps very different from what one is accustomed to in this culture, is very good. So with all of this stated above, looking at the issues that surround our lives now, with the increasing chaos and uncertainty, it becomes more than apparent that a repolarization of humanity's consciousness is greatly needed. People just have to wake up before things get a lot worse.

They (our brothers and sisters everywhere) need to become aware in the most direct and physical manner that there is a different way to live a life, a way that affords what every parent wants for their children, a way that foments and engenders a true ennobling of life— not just one life, but the ennobling of all life, and all that this implies. There needs to be a way that allows for our children to grow up remembering that they really are Divine and that they have taken incarnation to grow into and outpicture their Divine Nature here in this outer world. Every action one is involved in either enhances, is neutral, or diminishes the Light one receives from their I Am Presence in one's current lifetime and in subsequent lifetimes, not only on an individual basis but also collectively for all of humanity and the beautiful planet on which we live.

Our children (of all ages) need to understand that thought, word and deed are creative powers that do produce like fruit. That once the "heart's fire is ready" and this process of the Path is engaged, there is the quickening of the Sacred Fires of Love Divine within, which accelerates over time and leads to one's eventual freedom from karmic limitation in increasing plateaus of self-mastery. No small matter here as we are simply talking about the antidote for the Fall from Grace described in the sacred books of all Earth's cultures.

This is the sacred work of the Brotherhood of Light. This is the work of all the Great Masters who have come to instruct humanity over the ages, including those Great Ones who have had world religions established around their teachings.

Everywhere I Am, Father, I Am in Thee.
Everything I see and hear, Father, I Am in Thee.
Everything I think and feel, Father,
Everything I do and say, I Am in Thee.

Mighty I Am Presence, expand Thy Fire
in every cell of my being, in every facet of my affairs.

# 18 ~ A New Plateau

Now, building upon the Brotherhood's work of all that has come before, a new plateau of humanity's awakening has been reached, and the teaching of *The Presence of God Individualized! One God—One Presence—Many Sons—Many Daughters** has come forth—the Dawning Golden Age of Saint Germain comes quickly, is here. With this knowledge comes the taking of responsibility for what one has brought forth in their life, comes the empowerment to do so, and make the necessary changes in accordance with the Great Laws and one's own free will.

For one so hardened by physical-life experiences as myself, it's hard to adequately describe the sense of freedom, the joy, and the sheer excitement one experiences while fully engaged in one of the Temple's services as the Ascended Master's release is underway. Though there is "nothing new under the sun," the Masters always provide a new angle on the teachings, which while so simple is also so profound. How to say this? While registering the meaning of the words that one hears, there is a background-and-foreground charge of energy, a stream of electrical fire around and through the words that one hears, that paints elaborate thoughtforms within and that literally thrills the heart. During this experience, one knows that they've always known this—it's not new—but it's time to bring it forward into every part of one's life. Somehow you feel that you are home again.

One has the sense that the actual words that one hears are only conveying a tiny portion of what is being conveyed, that the streaming, electrical fire that is surging through one's being during the Master's teaching is what really contains what is being conveyed.

*Registered trademark ® of The Temple of The Presence

You know that you are involved in it, integrating it to some extent, but you can barely touch all that is there, let alone understand what is happening on all the levels upon which it's happening. Sometimes it's surrounded in so much love that you feel like a child, held in the arms of your loving mother or father. Sometimes there is a sense of joy that is so tangible you want to jump out of your skin. Sometimes the peace is so intense that you could just recline in that peace forever in such profound gratitude for being in this exact place at this exact moment and never wish to do anything else.

Oftentimes there is the sense that you are a 110-watt light bulb, but the current that you are plugged into is a million watts; your light bulb is surely going to blow with all the intensity that your Presence and the Master are releasing into your chaliced aura during that service, that initiation—and yet, you know your Presence will preserve and protect the upraised chalice or your life. For in such a state of prayer and meditation nothing save God's Will can ever come forth in one's life.

For truly when one is so engaged in the deepest meditation, and one's Christ Presence is directly overshadowing the physical, the physical vehicles are as a chalice and the Sacred Fire of one's Presence and the presiding Master is just pouring forth into your upraised chalice. This translates into a stretching action that purifies and accelerates one's physical, emotional, mental, and memory bodies, increasingly anchoring that great fire of one's Presence within and around you, and subsequently and progressively into all of one's affairs. This great charge of Light is also anchored into the actual Earth body in that area that you are located, creating more and more the momentum, the peace, of that perfection in one's life and into the physical location where one is thus engaged.

Monroe Shearer gave a wonderful teaching that summarizes this process when the Temple was located in Chelsea, Vermont. It's called the Blizzard Discourse and in it, Monroe referred to the state of attunement that a person is in when they are communing with their own I Am Presence. As many experience, when Monroe and the presiding Masters are engaged in a Discourse, the mechanics of what is being shared is experienced to a greater or lesser extent by those attending the service.

In this instance the topic described what happens as one draws nearer to their Presence in the deepest, most complete adoration in meditation. It was described that the Sacred Fire of one's Presence pours forth in greater and greater intensity, flowing through the expanding Crystal Cord, into one's Threefold Flame, ever expanding and intensifying. This radiance increasingly impacts everything in one's life, in one's experience. Monroe used the analogy of a blizzard, stating that during the blizzard, the snow coats everything facing the wind, with the snow impacting and building up on that windward surface.

Then he gave the teaching that in such complete communion with one's Presence, the Light pours forth and increasingly impacts, builds up, on and in everything in one's world with the Star Stuff Perfection of the Light of one's I Am Presence. This action radiating out, in increasingly greater circumference from one's Threefold Flame within the heart, increasingly purifying, transforming, and perfecting all of one's experience. The more one engages in this communion, the greater the intensity of Light, and the greater the distance from the Threefold Flame that is thus impacted by this ongoing pouring forth of the Light, including one's outer relationships, affairs and events—even those that have not yet happened in time and space.

This discourse (and so many others) are an absolute Treasure to those who are on the Path, for there is not only an intellectual understanding of the process conveyed, but as stated above, when the inner preparation is made, many participants actually experience some facet of this action ongoing during the actual Discourse. Again, the Discourses are usually a preparatory action preceding the Dictation by the presiding Master. Once again, words simply fail to convey the utter majesty of this profoundly sacred process that happens in every service at The Temple of The Presence, services that are freely given to all.

## *Attunement and Deciding for Yourself*

Conduct an experiment with the decrees, affirmations and praises from the Temple and decide for yourself if this works for you. A beginning set of decrees can be downloaded for free at: TempleOfThePresence.org/DecreeSample.pdf. You can purchase the *I AM Adorations, Affirmations, Fiats, and Rhythmic Decrees* directly from the Temple website. You can read Master Kuthumi's instruction on the Law of Invocation on this web page: TempleOfThePresence .org/Lawofinvocation.htm.

Plan on giving this exercise for at least two weeks so that you may experience the cumulative effect of this sacred action in your life. Set aside even fifteen minutes before you sleep or first thing in the morning, or both—the more often the better and the quicker the results. For the sake of this experiment, assume that the wonderful actions that these calls describe are really coming forth (because they are). Visualize your loved ones before you begin, seeing the Light pour forth over them. As you engage in this exercise, watch the images painted before your mind's eye, pause for a few moments after each call and note any changes in your vibration as you read these thought forms and ponder their meaning.

Understand that this is a cumulative action—the more you put into it, the longer that you engage in this, the greater return into your world. Engage in this dynamic meditation every day, throughout the day as you can, as stated for at least a two-week period. Remember that you are exercising spiritual muscles that you may not have used before. The sense of vibration at first will be very subtle, but as the Sacred Fire that you invoke does its perfect work you will begin to notice more and more the effects of this exercise in every facet of your life. It's like bathing in the Sacred Fire of your Presence, the more that you consciously do this, the more that the patina of lifetimes of karmic records that are less than perfection are washed away, and bit-by-bit, you will begin to feel lighter, happier, and more at peace.

A word to the wise here: It's always best to offer this entire exercise up to your I Am Presence to adjudicate. If the concept of your own I Am Presence is a bit too much for you to contemplate now, then offer it up to the Great Mother, or the Great Father, or to Jesus, to Gautama Buddha, or Mother Mary or the Great Light—anything that you associate with the Divine. The more sacred you make this exercise, the more powerful and sacred it becomes. As your momentum and the Sacred Fire increases, you will see how these thought forms that you are reading in these calls do produce the action that they describe.

Consider holding your loved ones in the sphere of your awareness as you give these calls. Visualize the Sacred Fire pouring from their own individualized I Am Presence, doing its perfect work in every facet of their lives. It is important to remember when so engaged that you are not the doer, not the healer—it is the I Am Presence that does the work through you, and the I Am Presence of your loved ones assisted by the Great Masters and Angels.

There are many dozens of inspired books available about the teachings of the Great Masters. At the end of this accounting is a Recommended Reading list of the very special ones (at least to me) that contain that tangible vibration of purity. However, as special as any of these books are, encountering a formal service with The Temple of The Presence—where the great Ascended Masters stand before you, before the world, and release the light of God, the light of their own Presence, and by this action, accelerate one's own consciousness, that we might experience the light of our own I Am Presence— is nothing short of miraculous, exhilarating, and empowering beyond what words can describe.

Simply put, imagine if CNN announced that Jesus or Buddha or Archangel Michael or Mother Mary was literally going to step through the veil from the higher worlds into the physical plane and address humanity. This is exactly what happens; however, only those who have the inner attunement or attainment, whose hearts are beginning to open and whose motives are increasingly pure would, to a greater or lesser degree, be able to feel, to hear, to see what was occurring.

How does one acquire the inner attainment? An overview of the process is described herein. If someone reading this accounting wants to experience the overwhelming reality of this immediately, then with all the Love for Life that they can muster, one must delve into the Science of the Spoken Word, giving the calls that are contained in *I AM Adorations, Affirmations, Fiats, and Rhythmic Decrees.* Do this so that the Sacred Fire that one invokes might bring forth the purification and acceleration of one's being, thus transmuting enough of the karma of lifetimes that is as a patina of smog obscuring the magnificence, the memory, and therefore, the empowerment of our Divine Threefold Flame within, which is the focus of our I Am Presence within this outer world.

According to the effort one engages in this process, according to the Will of God for each individual person, one will begin to see and feel the immensity of the Love of God increase in their life—this can become enhanced during a Temple service. As one becomes more comfortable with the process, one will begin to feel their heart opening. One may begin to experience all manner of profound mystical experiences that the mystics have recorded over humanity's long journey. All of this is determined by the Will of one's I Am Presence.

This is exactly what happens with hundreds and hundreds around the world who now participate in the ongoing releases of Sacred Fire that come forth from the Ascended Masters during every Temple service. This happens whether they participate in person, on location where these services are held in Tucson, Arizona, or whether they participate in the free, streaming audio and video Internet broadcasts that happen weekly. Can you imagine how many would be lined up to see for themselves as the word gets out that this is really happening? Of course, there would be many who could care less about this, but then they are not at a point yet where the awakening has begun in their lives.

The Path as described in this accounting is not for dilettantes (those who would sample of little of this and a little of that out of curiosity). The Path outlined by the Great Ones are for those whose hearts are already earnestly looking for the reason why, the answers to: Who am I? Why am I here?

It is always best to attend a live Temple service in person so that one can meet old and new friends and feel the intensity of the Sacred Fire (according to the Will of one's Presence) directly. However, in an absolutely remarkable dispensation of Mercy and Grace, for those who have done the inner preparation, joining in via the weekly Internet video broadcast is still the next best thing.

In fact, according to the Will of each one's I Am Presence, and the outer application of each one's striving, it is usual to be so engaged in the Sacred Fire that is being released in a Temple service, (whether it be live or pre-recorded) that one doesn't even register that they are participating over the Internet. It's almost like you're right there in person with those dearest to you, going through these blessed world-wide releases of Sacred Fire. You are aware that you are rendering this service to life. You are making your consciousness an upraised chalice for the Sacred Fire pouring forth from your Presence and the presiding Master.

This Sacred Fire is going forth from your heart and touching everything in your world—blessing, accelerating, purifying and protecting every aspect of one's life including one's loved ones. All manner of inner and outer mystical experiences may occur, again according to the Will of one's Presence.

It is for this reason that hundreds who are caught up in these ongoing services do not let anything get in the way of attending these weekly services or quarterly conclaves (in person or via the Internet). Simply put, as I shared with Carolyn and Monroe and many others over the past 15 years, it's by far "the greatest show on the planet," and in fact, nothing can even come close. Those who have not yet experienced a live or pre-recorded Temple service are in for a cumulative, life-changing experience.

### *Making It Happen*

It all starts right within your heart with the daily application of the calls, prayers and meditations followed by the delving into the teachings of the Ascended Masters conveyed in the ongoing live weekly services from the Temple as well as hundreds of pre-recorded services available online or in albums. The background and fundamentals of the Path are also contained in dozens of wonderfully inspired books on the teachings of the I Am Presence, the Masters and the Path that have been published over the past one-hundred-plus years. (*See Recommended Reading.*)

Remember to make your own attunement with your Presence before you begin, centering yourself with whatever affirmations, prayers, praises, or calls that are your favorites. Seek to establish an early-morning ritual before you engage in the affairs of the day, and then again at night before you go to sleep. Ask your Presence, and those Great Ones that you feel connected to, to multiply and expand this exercise so that others might benefit from the calls, prayers and meditations that you are about to engage in.

Saint Germain has stated that once you have your formal morning session, and then you take one minute every hour (throughout the day) to tune into your Presence, (giving a brief call) you will keep the Sacred Fire blazing in your aura. Hold your loved ones in your heart for their healing and protection and divine direction—and then hug yourself, for you are well on your way Home.

In the opening of this book, I laid out an overview of the daunting problems that beset our world. In this work, I have tried to establish, by relating this lifetime's experiences in search of the great mysteries of East and West, and encountering the teachings of the Great Masters, why one should consider this approach to living their life and what are the tremendous and innumerable benefits thereof.

Can you imagine not one, but many, initiates on the Path, bringing the full weight of their attainment, of the collective wisdom of the Christed Ones of All ages and of each one's own I Am Presence to bear, engaging in the teeth of these world problems? Again this is not a new idea—this is the very work of the great Ascended Masters, of Saint Germain, of Jesus, of Gautama Buddha, of countless others who serve Life. This is the sacred work of the Brotherhood of Light, and this is how the Great Golden Age comes forth.

With a slight, soft smile to every skeptic of what is presented here, know that by this life's experiences I myself, along with so many others, have proven again and again the great reality of the Path.

This work stands clearly as a challenge to you and to all who have read these words, or pondered these questions, and who have not yet in your outer consciousness made contact with your own Divine Presence and the great Ascended Masters. Will you sit back in your familiar, comfortable (or not so comfortable) life and wait for the closing chapters of this lifetime before you ask yourself these questions, hoping that illness and tragedy steer clear of you and your loved ones? Or have the fires of the heart been kindled enough by your life's experience and perhaps the cadence of these words to give it a try, see if there is really something Wonderful out there, rather right here Within You.

Over the years I would share with my children and friends "When you wish upon a Star you find out who you really are." We expand on this wisdom somewhat with this: When you focus upon and align yourself with the Star of your Presence all things become possible for you. You make a difference in life, in the lives of many by giving to life the sacred gift that only you can give, by bringing to life what you have been working on perfecting for many many lifetimes. There is a glory here that thrills the deepest part of one's heart.

As promised, this work does not leave those sincere of heart without a clear and scientifically detailed path by which each one might experience these untold, fathomless blessings for themselves and their loved ones—the beginning stages of which can be experienced within a few weeks' time, depending on the intensity of your heart's desire.

The chalice is either half full or half empty. "Is the heart's fire ready?"*

*From Aurobindo's poem, *The Dream Boat*

# ~ Musings on the Path

### *Getting Out of Your Head and Into Your Heart*

For me, I've known of this Path forever. I knew that I was to have a direct association with the Great Masters' work and that it was also my work, as I've been their student for a very long time.

As your heart takes you perhaps a bit deeper into the spiritual path with the Temple, I would share with you that there may be aspects of this experience that will be very different and or completely foreign to some. In fact, have effectively blocked too many from letting go of their frame of reference, their outer personalities long enough to quiet their hearts, which would allow them to feel, to begin to hear and to see what was really happening on the inner levels. As previously stated, if one can place their concerns on the shelf for a period and allow the Violet Fire to do its perfect work, oftentimes the concerns dissolve.

Mark Prophet, the first Messenger for The Summit Lighthouse, now the Ascended Master Lanello, referred to these outer personality characteristics as "peccadillos," meaning those personality traits of the ego that always seek to interfere with the awakening and purification of the heart, which are each one's personal stumbling blocks upon their Path. These "peccadillos" can allow for one to be offended or put off by the "perceived" activities, behaviors, or words of others, and this can take every form imaginable in life.

When it comes to understanding this situation, I shall convey here what I can recall of a wonderful Discourse from Monroe on the subject. He said that there will always be those things coming up for someone on the Path. These are those instances when someone's ego feels threatened or offended to the point where one's reactions would skew the Path for them. Monroe referenced an instance from Jesus' teachings in which Jesus said to someone, "What is that to you?" in response to seeing one of his disciples umbrage at the actions of another.

In this overwhelmingly complex life that we live, how can there not be numerous "peccadillos" in everyone's life that will come to the surface in all manner of instances, anytime one's frame of reference or experience is questioned? After all, this is the process of discernment that is key to a child becoming an adult. Still, on the Path, when one remembers Jesus' words that you find the kingdom by becoming "as a little child," we are reminded that there is a guileless innocence that is required on the Path.

The reason for this is that, in this carefree state, the heart of one's consciousness is freer to reflect, to remember, to experience the more refined, perfect worlds that exist immediately adjacent to this world, just at a much higher vibration so as to be invisible for someone who is caught up in the densification of the outer ego. This childlike outlook takes a lot of practice, and it's actually a practice of not doing or thinking anything, of being silent and refraining from criticism. As one's heart desires to become and to remember more and more of our native state of Divine Love, this process becomes easier.

For me, I was eventually able to ignore, or sometimes laugh at, my own peccadillos that were so familiar to me. Within the Temple, it was always so easy for me to not just see, but to also feel the immense perfection that was present at the very core of each service. I became aware at the onset of the Temple that a World Action was happening during each service. Sometimes I would catch a glimpse on the inner of the numberless numbers at inner levels who were orchestrating and assisting in the transmission of the Light into the very physical, emotional, and mental planes of the Earth body. It was almost as an inconsequential afterthought that the dozen or the hundreds who were in physical attendance just happened to be there, each of us going through our own process assimilating the intense

Love, the intense Light released throughout the service.

## *Step by Step*

Throughout this narrative I've used strong words in describing my experiences with the Path. It's appropriate here now to share what I have shared with many over the years both in an official capacity as a representative of the Temple, introducing the Teachings to those unfamiliar, and privately, doing the same with many friends and acquaintances. Everyone is at a different place on the Path, and because of this, everyone's experience is quite different.

The prerequisite for all who would experience a Temple service is an open heart. As Saint-Exupéry said in *The Little Prince*, "To see with the heart, to hear with the heart, to think with the heart, to speak with the heart..." is the surest way. When one is so prepared and engages in the preparatory group calls, the group momentum, and that of the presiding Great Ones, it adds a tremendous acceleration to all so enjoined, way beyond that which one might normally experience based on their own momentum and preparation.

Throughout the Discourse (from Monroe) or the Dictation (from Carolyn), there are often variations in the amount of Sacred Fire that is being released by the presiding Master and through one's individual's Presence. Sometimes this can be very intense, and the pressure of the Light can even feel uncomfortable; even when it is this intense, it is still so full of the most glorious love and purpose. It's helpful to remind oneself in such a state that nothing save the Will of your own I Am Presence can possibly come forth, and that the Will of your I Am Presence will adjust and adjudicate for you all that is coming forth, and it will always be Perfect and Good. The periods of discomfort are just the Sacred Fire of one's Presence doing its perfect work in the purification and acceleration of one's various bodies. If one can be still and surrender in this Sacred Fire, in faith, knowing that all is well, then a greater work may come forth during this initiation.

These periods of great intensity slowly diminish as the Master withdraws, the discomfort changes to a profound, loving peace, which oftentimes one wishes never to depart from, to move or be disturbed—one wishes to just bask in this Great Love. For this reason, after each service, the keynote musical meditation that the Master requests is played again and again for those sitting in meditation, while others eventually depart the sanctuary. It is not unusual for some people to remain in the sanctuary for 30 minutes or longer in meditation after the Master withdraws and the Messengers depart.

I discovered that I was as an upraised chalice when participating in these services, more so than in my daily meditations. I was aware that this Light was passing through my heart and going directly into the Earth body with the keynote of my Presence stamped upon it for a purpose that I can only faintly perceive.

During these experiences, I became aware I was able to go up and up into a higher level of the release, beyond the words that were spoken. With great effort to stay conscious, it was possible to open myself up to a greater extent to the intense Love and Light that was streaming forth. For me, the closest approximation that I can describe here is that it's like being in a great river of glorious Love and Light that contains everything.

By now, perhaps you've experienced the power and the joy of the Temple decrees and affirmations. When engaged in these calls with hundreds around the world, building the forcefield by which the Great Ones can step forth into the physical plane, it's an exhilarating joy in every sense of the word. Knowing that the karmic return of this action touches every aspect of one's life, blesses all of one's loved ones, infuses all of one's affairs. This karmic benefit is just an afterthought but is still part of the majesty of the Temple service.

I've shared this with many dozens of beautiful friends over the years, who were "old souls," and it's always been a sadness that some couldn't get past their own personalities, past their own "peccadillos" of their perceived limitations of the outer organization of the Temple long enough to just let go into that immense current of love that is just beyond the corner of one's outer personality. It's certainly true that everyone has their own Path but in my heart I felt that if they could have only let go for even a few moments, they would have been able to experience this amazing Divine Love.

For most of us, the outer personality, the ego has been in control of our lives. When one begins to accelerate upon the Path, there is often turmoil within as the hold that the ego has had for centuries of lifetimes is loosened and the Light and Love of the Presence draws nigh.

It has always been my desire to be able to couch this concept in some kind of descriptive words that would assist one in just getting out of themselves for long enough to touch this pure Sacred Fire of Love Divine. A person touching this, even just once, would find that it would change everything. They would know that they've finally arrived home.

## The Path and Air Traffic Control

In aviation, when you are in an Air Traffic Control (ATC) radar environment, ATC will call out possible traffic threats that the pilot does not see yet in order to provide greater safety. Everything happens so fast when flying and converging aircraft can be invisible one moment and then be literally right in front of you the next. A midair collision can really spoil your day.

The Path is like ATC. When one is fully involved with their daily attunement with their Presence, immersing themselves, repolarizing themselves, through prayer and meditation, and praises for the Gift of Life for themselves and their families and the world, a forcefield of protection is built up. The calls purify, accelerate and transmute a portion of the returning karma that is due to return on that day. As the karma is transmuted, very unfortunate things that were due to return to a person's life at that specific time can be dissolved, or lessened, so that one might go forward in their life without experiencing the full impact of that karmic return. This is exactly what happened in my Archangel Michael intervention in 1985. You could say that being on the Path is illumined self-interest.

### Children

Speaking of children, here's a bit of information that you might find interesting. I can only approximate the mechanics of this here, but there have been comments over the decades by the Great Ones through many different venues that the incarnating one's life circumstances are determined by that individuals karmic records—that before birth, one chooses the circumstances of their upcoming incarnation that will fulfill their karmic requirements and provide the best opportunity to grow more fully into their own unique Divine Plan to be outpictured in the coming lifetime.

So over the years, when associating with children, especially my defiant teenagers and their friends, I would often remind them that they came into this world to make it better. I assured them that it's okay not to like it, or the parental disciplines that they have to deal with. I would remind them that they chose their parents. (We parents certainly didn't choose them!) I would say to them, "You picked me as your father to remind you of what you already knew in previous lifetimes—so just do it!" This would quiet their protesting for a while as they considered what I was saying.

### The Physical Temple

Some have said that you are what you eat, but much more accurately, you are what you eat and also what you choose to put your attention upon—you become what you think, feel, say and do. If you eat processed junk foods and your attention is focused upon the materialistic fare that is streamed forth from the media, this will be your lot in life. You will reap the fruit of your free-will choices. However, if you decide to make more enlightened choices, then you have different experiences. More so, the choices that you make, in ignorance or in accordance with the Great Laws, will directly affect all those whom you interact with, including your children.

To provide a clearer picture of what is described herein I have included bits and pieces about my physical makeup, my drive, my lack of concern about the consequences that could befall me, during the period of my quest and thereafter, just so long as I was true to myself. I touched briefly upon those skills by which I made my way in the outer world—my decades in aviation, my scientific, engineering, and construction backgrounds, and I stated that the joy for me was always in my daily communion with my Presence and in sharing the Path with others.

To complete this picture, I need to fill out a few more details about the physical side of this lifetime. I still don't go to doctors except to get my flight physical so I can exercise my professional pilot certificates. I've always had the understanding that when you consecrate the food that you bring into your body and you exercise and strive to live like the Divine in All Life truly matters, then you keep this body healthy for as long as you need it. When it's time to move on, you move on. Experiencing the repeated instances of Archangel Michael's blessed intercession throughout this lifetime (most of which are detailed herein) only served to reinforce this for me—I was still here because I still had work to do.

That has been the way I've lived this life for the past four decades. Every morning after my long meditation, I still do many pushups in the Sun of my Presence that I started doing in south India all those years ago. I see the Fire of my Presence pouring through my physical, charging everything with the impetus of my Presence. Then, when I can do no more of this exercise, I visualize myself standing in the center of the Sun and begin deep breathing, intoning the great mantra, "I Am the Resurrection and the Life," on each in-breath. I visualize the Resurrection Fire pouring through these bodies (physical, emotional, mental, and memory) that are the vehicles of my Presence. I use the blessed decrees and affirmations that were written by the Great Masters from the Summit, the Temple, and earlier activities when doing long cardio workouts or biking, with similar visualizations.

This lifestyle has provided a physical body that is supple, strong, vibrant and healthy, capable of doing what needs doing—completely ignoring the dire predictions that the doctors told me I would be limited to—after I was "killed" in that head-on crash in 1985. The keys and origins to one's physical health is (as in everything else) a karmic situation. Actions one has engaged in during this lifetime and previous lifetimes determine everything, including one's physical predisposition.

The knowledge and application of the Path as outlined by the Brotherhood of Light is the swiftest way to understand and transmute (via the Violet Fire) old karmic patterns that have been limiting, not only to one's physical health, but also to all aspects of one's life. The incorporation of the calls, meditations and praises charges everything in a person's world with the Perfection of one's I Am Presence.

For me, the combined activity of physical exercise and inner visualization, using these blessed calls, assists in purifying, and transmuting the accumulation of lifetimes of karma that produce physical limitations including aging of the physical body. This sacred science is so profound that many on the Path look years younger than their actual physical age. There are wonderful stories from the mystical traditions of India where unascended Masters have retained youthful physical bodies for many, many decades, so that they could be of service to Life much longer.

As I describe the exercise that I've been doing daily for over 4 decades I wish to give a brief explanation of the call that I use in conjunction with this exercise that makes it ever more powerful.

The life-giving energy of the Sun not only nourishes the physical plane but all the planes of life. The Sun behind the Sun is well known and often invoked in all ancient spiritual practices. Helios and Vesta are the Hierarchs of our Sun, the Great Father, the Great Mother of our solar system. It is they who serve life in our system of worlds. I use this invocation to Helios and Vesta that I modified somewhat from the original "The New Day," published by the Summit Lighthouse.

Helios and Vesta, Helios and Vesta, Helios and Vesta,
Let the Light flow into our being,
Let the Light expand in the center of our hearts,
Let the Light expand in the center of the Earth
And let the Earth be transformed into the New Day.

Come into our heart, O Sun of God.
Come into our heart, O Sun of God.
Come into our heart, O Sun of God. *(repeated 3 times)*

B elow I've copied some magnificent sacred calls from The Summit Lighthouse that are a great gift to humanity's awakening. These calls assist in crystalizing and focusing the Sacred Fire in one's consciousness, one's entire being and world, when given during the morning prayer and meditation sessions or at any time throughout the day.

## Hymn to the Sun

O mighty Presence of God, I AM, in and behind the Sun:
I welcome thy Light, which floods all the Earth,
into my life, into my mind, into my spirit, into my soul.
Radiate and blaze forth thy Light!
Break the bonds of darkness and superstition!
Charge me with the great clearness
of thy white fire radiance!
I AM thy child, and each day I shall become
more of thy manifestation!

## I AM the Light of the Heart

I AM the Light of the Heart
Shining in the darkness of being
And changing all into the golden treasury
Of the Mind of Christ.

I AM projecting my Love out into the world
To erase all errors
And to break down all barriers.

I AM the power of Infinite Love,
Amplifying itself
Until it is victorious, world without end!

## *The Publishing Process Begins (October 3, 2012)*

Early this morning in the wee hours (4:30 am) I awoke thrilled through and through with this wonderful out-of-body experience I was remembering. I was with a large group of people, maybe a hundred or so, in some kind of amphitheater. On the stage was a beautifully choreographed dance of perhaps a few dozen people, ongoing as the backdrop of a person's discourse on some aspect of the Path.

I recall listening to this person and watching this choreographed dance become more elaborate and glorious as the discourse became more beautiful and powerful. Then I watched as the dancers actually levitated, no longer restrained by gravity. It was a fountain of joy, it was a promise. It appeared that the dancers were amazed at their new freedom from gravity. It was then that I realized that a Great Master was involved, was giving the discourse that the choreographed dance was depicting.

I moved to get closer to the Master, so that I might more clearly hear. I was perhaps fifty feet away now. The Master was either standing on a body of water or was moving in it. Then while feeling exultation at the Master's teaching and watching this glorious dance, the Master started walking toward me. As he approached, I recognized him as Saint Germain. His eyes were luminous as he looked at those who were gathered around with a soft smile on his face. He was about ten feet away when he looked directly at me. Then his actions from up to this point changed. I could feel him focusing his full attention upon me with that kind soft smile on his face, as our eyes locked, there was complete communication within and I said, "Thank you, thank you..."

There was an electric current of joy, of something wonderful being conveyed. Then he brought my attention to an empty crib nearby, and shrugged his shoulders as if asking where? What of this now? A woman to my side and back stepped forward with two young children in her arms. And now the experience dissolves away and I'm fully awake, with praises in my heart for waking to such a wonderful experience. At that moment, I didn't understand the part about the empty crib and the woman holding the two children. But then, at the conclusion of this writing period this morning, on Jesse's 18th birthday, I had the flash that the empty crib and Saint Germain looking at it and shrugging his shoulders as if to say what now, where are the children, was a thoughtform conveyed to me that now with Jesse 18, my twenty-nine years of direct parenting were concluded and it was time to fully engage in the mission of this lifetime.

I had already planned today on sending this story to my author friend who will do an informal editing of this work, using Jesse's birthday, and the start of the Temple's Fall conference cycle as auspicious events to commemorate the beginning of the publishing process. The advent of this wonderful experience early this morning is more than serendipitous. It's part and parcel of the entire process outlined in this story—a fitting push forward to get on with the plan.

## The Sacred Work of the Brotherhood and You

Throughout this accounting I have shared my adventures and experiences that may seem unusual to many who read these words. Again I used the analogy that when a person experiences something that is so foreign to the everyday concepts by which they live their lives, how could it be any different? Think how, in the past one hundred years, isolated cultures reacted when they saw their first airplane flying overhead.

I stated at the beginning of this work that various accountings of the Great Masters who comprise this sacred Brotherhood of Light first surfaced in the Western culture over the past 120 years. These accounts sprung up in North America, South America, Europe, and Asia, probably in Africa and Australia as well. (I'm just not familiar with those regions.)

Many of these books were published, seemingly without any connection between the various other groups or organizations that brought forth these books. Each contains a similar theme, that of an eternal sacred Brotherhood of Light that is comprised of all of the Great Ones of East and West, including Buddha, Jesus, Kuan Yin, Mother Mary, Zarathustra, Saint Germain, and many others whose very lives have demonstrated such truth, such love, wisdom, and power as to leave a permanent record in the consciousness of humanity that there is a higher way—and that it is the birthright of All.

What struck me in my early teens and then repeatedly growing up was the wonder of it all—that this sacred Brotherhood was not associated with any world religion or government—you couldn't go visit its location or any of its members. In fact, in the early days of my searching, it was difficult to find any reference to the Masters at all, but when I did, it filled me with an electric joy. Finally here was truth. Now, the intriguing piece of this was that it was they who would make their Presence known to those who sought truth. It was so refreshingly logical compared to the religious dogma that I was forcibly spoon fed as a child. Reading about these concepts made my heart soar that there really was a beautiful purpose behind everything. It began to make more and more sense to me.

I've detailed in this accounting my process of discovery. Now with tremendous gratitude to my Presence that I refer to in my heart as Father, with tremendous gratitude to those Great One who have assisted me all of these years and lifetimes. With tremendous gratitude for the wherewithal to bring forth this story, I pass it along to you that it might assist you in your journey and on whatever Path it may take you.

I have recommended to many that when they start reading the books or listening to any of the pre-recorded or live services from The Temple of The Presence (or any books about the Path), to ask your Divine Presence, or whatever great Master or Angel that you feel close to, to help you integrate what you are about to read—to be able to read between the lines that are written or spoken. If this is for you, then there is much additional material to share on this most ancient and most sacred of subjects. (See Recommended Reading.)

The key point here is to have your mind take a back seat—so that you can read with your heart, see with your heart, hear with your heart, feel with your heart, and act from your heart, not from your outer mind. Eventually this inner exercise will continue into more and more of your life's affairs as you become an Upraised Chalice of Divine Love, Wisdom, and Power to all. It is here in the Secret Chamber of the Heart where you will begin to hear the gentle voice of your God Presence.

It is time for many who already know of this on the inner to wake up to this knowledge consciously. I'm not talking about a mere "intellectual" understanding of the concepts here. If any of this speaks to your Heart, then understand that you may be about to embark on a life-changing journey.

It may not involve quests to Jerusalem, the Himalayas and India, or near-death encounters—it may not be as dramatic or challenging as some of my adventures that you have read about here, but but if you are sincere and put your heart to this, your life will change for the better. For once you are touched by the ever-so-sweet, intense Love of your Presence, reminding you of Who You Really Are, it's like an electrical charge that brings a quickening that conveys the empowerment to live differently. The Path becomes the most Sacred and the most Real aspect of your Life. You become an Upraised Chalice. The Joy, the Peace, the Wisdom, and the Protection that this will afford you, your family, and your loved ones is beyond words to convey.

I commend you to Your Presence. May the Brotherhood of Light, Archangel Michael and his Legions guide and protect You and All on this sacred journey.

⊰•⊱ ⊰•⊱ ⊰•⊱

# ~ The Power of The Temple of The Presence Calls

What follows are a few very special selections from *The Temple of The Presence I AM Adorations, Affirmations, Fiats, and Rhythmic Decrees.* (This entire book can be ordered directly from the Temple website.)

These calls convey so very much. When read and recited as a sacred meditation, the concepts contained herein expand in one's awareness. Each time they are recited the actions depicted become stronger and more pervasive in one's world because of the sciences lightly touched upon in this story. These specific calls in themselves convey many aspects of these ancient sacred teachings by which aspiring ones, by their own free-will action, can free themselves from binding karmic momentums, revealing more and more of one's Divine Presence within.

These are presented here for those of you who wish to experience this sacred exercise now, so that you might have the record of this action in your consciousness as you move forward in your life. You can download a beginning set of decrees, affirmations, and praises from the Temple website here: TempleOfThePresence.org/DecreeSample.pdf.

## Calls for Protection

**Mighty I AM Presence!**

Your Authority is in Action in my world!

**Mighty I AM Presence** and Beloved Archangel Michael!

You and your Legions of Angels stand within my world right now! Release the Blue Lightning of ten Thousand Suns right now! Sweep into all astral and psychic opposition and human conditions in my world and annihilate them right now!

**Mighty I AM Presence!** Beloved Jesus, Beloved Archangel Michael and Beloved Archeia Faith:

Take command of me and of all appearances of imperfection and Unreality in my world. Beloved Archangel Michael: *Blaze (3x)* your Blue Lightning in, though, and around all opposition to The Victorious Achievement of each and every call I make today and the inner purposes of this Decree Service.

## Archangel Michael

Prince Michael Archangel
    And Legions of Light!
I need Thee, come quickly
    To banish all fright!

*Chorus:*
    *Blaze thy Blue Lightning! Release Cosmic Fire!*
        *Seize every appearance of human desire!*
    *Bolts of Blue Lightning! Descend from above!*
        *Shatter all darkness opposed to God's Love!*
    *Sword of Blue Flame and Sheets of White Fire!*
        *Raise record and memory higher and higher!*

Saint Michael Archangel,
    Great Whirlwind of Power!
Oh, Champion my Cause
    With each passing hour!

Lord Michael Archangel,
    Great Sword of Blue Flame!
Protect us, defend us
    In God's I AM Name!

*Coda:*
    *Sunder unreality!*
        *Reveal my fiery Destiny!*
    *Defend my Christ Identity!*
        *And Manifest my Victory (3x)*

Let There Be LIGHT! — By Archangel's Might.
Let There Be FAITH! — In All that is True.
Let There be POWER! — God Freedom to win.
Let There be JOY! — God Will to attend.

*(Note: the chorus is repeated after each of the 3 verses.)*

## Jesus' Resurrection Call

**I AM, I AM, I AM** the Resurrection and the Life of the Ascended Jesus Christ Consciousness in every atom, cell, and electron of my four lower bodies and all of my affairs now made manifest! *(3x, 9x, or 12x)*

## Violet Fire

In the Name of the **Beloved Mighty Presence** of **God, I AM** in me, and my very own **Beloved Holy Christ Presence**, by the Power and Authority of the Immortal, Victorious **Threefold Flame** blazing upon the Altar of my Heart, I call to Beloved Alpha and Omega in the **Great Central Sun**, Beloved Helios and Vesta in the Sun of our System, Beloved Saint Germain and Portia, Beloved Maha Chohan, Beloved Omritas, Beloved Archangel Zadkiel and Holy Amethyst, Beloved Mighty Elohim Arcturus and Victoria, Beloved Sanat Kumara, Lady Master Venus and the Seven Holy Kumaras, Beloved Jesus and Mother Mary, Beloved Kwan Yin, the Lords of Karma, and the Hierarchs of the Elements —Earth, Air, Fire, Water, and Akasha, to Blaze the Violet Transmuting Flame throughout my entire consciousness, being, and world. Expand that Flame to include all mankind and elemental life. To this end, I decree:

> I AM the Violet Fire
> > God's All Consuming Love.
> I AM the Violet Fire
> > Descending from Above!
>
> I AM the Violet Fire
> > So Crystalline and Bright.
> I AM the Violet Fire
> > Releasing Freedom's Might!
>
> I AM the Violet Fire
> > Transmuting Thru and Thru.
> I AM the Violet Fire
> > Making All Things New!

I AM the Violet Fire
>   Of Mist and Flame Supreme.
I AM the Violet Fire
>   Restoring Heaven's Dream!

I AM the Violet Fire
>   A Mighty Whirling Flame.
I AM the Violet Fire
>   Ascending Once Again!

I AM the Violet Fire
>   Transmuting Thru and Thru.
I AM the Violet Fire
>   Freeing Me and You!

When one begins to understand what is contained in the above calls, it's both a humbling and an empowering experience—humbling in the sense that the sacred action invoked is so very beautiful, so vast, and all-inclusive in scope, conveying such hope and promise of a glorious freedom only dreamt of—empowering in the sense that as one accelerates in this sacred decree, the majesty of one's own Presence giving this decree is truly experienced more and more—thus the decree becomes even more powerful.

And yet these are just a few calls; there are so many others. And then what of the breadth and depth of these teachings released through this sacred Brotherhood of Light, released through The Temple of The Presence? All one can do figuratively or actually is to fall to one's knees and thank God for this great gift of Freedom and all that this implies.

Now, to conclude these excerpts from the Temple calls, I include the following that is given as a fiat:

### Cry Freedom's Cosmic Light

Mighty Cosmic Light, blaze forth!
　　Ten Thousand Suns descend!
I AM the Cosmic Christ Command!
　　Earth's children to defend!

Mighty Cosmic Light, come forth!
　　Burn through the darkest night!
I AM the Pow'r makes all things new and
　　Wakes to dawning Light!

Mighty Cosmic Light, stand forth!
　　Transmute by my Decree!
I AM the Thundering Christ Command
　　Proclaiming all Life free!

Mighty Cosmic Light, shine forth!
　　From sea to shining sea!
I AM thy ALL-Consuming Love,
　　The Love that sets all free!

Nature's Cosmic Might, pour forth!
　　More Light! More Light to Thee!
I AM God Freedom to the Earth!
　　I AM her Liberty!
*(3x, 9x, 12x)*

When the above call was first given at a formal Temple service by Monroe, with many dozens joining him in its recitation, it reverberated throughout my entire being. In euphoria, I felt and saw the action of this call rolling across the surface of the Earth. It is so very powerful, especially when given in unison with others, which happens during each Temple service as part of the building of the forcefield that allows the Great Ones to step forth.

Some years later I carved this call into the eight panels that surround the large Tibetan prayer wheel that graces the very top of the floating pagoda temple depicted in this picture.

**The floating *Temple of the Sun***

*"All for the Love of God—Everywhere in Action."*

I first saw this temple in a meditation as my mother approached her transition. The area that I saw it superimposed upon was a forested, swampy area near our large, beautifully landscaped pond. Upon her passing, I began the building process. I had cleared the area of trees and excavated the pond the year before. Every day in meditation, I saw the building assignment for that day, never seeing the entire picture of the temple, just the construction details that I would be engaged in for that specific day.

Every day as I worked, I wrote mantras and calls on the various pieces of wood that I cut and assembled. The temple is in the middle of a 60-foot in diameter, heart-shaped pond. The only access would either be "by walking on water" or across the 20-foot freestanding, trussed, arched bridge. Throughout the spring summer and fall, it is surrounded by fragrant flowers, the tinkling of the waterfalls that feed into the pond, and the birds and frogs singing their choruses. When one walks into the temple, the first thing one sees (aside from the beauty of nature surrounding) is the first panel with my favorite mantra carved into it: "All for the Love of God—Everywhere in Action." It is a magical place for praises. ❧

# RECOMMENDED READING/WEBSITES

Here are some resources that you might find interesting:

*BOOKS:*

**Autobiography of a Yogi** (Self-Realization Fellowship, 1946)
Paramahansa Yogananda

**Unveiled Mysteries** (Saint Germain Series, Vol. 1, 1934)
Godfré Ray King

**The Magic Presence** (Saint Germain Series, Vol. 2, 1935)
Godfré Ray King

**The "I AM" Discourses** (Saint Germain Series, Vol. 3, 1935)
Godfré Ray King

**Life and Teaching of the Masters of the Far East** (Vols. 1–4,1924)
Baird T. Spalding

**The Aquarian Gospel of Jesus the Christ, The Christ of the Piscean Age**
Levi H. Dowling (1908)

**The Masters and the Path** (The Theosophical Society, 1925)
Charles W. Leadbeater

**At the Feet of the Master** (The Theosophical Society, 1910)
Jiddu Krishnamurti

**The Agni Yoga Series** (Agni Yoga Society, 17 titles: 1923–1941)
Nicholas and Helena Roerich

**Prayer and Meditation** (The Summit Lighthouse, 1978)
Jesus and Kuthumi

**Climb the Highest Mountain** (The Summit Lighthouse, 1972)
Mark and Elizabeth Prophet

**Studies of the Human Aura** (The Summit Lighthouse, 1975)
Mark Prophet

**A Dweller on Two Planets** (through Frederick S. Oliver, 1905)
Phylos the Thibetan

**The Bridge to Freedom Dispensation** (Over 70 titles: 1952–1961)
Geraldine Innocente (Ascended Master Teaching Foundation)

*Wisdom from White Eagle*
(White Eagle Lodge, plus over 50 titles, 1936–1979)
Grace Cooke

**The Complete Works of Aurobindo** (Lotus Press, 24 titles)
including **The Life Divine** (1939) and
**The Synthesis of Yoga** (1940)

*WEBSITES:*

**Roop Verma's Sacred Music**
Information about Roop's concerts and seminars as well as
CDs of his recordings are available at RoopVerma.com

**Ascension Research Center**, an independent student research
project on the Ascended Master Teachings,
at Ascension-Research.org

**The Temple of The Presence**
Live broadcasts and recorded discourses and dictations by
Monroe and Carolyn Shearer, at TempleOfThePresence.org

**An Upraised Chalice**
More info, blog commentaries on the Path, color prints of
the cover artwork, and additional copies of this book.
UpraisedChalice.com

Made in the USA
Middletown, DE
08 August 2023

36341023R00149